Computational Models of Language Evolution

Editors: Luc Steels, Remi van Trijp

In this series:

1. Steels, Luc. The Talking Heads Experiment: Origins of words and meanings.

2. Vogt, Paul. How mobile robots can self-organize a vocabulary.

3. Bleys, Joris. Language strategies for the domain of colour.

4. van Trijp, Remi. The evolution of case grammar.

5. Spranger, Michael. The evolution of grounded spatial language.

ISSN: 2364-7809

How mobile robots can self-organise a vocabulary

Paul Vogt

language
science
press

Paul Vogt. 2015. *How mobile robots can self-organise a vocabulary* (Computational Models of Language Evolution 2). Berlin: Language Science Press.

This title can be downloaded at:
http://langsci-press.org/catalog/book/50
© 2015, Paul Vogt
Published under the Creative Commons Attribution 4.0 Licence (CC BY 4.0):
http://creativecommons.org/licenses/by/4.0/
ISBN: 978-3-944675-43-5 (Digital)
   978-3-946234-00-5 (Hardcover)
   978-3-946234-01-2 (Softcover)
ISSN: 2364-7809

Cover and concept of design: Ulrike Harbort
Typesetting: Felix Kopecky, Sebastian Nordhoff, Paul Vogt
Proofreading: Felix Kopecky
Fonts: Linux Libertine, Arimo, DejaVu Sans Mono
Typesetting software: X∃LATEX

Language Science Press
Habelschwerdter Allee 45
14195 Berlin, Germany
langsci-press.org

Storage and cataloguing done by FU Berlin

Language Science Press has no responsibility for the persistence or accuracy of URLs for external or third-party Internet websites referred to in this publication, and does not guarantee that any content on such websites is, or will remain, accurate or appropriate. Information regarding prices, travel timetables and other factual information given in this work are correct at the time of first publication but Language Science Press does not guarantee the accuracy of such information thereafter.

Contents

Preface	vii
Acknowledgments	xi

1 Introduction — 1
- 1.1 Symbol grounding problem — 3
  - 1.1.1 Language of thought — 3
  - 1.1.2 Understanding Chinese — 5
  - 1.1.3 Symbol grounding: philosophical or technical? — 8
  - 1.1.4 Grounding symbols in language — 11
  - 1.1.5 Physical grounding hypothesis — 12
  - 1.1.6 Physical symbol grounding — 14
- 1.2 Language origins — 18
  - 1.2.1 Computational approaches to language evolution — 19
  - 1.2.2 Steels' approach — 20
- 1.3 Language acquisition — 24
- 1.4 Setting up the goals — 26
- 1.5 Contributions — 28
- 1.6 The book's outline — 31

2 The sensorimotor component — 33
- 2.1 The environment — 33
- 2.2 The robots — 34
  - 2.2.1 The sensors and actuators — 35
  - 2.2.2 Sensor-motor board II — 38
- 2.3 The Process Description Language — 41
- 2.4 Cognitive architecture in PDL — 47
- 2.5 Summary — 51

3 Language games — 53
- 3.1 Introduction — 53

Contents

	3.2	The language game scenario	54
	3.3	PDL implementation	56
	3.4	Grounded language games	61
		3.4.1 Sensing, segmentation and feature extraction	62
		3.4.2 Discrimination games	71
		3.4.3 Lexicon formation	83
	3.5	Coupling categorisation and naming	94
4	**Experimental results**		**99**
	4.1	Measures and methodology	99
		4.1.1 Measures	99
		4.1.2 Statistical testing	103
		4.1.3 On-board versus off-board	104
	4.2	Sensory data	105
	4.3	The basic experiment	107
		4.3.1 The global evolution	108
		4.3.2 The ontological development	113
		4.3.3 Competition diagrams	115
		4.3.4 The lexicon	120
		4.3.5 More language games	123
	4.4	Summary	124
5	**Varying methods and parameters**		**125**
	5.1	Impact from categorisation	125
		5.1.1 The experiments	126
		5.1.2 The results	127
		5.1.3 Discussion	130
	5.2	Impact from physical conditions and interactions	131
		5.2.1 The experiments	132
		5.2.2 The results	133
		5.2.3 Discussion	139
	5.3	Different language games	140
		5.3.1 The experiments	140
		5.3.2 The results	140
		5.3.3 Discussion	143
	5.4	The observational game	145
		5.4.1 The experiments	145
		5.4.2 The results	146
		5.4.3 Discussion	148

5.5	Word-form creation		150
	5.5.1	The experiments	150
	5.5.2	The results	150
	5.5.3	Discussion	152
5.6	Varying the learning rate		153
	5.6.1	The experiments	153
	5.6.2	The results	153
	5.6.3	Discussion	157
5.7	Word-form adoption		157
	5.7.1	The experiments	157
	5.7.2	The results	158
	5.7.3	Discussion	159
5.8	Summary		159

6 The optimal games — 163

6.1	The guessing game		163
	6.1.1	The experiments	163
	6.1.2	The results	164
	6.1.3	Discussion	170
6.2	The observational game		177
	6.2.1	The experiment	177
	6.2.2	The results	177
	6.2.3	Discussion	177
6.3	Summary		183

7 Discussion — 185

7.1	The symbol grounding problem solved?		186
	7.1.1	Iconisation	187
	7.1.2	Discrimination	189
	7.1.3	Identification	193
	7.1.4	Conclusions	195
7.2	No negative feedback evidence?		197
7.3	Situated embodiment		200
7.4	A behaviour-based cognitive architecture		201
7.5	The Talking Heads		203
	7.5.1	The differences	203
	7.5.2	The discussion	208
	7.5.3	Summary	211
7.6	Future directions		212
7.7	Conclusions		215

Contents

Appendix A: Glossary 217

Appendix B: PDL code 221

Appendix C: Sensory data distribution 241

Appendix D: Lexicon and ontology 245

References 253

Indexes 265
    Name index 265
    Subject index 268

Preface

You are currently reading the book version of my doctoral dissertation which I successfully defended at the Vrije Universiteit Brussel on 10th November 2000, slightly more than 15 years ago at the time of writing this preface. I feel privileged to have been the very first to implement Luc Steels' language game paradigm on a robotic platform. As you will read, the robots I used at that moment were very limited in their sensing, computational ressources and motor control. Moreover, I spent much time repairing the robots, as they were built from LEGO parts (not LEGO Mindstorms, which was not yet available at the start of my research) and a homemade sensorimotor board. As a result, the experimental setup and the evolved lexicons were also very limited. Nevertheless, the process of implementing the model, carrying out the experiments and analysing these, has provided a wealth of insights and knowledge on lexicon grounding in an evolutionary context, which, I believe, are still relevant today.

Much progress has been made since the writing of this dissertation. First, the language game paradigm has been implemented in more advanced robots, starting with the Talking Heads (Steels et al. 2002) and the Sony Aibo (Steels & Kaplan 2000), which emerged while I was struggling with the LEGO robots, then soon followed by various humanoid platforms, such as Sony's Qrio (see, e.g. Steels 2012 and this book series). Second, the cognitive architecture has become much more advanced through the development of FCG (Steels & De Beule 2006), which allowed for more complex languages to emerge, resembling more closely natural languages. Third, the underlying processes of language games, in particular of the naming game, and the resulting dynamics in an evolutionary context have been widely studied using methods stemming from statistical mechanics (e.g., Baronchelli et al. 2006).

During the first years after the completion of my dissertation, I have published various studies from this book as journal articles (Vogt 2000a; 2002; 2003a). A broader review of using robots in studies of language evolution has appeared in Vogt 2006. Building further on the work presented in this book, I formulated the PHYSICAL SYMBOL GROUNDING HYPOTHESIS (Vogt 2002). This hypothesis essentially states that Harnad's (1990) symbol grounding problem is not a philosophical problem, but a technical problem that needs to be addressed by (virtual) robotic agents situated in a (virtual) environment, provided we adopt Peirce's semiotics, because according to this view, symbols have per definition meaning. As physical symbol grounding can in principle be achieved by individual agents, the ability to develop a shared symbolic communication system is a (much) harder challenge. This challenge, which I have called SOCIAL SYMBOL GROUNDING (Vogt & Divina 2007), has remained my primary research focus.

The fact that I worked in a lab without robotic platforms forced me to continue my research in simulations. Although simulations move away from the advantages of studying physically situated language development, it allowed me to scale up and, not unimportantly, speed up the research. Together with Hans Coumans, I reimplemented the three types of language games studied in this book (the observational game, the guessing game and what I then called the selfish game) in a simulation to demonstrate that the selfish game can work properly (Vogt & Coumans 2003), despite the results presented in this book. In my dissertation, the term "selfish game" was used to indicate that the hearer had to interpret an utterance solely based on the utterance and the context without receiving additional cues through joint attention or feedback. I later discovered that the statistical learning method I implemented is known as CROSS-SITUATIONAL LEARNING (Pinker 1984; Siskind 1996). As I have worked a lot on cross-situational learning (XSL) over the past decade, I have decided to change the term "selfish game" into XSL game. Apart from a few small typos, this is the only change made with respect to the original dissertation.

Over the years, I have become convinced that XSL is the basic learning mechanism that humans use to learn word-meaning mappings. XSL learning allows the learner to infer the meaning of a word by using the covariation of meanings that occur in the contexts of different situations. In Smith et al. (2006), we have shown that XSL can be highly robust under large amounts of referential uncertainty (i.e. a lexicon can be learned well even when an agent hears a word in contexts containing many possible meanings). However, this was shown using a mathematical model containing many unrealistic assumptions. When relaxing such assumptions, such as using a robot (cf. this book), having many agents in the population (Vogt & Coumans 2003) or assuming that words and meanings occur following a Zipfian distribution (Vogt 2012), XSL is no longer that powerful. To resolve this, a learner requires additional cues to learn a human-size lexicon, such as joint attention or corrective feedback.

These ideas were further elaborated in the EU funded New Ties project (Gilbert et al. 2006), in which we aimed to set up a large scale ALife simulation, containing thousands of agents who "lived" in a complex environment containing all sorts of objects, who could move around, and who would face all sorts of challenges in order to survive. The agents would learn to survive through evolutionary adaptation based on genetic transmission, individual learning and social learning of skills and language. Although we only succeeded partially, an interesting modification of the language game was implemented. In this implementation, agents could engage in a more dialogue-like interaction requesting additional cues or testing learnt vocabulary. They could also pass on learnt skills to other agents using the evolved language. The interactions could involve both joint attention and corrective feedback to reduce referential uncertainty, while learning was achieved through xsl (Vogt & Divina 2007; Vogt & Haasdijk 2010).

Another line of research that I have carried out after writing this book, combined the language game paradigm with Kirby and Hurford's 2002 ITERATED LEARNING MODEL, studying the emergence of compositional structures in language (Vogt 2005b,a). This hybrid model, implemented in the simulation toolkit THsim (Vogt 2003b), simulates the Talking Heads experiment.[1] These studies have provided fundamental insights on how compositionality might have evolved through cultural evolution by means of social interactions, social learning and self-organisation. Population dynamics, transmission over generations, and the active acquisition of language and meaning were considered crucial ingredients of this model (for an overview of the results, see Vogt 2007).

While I was making good progress with all this modelling work, providing interesting and testable predictions on language evolution and language acquisition, I increasingly realised the importance of validating these predictions with empirical data from studies with humans (or other animals). Together with Bart de Boer, we organised a week-long meeting in which language evolution modellers working on various topics were coupled to researchers working on empirical data from various fields, such as child language acquisition, animal communication, cognitive linguistics, etc. In this workshop, novel approaches to compare our models as closely as possible to empirical findings were developed (Vogt & de Boer 2010).

As there is virtually no empirical data on the evolution of word-meaning mappings, the most straightforward comparison that could be made with my modelling research was to compare to child language acquisition (Vogt & Lieven 2010). Although there is a wealth of data on child language acquisition, none was found that captured the data needed to make a reliable comparison. Therefore, I decided to collect the data myself. This resulted in a project on which I have worked

---

[1] Downloadable from http://ilk.uvt.nl/~pvogt/thsim.html.

for over the past five years. Its aim is to develop longitudinal corpora of children's interactions with their (social) environment from different cultures (the Netherlands and Mozambique), together with parental estimates of the children's vocabulary size at different ages during children's second year of life. In these corpora, recordings of naturalistic observations are annotated based on the type of interactions (e.g. dyadic vs. triadic interactions), the use of gestures such as pointing, the use of feedback, the child-directed speech and the children's social network of interactions. The resulting corpora contain statistical descriptions of the types of interactions and stimuli which the children from the different cultures encounter. The idea is that these corpora can be used to set the parameters of language game simulations similar to the one described in Vogt & Haasdijk (2010). The aim is to simulate observed naturalistic interactions and to compare the lexicon development of the artificial agents with that of the simulated children. If the predictions from the simulations match the observed development of the children, then we may be confident that the model is an accurate (or at least highly plausible) theory of children's language acquisition. Development of the ultimate model, however, may take another 15 years. (For more details on this approach, consult Vogt & Mastin 2013.)

Now, let us move on to where it all started for me. Before going there, however, I would like to apologise for any mistake that you may encounter, or visions I may no longer adhere to, and which could easily have been repaired if I would have had the time. Enjoy the rest of the journey.

Paul Vogt
Tilburg, November 2013.

Acknowledgments

In 1989 I started to study physics at the University of Groningen, because at that time it seemed to me that the working of the brain could best be explained with a physics background. Human intelligence has always fascinated me, and I wanted to understand how our brains could establish such a wonderful feature of our species. After a few years I got disappointed in the narrow specialisation of a physicist. In addition, it did not provide me the answers to the question I had. Fortunately, the student advisor of physics, Professor Hein Rood introduced to me a new study, which would start in 1993 at the University of Groningen (RuG). This study was called "cognitive science and engineering", which included all I was interested in. Cognitive science and engineering combined physics (in particular biophysics), artificial intelligence, psychology, linguistics, philosophy and neuroscience in an technical study in intelligence. I would like to thank Professor Rood very much for that.

This changed my life. After a few years of study, I became interested in robotics, especially the field of robotics that Luc Steels was working on at the AI lab of the Free University of Brussels. In my last year I had to do a research project of six months resulting in a Master's thesis. I was pleased to be able to do this at Luc Steels' AI lab. Together we worked on our first steps towards grounding language on mobile robots, which formed the basis of the current PhD thesis. After receiving my MSc degree (*doctoraal* in Dutch) in cognitive science and engineering, Luc Steels gave me the opportunity to start my PhD research in 1997.

I would like to thank Luc Steels very much for giving me the opportunity to work in his laboratory. He gave me the chance to work in an extremely motivating research environment on the top floor of a university building with a wide view over the city of Brussels and with great research facilities. In addition, his ideas and our fruitful discussions showed me the way to go and inspired me to express my creativity.

Many thanks for their co-operation, useful discussions and many laughs to my friends and (ex-)colleagues at the AI lab Tony Belpaeme, Karina Bergen, Andreas Birk, Bart de Boer, Sabine Geldof, Edwin de Jong, Holger Kenn, Dominique Osier, Peter Stuer, Joris Van Looveren, Dany Vereertbrugghen, Thomas Walle and all those who have worked here for some time during my stay. I cannot forget to thank my colleagues at the Sony CSL in Paris for providing me with a lot of interesting ideas and the time spent during the inspiring off-site meetings: Frédéric Kaplan, Angus McIntyre, Pierre-Yves Oudeyer, Gert Westermann and Jelle Zuidema.

Students Björn Van Dooren and Michael Uyttersprot are thanked for their very helpful assistance during some of the experiments. Haoguang Zhu is thanked for translating the title of this thesis into Chinese.

The teaching staff of cognitive science and engineering have been very helpful for giving me feedback during my study and my PhD research, especially thanks to Tjeerd Andringa, Petra Hendriks, Henk Mastebroek, Ben Mulder, Niels Taatgen and Floris Takens. Furthermore, some of my former fellow students from Groningen had a great influence on my work through our many lively discussions about cognition: Erwin Drenth, Hans Jongbloed, Mick Kappenburg, Rens Kortmann and Lennart Quispel. Also many thanks to my colleagues from other universities that have provided me with many new insights along the way: Ruth Aylett, Dave Barnes, Aude Billard, Axel Cleeremans, Jim Hurford, Simon Kirby, Daniel Livingstone, Will Lowe, Tim Oates, Michael Rosenstein, Jun Tani and those many others who gave me a lot of useful feedback.

Thankfully I also have some friends who reminded me that there was more in life than work alone. For that I would like to thank Wiard, Chris and Marcella, Hilde and Gerard, Herman and Xandra and all the others who somehow brought lots of fun in my social life.

I would like to thank my parents very much for their support and attention throughout my research. Many thanks to my brother and sisters and inlaws for being there for me always. And thanks to my nieces and nephews for being a joy in my life

Finally, I would like to express my deepest gratitude to Miranda Brouwer for bringing so much more in my life than I could imagine. I thank her for the patience and trust during some hard times while I was working at a distance. I dedicate this work to you.

Brussels, November 2000

1 Introduction

L'intelligence est une adaptation.
(Piaget 1996)

One of the hardest problems in artificial intelligence and robotics is what has been called the SYMBOL GROUNDING PROBLEM (Harnad 1990). The question how "seemingly meaningless symbols become meaningful" (Harnad 1990) is a question that also holds grip of many philosophers for already more than a century, e.g. Brentano (1874), Searle (1980) and Dennett (1991).[1] With the rise of artificial intelligence (AI), the question has become very actual, especially within the symbolic paradigm (Newell 1990).[2] The symbol grounding problem is still a very hard problem in AI and especially in robotics (Pfeifer & Scheier 1999).

The problem is that an agent, be it a robot or a human, perceives the world in analogue signals. Yet humans have the ability to categorise the world in symbols that they, for instance may use for language. The perception of something, like e.g. the colour red, may vary a lot when observed under different circumstances. Nevertheless, humans are very good at recognising and naming this colour under these different conditions. For robots, however, this is extremely difficult. In many applications the robots try to recognise such perceptions based on the rules that are pre-programmed. But there are no singular rules that guide the conceptualisation of red. The same argument holds for many, if not all perceptions. A lot of solutions to the symbol grounding problem have been proposed, but there are still many limitations on these solutions.

Intelligent systems or, as Newell (1980) called them, "physical symbol systems" should amongst others be able to use symbols, abstractions and language. These symbols, abstractions and language are always about something. But how do they become that way? There is something going on in the brains of language users that give meaning to these symbols. What is going on is not clear. It is clear from neuroscience that active neuronal pathways in the brain activate mental

---

[1] In philosophy the problem is usually addressed with the term "intentionality", introduced by Brentano (1874).
[2] In the classical and symbolic AI the problem has also been addressed in what is known as the "frame problem" (Pylyshyn 1987).

1 Introduction

states. But how does this relate to objects and other things in the real world? According to Maturana & Varela (1992) there is a structural coupling between the things in the world and an organism's active pathways. Wittgenstein (1958) stresses the importance of how language is used to make a relation with language and its meaning. The context of what he called a language game and the purpose of the language game establishes the meaning of it. According to these views, the meaning of symbols is established for a great deal by the interaction of an agent with its environment and is context dependent. A view that has been adopted in the field of pragmatics and situated cognition (Clancey 1997).

In traditional AI and robotics the meaning of symbols was predefined by the programmer of the system. Besides that these systems have no knowledge about the meaning of these symbols, the symbols' meanings were very static and could not deal with different contexts or varying environments. Early computer programs that modelled natural language, notably SHRDLU (Winograd 1972) were completely pre-programmed, and hence could not handle the complete scope of a natural language. It could only handle that part of the language that was pre-programmed. SHRDLU has been programmed *as if* it were a robot with an eye and arm that was operating in a blocks world. Within certain constrictions, SHRDLU could manipulate English input such that it could plan particular goals. However, the symbols that SHRDLU was manipulating had no meaning for the virtual robot. Shakey, a real robot operating in a blocks world, did solve the grounding problem. But Shakey was limited to the knowledge that had been pre-programmed.

Later approaches to solve the grounding problem on real world multi-agent systems involving language have been investigated by Yanco & Stein (1993) and Billard & Hayes (1997). In the work of Yanco and Stein the robots learned to communicate about actions. These actions, however, were pre-programmed and limited, and are therefore limited to the meanings that the robots had. In Billard & Hayes (1997) one robot had pre-programmed meanings of actions, which were represented in a neural network architecture. A student robot had to learn couplings between communicated words and actions it did to follow the first robot. In this work the student robot learned to ground the meaning of its actions symbolically by associating behavioural activation with words. However, the language of the teacher robot was pre-programmed and hence the student could only learn what the teacher knows.

In the work of Billard and Hayes, the meaning is grounded in a situated experiment. So, a part of the meaning is situated in the context in which it is used. However, the learned representation of the meaning is developed through bodily experiences. This is conform with the principle of EMBODIMENT (Lakoff 1987), in which the meaning of something is represented according to bodily experiences. The meaning represented in someone's (or something's) brain depends on previous experiences of interactions with such meanings. The language that emerges is therefore dependent on the body of the system that experiences. This principle is made clear very elegantly by Thomas Nagel in his famous article *What is it like to be a bat?* (Nagel 1974). In this article Nagel argues that it is impossible to understand what a bat is experiencing because it has a different body with different sensing capabilities (a bat uses echolocation to navigate). A bat approaching a wall must experience different meanings (if it has any) than humans would have when approaching a wall. Thus a robot that has a different body than humans will have different meanings. Moreover, different humans have different meaning representations because they encountered different experiences.

This book presents a series of experiments in which two robots try to solve the symbol grounding problem. The experiments are based on a recent approach in AI and the study of language origins, proposed by Luc Steels (1996c). In this new approach, behaviour-based AI (Steels & Brooks 1995) is combined with new computational approaches to the language origins and multi-agent technology. The ideas of Steels have been implemented on real mobile robots so that they can develop a grounded lexicon about objects they can detect in their real world, as reported first in Steels & Vogt 1997. This work differs from the work of Yanco & Stein (1993) and Billard & Hayes (1997) in that no part of the lexicon and its meaning has been programmed. Hence their representation is not limited due to pre-programmed relations.

The next section introduces the symbol grounding problem in more detail. This section first discusses some theoretical background on the meaning of symbols after which some practical issues on symbol grounding are discussed. The experiments are carried out within a broader research on the origins of language, which is presented in Section 1.2. A little background on human language acquisition is given in Section 1.3. The research goals of this book are defined in Section 1.4. The final section of this chapter presents the outline of this book.

1.1 Symbol grounding problem

1.1.1 Language of thought

Already for more than a century philosophers ask themselves how is it possible that we seem to think in terms of symbols which are *about* something that is in the real world. So, if one manipulates symbols as a mental process, one

1 Introduction

could ask what is the symbol (manipulation) about? Most explanations in the literature are however in terms of symbols that again are about something, as in folk-psychology intentionality is often explained in terms of beliefs, desires etc. For instance, according to Jerry Fodor (1975), every concept is a propositional attitude. Fodor hypothesises a "Language of Thought" to explain why humans tend to think in a *mental* language rather than in natural language alone.

Fodor argues that concepts can be described by symbols that represent propositions towards which attitudes (like beliefs or desires) can be attributed. Fodor calls these symbols "propositional attitudes". If P is a proposition, then the phrase "I belief that P" is a propositional attitude. According to Fodor, all mental states can be described as propositional attitudes, so a mental state is a belief or desire *about* something. This *something*, however, is a proposition, which according to Fodor is *in the head*. But mental states should be about something that is in the real world. That is the essence of the symbol grounding problem. The propositions are symbol structures that are represented in the brain, sometimes called "mental representations". In addition, the brain consists of rules that describe how these representations can be manipulated. The language of thought, according to Fodor, is constituted by symbols which can be manipulated by applying existing rules. Fodor further argues that the language of thought is innate, and thus resembles Chomsky's universal grammar very well.

Concepts are in this Computational Theory of Mind (as Fodor's theory sometimes is called) constructed from a set of propositions. The language of thought (and with that concepts) can, however, not be learned according to Fodor, who denies:

> [r]oughly, that one can learn a language whose expressive power is greater than that of a language that one already knows. Less roughly, that one can learn a language whose predicates express extensions not expressible by those of a previously available representational system. Still less roughly, that one can learn a language whose predicates express extensions not expressible by predicates of the representational system *whose employment mediates the learning*. (Fodor 1975: 86, Fodor's italics)

According to this, the process of concept learning is the testing of hypotheses that are already available at birth. Likewise, Fodor argues that perception is again the formulating and testing of hypotheses, which are already available to the agent. So, Fodor argues that, since one cannot learn a concept if one does not have the conceptual building blocks of this concept, and since perception needs such building blocks as well, concept learning does not exist and therefore concepts must be innate. This is a remarkable finding, since it roughly implies that all that we know is actual innate knowledge. Fodor called this innate inner language "Mentalese". It must be clear that it is impossible to have such a language. As Patricia S. Churchland puts it:

> [The Mentalese hypothesis] entails the ostensibly new concepts evolving in the course of scientific innovation – concepts such as atom, force field, quark, electrical charge, and gene – are lying ready-made in the language of thought, even of a prehistoric hunter-gatherer... The concepts of modern science are defined in terms of the theories that embed them, not in terms of a set of "primitive conceptual atoms," whatever those may be. (Churchland 1986: 389)

Although the Computational Theory of Mind is controversial, there are still many scientist who adheres to this theory and not the least many AI researchers. This is not surprising, since the theory tries to model cognition computationally, which of course is a nice property since computers are computational devices. It will be shown however that Fodor's Computational Theory of Mind is not necessary for concept and language learning. In particular it will be shown that robots can be developed that can acquire, use and manipulate symbols which are about something that exists in the real world, *and* which are initially not available to the robots.

1.1.2 Understanding Chinese

This so-called symbol grounding problem was made clear excellently by John R. Searle with a gedankenexperiment called the "Chinese Room" (Searle 1980). In this experiment, Searle considers himself standing in a room in which there is a large data bank of Chinese symbols and a set of rules how to manipulate these symbols. Searle, while in the room receives symbols that represent a Chinese expression. Searle, who does not know any Chinese, manipulates these symbols according to the rules such that he can output (other) Chinese symbols as if it was responding correctly in a human like way, but only in Chinese. Moreover, this room passes the Turing test for speaking and understanding Chinese.

Searle claims that this room cannot understand Chinese because he himself does not. Therefore it is impossible to build a computer program that can have mental states and thus being what Searle calls a "strong AI".[3] It is because Searle

---
[3] It is not the purpose of this book to show that computer programs can have mental states, but to show that symbols in a robot can be about something.

1 Introduction

inside the room does not know what the Chinese symbols are about that Searle concludes that the room does not understand Chinese. Searle argues with a logical structure by using some of the following premises (Searle 1984: 39):

(1) Brains cause minds.

(2) Syntax is not sufficient for semantics.

(3) Computer programs are entirely defined by their formal, or syntactical, structure.

(4) Minds have mental contents; specifically, they have semantic contents.

Searle draws his conclusions from these premises in a correct logical deduction, but, for instance, premise (1) seems incomplete. This premise is drawn from Searle's observation that:

> [A]ll mental phenomena [...] are caused by processes going on in the brain. (Searle 1984: 18)

One could argue in favour of this, but Searle does not mention what causes these brain processes. Besides metabolic and other biological processes that are ongoing in the brain, brain processes are caused by sensory stimulation and maybe even by *sensorimotor* activity as a whole. So, at least some mental phenomena are to some extent caused by an agent's[4] interaction with its environment.

Premise (3) states that computer programs are entirely defined by their formal structure, which is correct. Only Searle equates formal with syntactical, which is correct when syntactic means something like "manipulating symbols according to the rules of the structure". The appearance of *symbols* in this definition is crucial, since they are by definition about something. If the symbols in computer programs are about something, the programs are also defined by their semantic structure.

Although Searle does not discuss this, it may be well possible that he makes another big mistake in assuming that he (the central processing unit) is the part where all mental phenomena should come together. An assumption which is debatable (see, e.g. Dennett 1991; Edelman 1992). It is more likely that consciousness is more distributed. But it is not the purpose here to explain consciousness,

---

[4] I refer to an agent when I am talking about an autonomous agent in general, be it a human, animal, robot or something else.

instead the question is how are symbols about the world. The Chinese Room is presented to make clear what the problem is and how philosophers deal with it.

Obviously Searle's Chinese Room argument found a lot of opposition in the cognitive science community. The critique presented here is in line with what has been called the "system's reply" and to a certain extend the "robot's reply".[5] The system's reply holds that it is not the system who does not understand Chinese, but it is *Searle* who does not. The system as a whole does, since it passed the Turing test.

The robot's reply goes as follows: The Chinese Room as a system does not have any other input than the Chinese symbols. So the system is a very unlikely cognitive agent. Humans have perceptual systems that receive much more information than only linguistic information. Humans perceive visual, tactile, auditory, olfactory and many other information; the Chinese Room does, as it seems, not. So, what if we build a device that has such sensors and like humans has motor capacities? Could such a system with Searle inside understand Chinese?

According to Searle in his answer to both the system's as robot's reply (Searle 1984), his argument still holds. He argues that both the system's reply and the robot's reply do not solve the syntax vs. semantics argument (premise 2). But the mistake that Searle makes is that premise (3) does not hold, thus making premise (2) redundant. Furthermore, in relation to the robot's reply, Searle fails to notice the fact that brain processes are (partly) caused by sensory input and thus mental phenomena are indirectly caused by sensory stimulation.

And even if Searle's arguments are right, in his answer to the robot's reply he fails to understand that a robot is actually a *machine*. It is not just a computer that runs a computer program. And as Searle keeps on stressing:

> "Could a machine think?" Well, in one sense, of course, we are all machines. [...] [In the] sense in which a machine is just *a physical system which is capable of performing certain kinds of operations* in that sense we are all machines, and we can think. So, trivially there are machines that can think. (Searle 1984: 35, my italics)

The reason why the phrase "a physical system which is capable of performing certain kinds of operations" is emphasised is because it is exactly that what a robot is. A robot is more than a computer that runs a computer program.

A last point that is made in this section is that Searle does not speak about development. Could Searle learn to understand Chinese if it was in the room

---

[5] See for instance the critiques that appeared in the open peer commentary of Searle's 1980 article in the *Behavioural and Brain Sciences*.

from its birth and that he learned to interpret and manipulate the symbols that were presented to him? It is strange that a distinguished philosopher like Searle does not understand that it is possible to develop computer programs which can learn.

The Chinese Room introduced the symbol grounding problem as a thought experiment that inspired Stevan Harnad to define his version of the problem (Harnad 1990). Although controversial, the Chinese Room experiment showed that there are nontrivial problems arising when one builds a cognitive robot that should be able to acquire a meaningful language system. The arguments presented against the Chinese Room are the core of the argument why robots can ground language. As shall become clear, there's more to language than just symbol manipulation according to some rules.

1.1.3 Symbol grounding: philosophical or technical?

Although it might seem very philosophical up to now, this book in no way tries to solve the philosophical problem of what is meaning. In fact there is no attempt being made in solving any philosophical problem. The only thing that is done here is to translate a philosophical problem into a technical problem, which will be tackled in this work. The solution to the technical problem could then be the meat for the philosophers to solve their problem.

Before discussing the symbol grounding problem in more technical detail, it is useful to come up with a working definition of what is meant with a symbol. Harnad's definition of a symbol is very much in line with the standard definition used in artificial intelligence. This definition is primarily based on physical symbol systems introduced by Newell and Simon Newell (1980; 1990). According to Harnad symbols are basically a set of arbitrary tokens that can be manipulated by rules made of tokens; the tokens (either atomic or composite) are "semantically interpretable" (Harnad 1990).

In this book a definition taken from semiotics will be adopted. Following Charles Sanders Peirce and Umberto Eco (1976; 1986) a symbol will be equalled with a SIGN. Using a different, but more familiar terminology than Peirce Nöth (1990), a sign consists of three elements (Chandler 1994):[6]

Representamen The form which the sign takes (not necessarily material).

Interpretant The sense made of the sign.

---

[6] An instructive introduction into the theory of semiotics can be found on the world-wide web (Chandler 1994). The work of Peirce is collected in Peirce 1931–1958.

Object To which the sign refers.

Rather than using Peirce's terms, the terms adopted in this book are FORM for representamen, MEANING for interpretant and REFERENT for object. The adopted terminology is in line with Steels' terminology (Steels 1999). It is also interesting to note that the Peircean sign is not the same as the Saussurean sign (de Saussure 1974). De Saussure does not discuss the notion of the referent. In de Saussure's terminology the form is called "signifier" and the meaning is called the "signified".

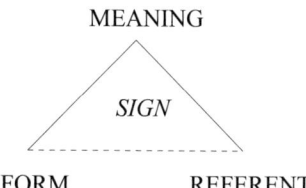

Figure 1.1: A semiotic triangle shows how a referent, meaning and form are related as a sign.

How the three units of the sign are combined is often illustrated with the semiotic triangle (Figure 1.1). According to Peirce, a sign becomes a "symbol" when its form, in relation to its meaning "is arbitrary or purely conventional – so that the relationship must be learnt" (Chandler 1994). The relation can be conventionalised in language. According to the semiotic triangle and the above, a symbol is *per definition* grounded.

In the experiments reported in this book, the robots try to develop a shared and grounded lexicon about the real world objects they can detect. They do so by communicating a name of the categorisation of a real world object. In line with the theory of semiotics, the following definitions are made:

Referent The referent is the real world object that is subject of the communication.

Meaning The meaning is the categorisation that is made of the real world object and that is used in the communication.

Form The form is the name that is communicated. In principle its shape is arbitrary, but in a shared lexicon it is conventionalised through language use.

1 Introduction

Symbol A symbol is the relation between the referent, the meaning and the form as illustrated in the semiotic triangle.

This brings us to the technically hard part of the symbol grounding problem that remains to be solved: How can an agent construct the relations between a form, meaning and referent? In his article Harnad (1990) recognises three main tasks of grounding symbols:

Iconisation Analogue signals need to be transformed to ICONIC REPRESENTATION (or icons).[7]

Discrimination "[The ability] to judge whether two inputs are the same or different, and, if different, how different they are." Note that in Harnad's article, discrimination is already pursued at the perceptual level. In this book, discrimination is done at the categorical level.

Identification "[The ability] to be able to assign a unique (usually arbitrary) response – a "name" – to a class of inputs, treating them all as equivalent or *invariant* in some respect." (Harnad 1990, my italics)

So, what is the problem? Analogue signals can be iconised (or recorded) rather simple with meaningless sub-symbolic structures. The ability to discriminate is easy to implement just by comparing two different sensory inputs. The ability to identify requires to find *invariant* properties of objects, events and state of affairs. Since finding distinctions is rather easy, the big problem in grounding actually reduces to identifying

> invariant features of the sensory projection that will reliably distinguish a member of a category from any non-members with which it could be confused. (Harnad 1990)

Although people might disagree, for the roboticists this is not more than a technical problem. The question is whether or not there exist real invariant features of a category in the world. This probably could be doubted quite seriously (see e.g.Harnad 1993). For the time being it is assumed that there are invariant properties in the world and it will be shown that these invariants can be found if an embodied agent is equipped with the right physical body and control. The latter inference is in line with the PHYSICAL GROUNDING HYPOTHESIS (Brooks 1990), which will be discussed below.

---

[7] The terms "icon" and "iconisation", as they are used by Harnad and will be adopted here, should not be confused with Peirce's notion of these terms.

Stevan Harnad proposes that the SGP for a robot could possibly be solved by invoking (hybrid) connectionist models with a serious interface to the outside world in the form of TRANSDUCERS (or sensors) (Harnad 1993). Harnad, however admits that the symbol grounding problem also might be solved with other than connectionist architectures.

1.1.4 Grounding symbols in language

In line with the work of Luc Steels the symbols are grounded in language (see e.g. Steels 1997b; 1999). Why grounding symbols in language directly and not ground the symbols first and develop a shared lexicon afterwards? Associating the grounded symbols with a lexicon is then a simple task, (see e.g. Oliphant 1997; Steels 1996c). However, as Wittgenstein (1958) pointed out, the meaning of something depends on how it is used in language. It is situated in the environment of an agent and depends on the bodily experience of it. Language use gives feedback on the appropriateness of the sense that is made of a referent. So, language gives rise to the construction of meanings and the construction of meaning gives rise to language development. Hence, meaning co-evolves with language.

That this approach seems natural can be illustrated with Roussau's paradox. Although for communication, categorisation of reality needs to be similar to different language users, different languages do not always employ the same categorisations. For instance, there are different referential frames to categorise spatial relations in different language communities. In English there are spatial relations like *left*, *right*, *front* and *back* relative to some axis. However in Tzetal, a Mayan language, this frame of reference is not used. The Tzetal speakers live in an area with mountains and their frame of reference is absolute in relation to the mountain they are on. The spatial relations in this language can be translated with 'uphill', 'downhill' and 'across'. If something is higher up the mountain in relation to the speaker, they can say "this something is uphill of me".

So, if a novel language user enters a language society, how would it know how to categorise such a spatial relation? To know this, the new language user has to learn how to categorise the reality in relation to the language that is used by the particular language society. Therefore it is thought to be necessary to ground meaning in language. How lexicon development interacts with the development of meaning will become clearer in the remainder of this book.

1 Introduction

1.1.5 Physical grounding hypothesis

Another approach to grounding is physical grounding. In his article *Elephants Don't Play Chess*, Rodney Brooks (1990) proposed the physical grounding hypothesis as an additional constraint to the physical symbol system hypothesis.

> The physical grounding hypothesis states that to build a system that is intelligent it is necessary to have its representations grounded in the physical world. (Brooks 1990)

The advantage of the physical grounding hypothesis over physical symbol system hypothesis is that the system (or agent) is directly coupled to the real world through its set of sensors and actuators.

> Typed input and output are no longer of interest. They are not physically grounded. (Brooks 1990)

In Brooks' approach symbols are not a necessary condition for intelligent behaviour anymore (Brooks 1990; 1991). Intelligent behaviour can emerge from a set of simple couplings of an agent's sensors with its actuators,[8] as is also shown in e.g. Steels & Brooks 1995, Steels 1994a, and Steels 1996b. An example is "wall following". Suppose a robot has two simple behaviours: (1) the tendency to move towards the wall and (2) the tendency to move away from the wall. If the robot incorporates both behaviours at once, then the resulting *emergent* behaviour is wall following. Note that agents designed from this perspective have no cognitive abilities. They are reactive agents, like e.g. ants are, rather than cognitive agents that can manipulate symbolic meanings.

The argument that Brooks uses to propose the physical grounding hypothesis is that

> [evolution] suggests that problem solving behaviour, language, expert knowledge and application, and reason, are all rather simple once the essence of being and reacting are available. That essence is the ability to move around in a dynamic environment, sensing the surroundings to a degree sufficient to achieve the necessary maintenance of life and reproduction. (Brooks 1990)

This rapid evolution is illustrated in Figure 1.2. Brooks also uses this argument of the rapid evolution of human intelligence as opposed to the slow evolution of life on earth in relation to symbols.

---

[8] Note that Brooks' approach does not necessarily invoke connectionist models.

1.1 Symbol grounding problem

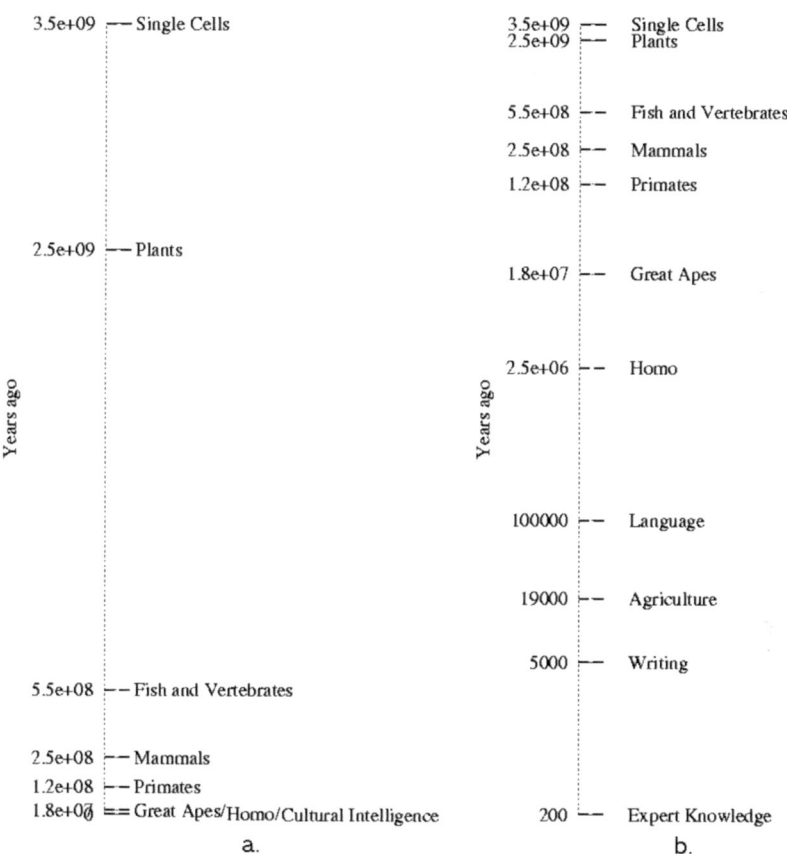

Figure 1.2: (a) The evolutionary time-scale of life and cognitive abilities on earth. After the entrance of the great apes, evolution of man went so fast that it cannot be shown on the same plot, unless it is shown in logarithmic scale (see b). It appears from the plot that cultural evolution works much faster than biological evolution. Time-scale is adapted from Brooks (1990).

1 Introduction

> [O]nce evolution had symbols and representations things started moving rather quickly. Thus symbols are the key invention … Without a carefully built physical grounding any symbolic representation will be mismatched to its sensors and actuators. (Brooks 1990)

To explore the physical grounding hypothesis, Brooks and his co-workers at the MIT AI Lab developed a software architecture called the SUBSUMPTION ARCHITECTURE (Brooks 1986). This architecture is designed to connect a robot's sensors to its actuators so that it "embeds the robot correctly in the world" (Brooks 1990). The point made by Brooks is that intelligence can emerge from an agent's physical interactions with the world. So, the robot that needs to be built should be both embodied and situated. The approach proposed by Brooks is also known as "behaviour-based AI".

1.1.6 Physical symbol grounding

The physical grounding hypothesis (Brooks 1990) states that intelligent agents should be grounded in the real world. However, it also states that the intelligence need not to be represented with symbols. According to the physical symbol system hypothesis the thus physically grounded agents are no cognitive agents. The physical symbol system hypothesis (Newell 1980) states that cognitive agents are *physical symbol systems* with the following features (Newell 1990: 77):

Memory
- Contains structures that contain symbol tokens
- Independently modifiable at some grain size

Symbols
- Patterns that provide access to distal structures
- A symbol token is the occurrence of a pattern in a structure

Operations Processes that take symbol structures as input and produce symbol structures as output

Interpretation Processes that take symbol structures as input and execute operations

Capacities
- Sufficient memory and symbols
- Complete compositionality
- Complete interpretability

1.1 Symbol grounding problem

Clearly, an agent that uses language is a physical symbol system. It should have a memory to store an ontology and lexicon. It has symbols. The agent makes operations on the symbols and interprets them. Furthermore, it should have the capacity to do so. In this sense, the robots of this book are physical symbol systems.

A physical symbol system somehow has to represent the symbols. Hence the physical grounding hypothesis is not the best candidate. But since the definition of a symbol adopted in this book has an explicit relation to the referent, the complete symbol cannot be represented inside a robot. The only parts of the symbols that can be represented are the meaning and the form. Like in the physical grounding hypothesis, a part of the agent's knowledge is in the world. The problem is: how can the robot *ground* the relation between internal representations and the referent? Although Newell (1990) recognises the problem, he does not investigate a solution to it.

This problem is what Harnad (1990) called the symbol grounding problem. Because there is a strong relation between the physical grounding hypothesis (that the robot has its knowledge grounded in the real world) and the physical symbol system hypothesis (that cognitive agents are physical symbol systems) it is useful to rename the symbol grounding problem in the PHYSICAL SYMBOL GROUNDING PROBLEM.

The physical symbol grounding problem is very much related to the FRAME PROBLEM (Pylyshyn 1987). The frame problem deals with the question how a robot can represent things of the dynamically changing real world and operate in it. In order to do so, the robot needs to solve the symbol grounding problem.

As mentioned, this is a very hard problem. Why is the physical symbol grounding problem so hard? When sensing something in the real world under different circumstances, the physical sensing of this something is different as well. Humans are nevertheless very good at identifying this something under these different circumstances. For robots this is different. The one-to-many mappings of this something unto the different perceptions needs to be interpreted so that there is a more or less one-to-one mapping between this something and a symbol, i.e. the identification needs to be invariant. Studies have shown that this is an extremely difficult task for robots.

Already numerous systems have been physically grounded (see e.g. Brooks 1990; Steels 1994a; Barnes et al. 1997; Kröse et al. 1999; Tani & Nolfi 1998; Berthouze & Kuniyoshi 1998; Pfeifer & Scheier 1999; Billard & Hayes 1997; Rosenstein & Cohen 1998a; Yanco & Stein 1993 and many more). However, a lot of these systems do not ground symbolic structures because they have no form (or arbi-

1 Introduction

trary label) attached. These applications ground "simple" physical behaviours in the Brooksean sense. Only a few physically grounded systems mentioned above grounded symbolic structures, for instance in the case of Yanco & Stein (1993), Billard & Hayes (1997), and Rosenstein & Cohen (1998a).

Yanco & Stein developed a troupe of two robots that could learn to associate certain actions with a pre-defined set of words. One robot would decide what action is to be taken and communicates a relating signal to the other robot. The learning strategy they used was reinforcement learning where the feedback in their task completion was provided by a human instructor. If both robots performed the same task, a positive reinforcement was given, and when both robots did not, the feedback consisted of a negative reinforcement.

The research was primarily focussed on the learning of associations between word and meaning on physical robots. No real solution was attempted to solve the grounding problem and only a limited set of word-meaning associations were pre-defined. In addition, the robots learned by means of supervised learning with a human instructor. Yanco & Stein showed, however, that a group of robots could converge in learning such a communication system.

In Billard & Hayes (1997) two robots grounded a language by means of imitation. The experiments consisted of a teacher robot, which had a pre-defined communication system, and a student robot, which had to learn the teacher's language by following it. The learning mechanism was provided by an associative neural network architecture called DRAMA. This neural network learned associations between communication signals and sensorimotor couplings. Feedback was provided by the student's evaluation if it was still following the teacher.

So, the language was grounded by the student using this neural network architecture, which is derived from Wilshaw networks. Associations for the teacher robot were pre-defined in their couplings and weights. The student could learn a limited amount of associations of actions and perceptions very rapidly (Billard 1998).

Rosenstein & Cohen (1998a) developed a robot that could ground time series by using the so-called method of delays, which is drawn from the theory of non-linear dynamics. The time series that the robots produce by interacting in their environment are categorised by comparing their delay vectors, which is a low-dimensional reconstruction of the original time series, with a set of prototypes. The concepts the robots thus ground could be used for grounding word-meanings (Rosenstein & Cohen 1998b).

The method proposed by Rosenstein & Cohen has been incorporated in a language experiment where two robots play FOLLOW ME GAMES to construct an ontology and lexicon to communicate their actions (Vogt 1999; 2000b). This was a preliminary experiment, but the results appear to be promising.

A similar experiment on language acquisition on mobile robots has been done by the same group of Rosenstein & Cohen at the University of Massachusetts (Oates, Eyler-Walker & Cohen 1999). The time series of a robot's actions are categorised using a clustering method for distinctions (Oates 1999). Similarities between observed time series and prototypes are calculated using dynamical time warping. The thus conceptualised time series are then analysed in terms of human linguistic interactions, who describe what they see when watching a movie of the robot operating (Oates, Eyler-Walker & Cohen 1999).

Other research propose simulated solutions to the symbol grounding problem, notably Cangelosi & Parisi (1998) and Greco, Cangelosi & Harnad (1998). In his work Angelo Cangelosi created an ecology of edible and non-edible mushrooms. Agents that are provided with neural networks learn to categorise the mushrooms from "visible" features into the categories of edible and non-edible mushrooms.

A problem with simulations of grounding is that the problem cannot be solved in principle, because the agents that "ground" symbols do not do so in the *real world*. However, these simulations are useful in that they can learn us more about how categories and words could be grounded. One of the important findings of Cangelosi's research is that communication helps the agents to improve their categorisation abilities (Cangelosi, Greco & Harnad 2000).

Additional work can be found in *The grounding of word meaning: Data and models* (Gasser 1998), the proceedings of a joint workshop on the grounding of word meaning of the AAAI and Cognitive Science Society. In these proceedings, grounding of word meaning is discussed among computer scientists, linguistics and psychologists.

So, the problem that is tried to be solved in this book is what might be called the physical symbol grounding problem. This problem shall not be treated philosophically but technically. It will be shown that the quality of the physically grounded interaction is essential to the quality of the symbol grounding. This is in line with Brooks' observation that a.o. language is

> rather easy once the essence of being and reacting are available.
> (Brooks 1990)

Now that it is clear that the physical symbol grounding problem in this work is considered to be a technical problem, the question rises how it is solved. In 1996, Luc Steels published a series of papers in which some simple mechanisms were

1 Introduction

introduced by which autonomous agents could develop a "grounded" lexicon (Steels 1996c,d,a,e, for an overview see Steels 1997c). Before this work is discussed, a brief introduction in the origins of language is given.

1.2 Language origins

Why is it that humans have language and other animals cannot? Until not very long ago, language has been ascribed as a creation of God. Modern science, however, assumes that life as it currently exists has evolved gradually. Most influencing in this view has been the book of Charles Darwin *The origins of species* (1968). In the beginning of the existence of life on earth, humans were not yet present. Modern humans evolved only about 100,000 to 200,000 years ago. With the arrival of homo sapiens, language is thought to have emerged. So, although life on earth is present for about 3.5 billion years, humans are on earth only a fraction of this time.

Language is exclusive to humans. Although other animals have communication systems, they do not use a complex communication system like humans do. At some point in evolution, humans must have developed language capabilities. These capabilities did not evolve in other animals. It is likely that these capabilities evolved biologically and are present in the human brain. But, what are these capabilities? They are likely to be the initial conditions from which language emerged. Some of them might have co-evolved with language, but most of them were likely to be present before language originated. This is likely because biological evolution is very slow, whereas language on the evolutionary time scale evolved very fast.

The capabilities include at least the following things: (1) The ability to associate meanings of things that exist in the world with arbitrary word-forms. (2) The ability to communicate these meaningful symbols to other language users. (3) The ability to vocalise such symbols. (4) The ability to map auditory stimuli of such vocalisations to the symbols. And (5) the ability to use grammatical structures. These abilities must have evolved somehow, because they are principle features of human language. There are probably more capabilities, but they serve to accomplish the five capabilities mentioned. In line with the symbol grounding problem this book concentrates on the first two principle capabilities.

Until the 1950s there was very little research going on about the evolution and origins of language. Since Noam Chomsky wrote his influential paper on syntactic structures (Chomsky 1956), linguistic research and research on the evolution of language boomed. It took until 1976 for the first conference on the origins

1.2 Language origins

and evolution of language to be held (Harnad, Steklis & Lancaster 1976). Most papers of this conference involved empirical research on ape studies, studies on gestural communication and theoretical and philosophical studies. Until very recently, many studies had a high level of speculation and some strange theories were proposed. For an overview of theories that were proposed on the origins and evolution of language until 1996, see Aitchison (1996).

1.2.1 Computational approaches to language evolution

With the rise of advanced computer techniques in artificial intelligence (AI) and Artificial Life (ALife), it became possible to study the origins and evolution of language computationally. In the 1990s many such studies were done. It is probably impossible to say with this approach exactly how language originated, but the same is probably true for all other investigations. The only contribution computer techniques can bring is a possible scenario of language evolution. Possible initial conditions and hypotheses can be validated using computer techniques, which may shed light on how language may have emerged. Furthermore, one can rule out some theories, because they do not work on a computer.

Many early (and still very popular) scenarios were investigated based on Chomsky's theory about a UNIVERSAL GRAMMAR, which are supposed to be innate.[9] According to Chomsky, the innate universal grammar codes "principles" and "parameters" that enable infants to learn any language. The principles encode universals of languages as they are found in the world. Depending on the language environment of a language learner, the parameters are set, which allows the principles of a particular language to become learnable. So, the quest for computer scientist is to use evolutionary computation techniques to come up with a genetic code of the universal grammar. That this is difficult can already be inferred from the fact that up to now not one non-trivial universal tendency of language is found which is valid for every language.

In the early nineties a different approach gained popularity. This approach is based on the paradigm that language is a complex dynamical adaptive system. Here it is believed that universal tendencies of language are learned and evolve culturally.

Agent based simulations were constructed in which the agents tried to develop (usually an aspect of) language. The agents are made adaptive using techniques taken from AI and adaptive behaviour (or ALife). The main approach taken is

---

[9] One of the reasons why Chomsky's theory is still very popular amongst computational linguistics is that the theory has a computational approach.

1 Introduction

a bottom-up approach. In contrast to the top-down approach, where the intelligence is modelled and implemented in rules, the bottom-up approach starts with implementing simple *sensorimotor* interfaces and learning rules, and tries to increase the complexity of the intelligent agent step by step.

Various models have been built by a variety of computer scientists and computational linguists to investigate the evolution of language and communication (e.g. Cangelosi & Parisi 1998; Kirby & Hurford 1997; MacLennan 1991; Oliphant 1997; Werner & Dyer 1991). It goes beyond the scope of this book to discuss all this research, but there is one research that is of particular interest for this book, namely the work of Mike Oliphant (1997; 1998; 1999).

Oliphant simulates the learning of a symbolic communication system in which a fixed number of signals are matched with a fixed number of meanings. The number of signals that can be learned is equal to the number of meanings. Such a coherent mapping is called a Saussurean sign (de Saussure 1974) and is the idealisation of language. The learning paradigm of Oliphant is an *observational* one and he uses an associative network incorporating Hebbian learning. With observational is meant that the agents during a language game have access to both the linguistic signal and its meaning.

As long as the communicating agents are aware of the meaning they are signalling, the Saussurean sign can be learned (Oliphant 1997; 1999). The awareness of the meaning meant by the signal should be acquired by observation in the environment. Oliphant further argues that reinforcement types of learning as used by Yanco & Stein (1993) and Steels (1996c) are not necessary and unlikely (see also the discussion about the no negative feedback evidence in Section 1.3). But he does not say they are not a possible source of language learning (Oliphant 1999).

The claim Oliphant makes has implications on why only humans can learn language. According to Oliphant (1998), animals have difficulty in matching a signal to a meaning when it is not an innate feature of the animal. Although this is arguable (Oliphant refers here to e.g. Gardner & Gardner 1969 and Premack 1971), he observes the fact that in these animal learning the communication is explicitly taught by the researchers.

1.2.2 Steels' approach

This adaptive behaviour based approach has also been adopted by Luc Steels (e.g. Steels 1996c,d; 1997c). The work of Steels is based on the notion of LANGUAGE GAMES (Wittgenstein 1958). In language games agents construct a lexicon through cultural interaction, individual adaptation and self-organisation. The view of Wittgenstein is adopted that language gets its meaning through its use and should be investigated accordingly. The research presented in this book is in line with the work done by Luc Steels. This research is part of the ongoing research done at the Sony Computer Science Laboratory in Paris and at the Artificial Intelligence Laboratory of the Free University of Brussels (VUB), both directed by Luc Steels.

The investigation in Paris and Brussels is done on both simulations and grounded robots. It focuses on the origins of sound systems, in particular in the field of phonetics (de Boer 1997; 1999; Oudeyer 1999), the origins of meaning (Steels 1996d; Steels & Vogt 1997; de Jong & Vogt 1998; Vogt 1998a; de Jong & Steels 1999), the emergence of lexicons (Steels 1996c; Steels & Kaplan 1998; Kaplan 2000; Vogt 1998b; Van Looveren 1999), the origins of communication (de Jong 1999a; 2000) and the emergence of syntax (Steels 2000). Within these subjects various aspects of language like stochasticity (Steels & Kaplan 1998; Kaplan 2000), dynamic language change (Steels 1997a; Steels & McIntyre 1999; de Boer & Vogt 1999), multi-word utterances (Van Looveren 1999), situation concepts (de Jong 1999b) and grounding (Belpaeme, Steels & van Looveren 1998; Steels & Vogt 1997; Steels 1999; Kaplan 2000) are investigated.

Bart de Boer of the VUB AI Lab has shown how agents can develop a human-like vowel system through self-organisation (de Boer 1997; 1999). These agents were modelled with a human like vocal tract and auditory system. Through cultural interactions and imitations the agents learned vowel systems as they are found prominently among human languages.

First in simulations (Steels 1996c,d) and later in grounded experiments on mobile robots (Steels & Vogt 1997; Vogt 1998a,b; de Jong & Vogt 1998) and on the Talking Heads (Belpaeme, Steels & van Looveren 1998; Kaplan 2000; Steels 1999) the emergence of meaning and lexicons have been investigated. Since the mobile robots experiment is the issue of the current book, only the other work will be discussed briefly here.

The simulations began fairly simple by assuming a relative perfect world (Steels 1996c,d). Software agents played naming and discrimination games to create lexicons and meaning. The lexicons were formed to name predefined meanings and the meanings were created to discriminate predefined visual features. In later experiments more complexity was added to the experiments. From findings of the mobile robots experiments (Vogt 1998a) it was found that the ideal assumptions of the naming game, for instance, considering the topic to be known by the hearer, were not satisfied. Therefore a more sophisticated naming game was developed that could handle noise of the environment (Steels & Kaplan 1998).

1 Introduction

Figure 1.3: The Talking Heads as it is installed at Sony CSL Paris.

For coupling the discrimination game to the naming game, which first has been done in Steels & Vogt (1997), a new software environment was created: the GEOM world (Steels 1999). The GEOM world consisted of an environment in which geometric figures could be conceptualised through the discrimination game. The resulting representations could then be lexicalized using the naming game. The Talking Heads are also situated in a world of geometrical shapes that are pasted on a white board the cameras of the heads look at (Figure 1.3).

The Talking Heads consist of a couple of installations that are distributed around the world. Installations currently exist in Paris at the Sony CSL, in Brussels at the VUB AI Lab, in Amsterdam at the Intelligent Autonomous Systems laboratory of the University of Amsterdam. Temporal installations have been operational in Antwerp, Tokyo, Laussane, Cambridge, London and at another site in Paris. Agents can travel the world through the internet and embody themselves into a Talking Head. A Talking Head is a pan-tilt camera connected to a computer. The Talking Heads play language games with the cognitive capaci-

1.2 Language origins

ties and memories that each agent has or has acquired. The language games are similar to the ones that are presented in the subsequent chapters. The main difference is that the Talking Heads do not move from their place, which the mobile robots do. The Talking Heads have cameras as their primary sensory apparatus and there are some slight differences in the cognitive capabilities as will become clear in the rest of this book.

All these experiments show similar results. Label-representation (or form-meaning) pairs can be grounded in sensorimotor control, for which (cultural) interactions, individual adaptation and self-organisation are the key mechanisms. A similar conclusion will be drawn at the end of this book. The results of the experiments on mobile robots will be compared with the Talking Heads as reported mainly in Steels 1999. Other findings based on the different variations of the model, which inspects the different influences of the model will be compared with the PhD thesis of Frédéric Kaplan of Sony CSL in Paris (Kaplan 2000).[10]

A last set of experiments that will be brought to the reader's attention is the work done by Edwin de Jong of the VUB AI Lab. De Jong has done an interesting experiment in which he showed that the communication systems that emerged under the conditions by which language research is done in Paris and Brussels are indeed complex dynamical systems (de Jong 2000). The communication systems of his own experiments all evolved towards an attractor and he showed empirically that the system was a complex dynamical system.

Using simulations, de Jong studied the evolution of communication in experiments in which agents construct a communication system about situation concepts (de Jong 1999b). In his simulation, a population of agents were in some situation that required a response in the form of an action. I.e. if one of the agents observed something (e.g. a predator), all the agents needed to go in some save state. De Jong investigated if the agents could benefit from communication, by allowing the agents to develop a shared lexicon that is grounded in this simulated world. The agents were given a mechanism to evaluate, based on their previous experiences, whether to trust on their observations or on some communicated signal. The signal is communicated by one of the agents that had observed something.

While doing so, the agents developed an ontology of situation concepts and a lexicon in basically the same way as in the work of Luc Steels. This means that the robots play discrimination games to build up the ontology and naming games

---

[10] Currently Frédéric Kaplan is working on human-machine interaction on the AIBO robot that looks like a dog and which has been developed by Sony CSL in Tokyo. Naturally, the AIBO learns language according to the same principles advocated by our labs.

to develop a language. A major difference is that the experiments are situated in a task oriented approach. The agents have to respond correctly to some situation. To do so, the agents can evaluate their success based on the appropriateness of their actions. As will be discussed in Chapter 3, de Jong used a different method for categorisation, called the ADAPTIVE SUBSPACE METHOD (de Jong & Vogt 1998).

One interesting finding of de Jong was that it is not necessary that agents use feedback on the outcome of their linguistic interactions to construct a coherent lexicon, provided that the robots have access to the meaning of such an interaction and lateral inhibition was assured. Hence this confirms the findings of Mike Oliphant (1998). Questions about the feedback on language games are also issued in the field of human language acquisition.

1.3 Language acquisition

Although children learn an existing language, lessons from the language acquisition field may help to understand how humans acquire symbols. This knowledge may in turn help to build a physically grounded symbol system. In the experiments presented in the forthcoming, the robots develop only a lexicon by producing and understanding one word utterances. In the literature of language acquisition, this period is called EARLY LEXICON DEVELOPMENT. Infants need to learn how words are associated with meanings. How do they do that?

In early lexicon development it is important to identify what cues an infant receives of the language it is learning. These cues not only focus on the linguistic information, but also on the extra-linguistic information. It is not hard to imagine that when no linguistic knowledge is available about a language, it seems impossible to learn such a language without extra-linguistic cues such as pointing or feedback about whether one understands a word correctly. (Psycho-) linguists have not agreed upon what information is available to a child and to what extend.

The POVERTY OF THE STIMULUS argument led Chomsky to propose his linguistic theory. Although an adult language user can express an unlimited number of sentences, a language learner receives a limited amount of linguistic information to master the language. With this argument Chomsky concluded that linguistic structures must be innate. But perhaps there are other mechanisms that allow humans to learn language. Some might be learned and some might be innate.

A problem that occupies the nativist linguists is the so-called NO NEGATIVE FEEDBACK EVIDENCE (e.g. Bowerman 1988). The problem is that in the innate approach language can only be learned when both positive and negative feedback on language is available to a language learner. However, psychological research has shown that no negative feedback is provided by adult language users (Braine 1971). Demetras and colleagues, however showed that there is more negative feedback provided than assumed (Demetras, Nolan Post & Snow 1986). In addition, it is perhaps underestimated how much feedback a child can evaluate itself from its environment. Furthermore, feedback is thought to be an important principle in cognitive development (see e.g. Clancey 1997).

One alternative for the feedback, which is assumed to be provided after the linguistic act, is the establishment of joint attention *prior* to the linguistic communication. Do children really receive such input? Early studies of Tomasello showed that children can learn better when joint attention is established, as long as this is done spontaneously by the child (Tomasello, Mannle & Kruger 1986, cited in Barrett 1995). Explicit drawing of attention seemed to have a negative side effect. Although it has been assumed that pointing was a frequently used method to draw a child's attention, later studies have argued against such this assumption. Tomasello reported in a later studies that pointing is not necessary for learning language, *provided* there is explicit feedback (Tomasello & Barton 1994).

In this article, Tomasello and Barton report on experiments where children learn novel words under two different conditions. In one condition, children do not receive extra-linguistic cues when the word-form is presented. There is a so-called "nonostensive" context. When at a later moment the corresponding referent is shown, a positive feedback is given if the child correctly relates the referent with given word-form. If the child relates the word-form to an incorrect referent, negative feedback is given. In the second condition, joint attention is established simultaneous with the presentation of the word-form. In this condition the child receives a so-called "ostensive" context. Tomasello & Barton (1994) showed in their experiments that children could equally well learn novel word-meaning relations in both condition.

Yet another strategy is proposed by Eve Clark (1993). She argues that children can fill in knowledge gaps when receiving novel language, provided the context was known.

So, a lot of strategies appear to be available to a language learner, and there may be more. It is not unlikely that a combination of the available strategies is used; perhaps some more frequent than others. A natural question rises: Which strategies work and which do not? In this book experiments are presented that investigate both the role of feedback and joint attention.

1 Introduction

1.4 Setting up the goals

This book presents the development and results of a series of experiments where two mobile robots develop a grounded lexicon. The experiments are based on language games that have first been implemented on mobile robots in Steels & Vogt (1997) and Vogt (1997). The goal of the language games is to construct an ontology and lexicon about the objects the robots can detect in their environment.

The sensory equipment with which the robots detect their world is kept simple, namely sensors that can only detect light intensities. One of the goals was to develop the experiments without changing the simplicity of the robots very much and to keep the control architecture within the behaviour-based design. Luc Steels (1996c) hypothesises three basic mechanisms for language evolution, which have been introduced above: individual adaptation, cultural evolution and self-organisation.

In a language game, robots produce a sensorimotor behaviour to perceive their environment. The environment consists of a set of light sources, which are distinguishable in height. The raw sensory data that results from this sensing is segmented, yielding a set of segments of which each segment relates to the detection of a light source. These segments can be described by features, which are categorised by the individual robots. The categorisation is processed by so-called DISCRIMINATION GAMES (Steels 1996d). In this process the robots try to develop categories that discriminates one segment from another. The lexicon is formed based on an interaction and adaptation strategy modelled in what has been called NAMING GAMES (Steels 1996c). In a naming game one robot has the role of a speaker and the other robot has the role of the hearer. The speaker tries to name the categorisation (or meaning) of a segment it has chosen to be the topic. The hearer tries to identify the topic using both linguistic and extra-linguistic information when available.

The language game is adaptive in that the robots can adapt either their ontology or lexicon when they fail to categorise of name the topic. This way they may be successful in future games. In addition, the robots can adapt association strengths that they use to select elements of their ontology or lexicon. The selection principle is very much based on natural selection as proposed by Charles Darwin (1968), but the evolution is not spread over generations of organisms, but over "generations" of language games. The principle is that the most effective elements are selected more and ineffective ones are selected less frequently, or even not at all. This way the most effective elements of the language are spread in the language community, thus leading to a cultural evolution.

The idea of cultural evolution has best been described by Richard Dawkins in his book *The Selfish Gene* (1976). In this book Dawkins proposes the notion of MEMES. Memes are elements that carry the notion of ideas, like the idea of a wheel. Like genes, memes are generated as varieties of previous ideas and possibly as complete new ideas. The memes are spread in the society by cultural interactions. The evolution of memes is similar to that of genetic evolution and good memes survive, whereas bad memes do not. However, the cultural evolution is much faster than biological evolution and several generations of memes can occur in a society within the lifetime of an organism. When changing the notion of memes into language elements, a cultural evolution of language arrives. The emergence of language through cultural evolution is based on the same principle as biological evolution, namely self-organisation.

Three main research questions are raised in this book:

1. Can the symbol grounding problem be solved with these robots by constructing a lexicon through individual adaptation, (cultural) interaction and self-organisation? And if so, how is this accomplished?

2. What are the important types of extra-linguistic information that agents should share when developing a coherent communication system?

3. What is the influence of the physical conditions and interaction of the robots on developing a grounded lexicon?

The first question is an obvious one and can be answered with yes, but to a certain extend. As argued in Section 1.1.3, the symbol grounding problem is solved when the robots are able to construct a semiotic sign of which the form is either arbitrary or conventionalised. Since the robots try to ground a shared lexicon, the form has to be conventionalised. Therefore the robots solve the symbol grounding problem when they successfully play a language game. I.e. when both robots are able to identify a symbol with the same form that stands for the same referent.

Throughout the book the model that accomplishes the task is presented and revised to come up with two language game models that work best. Although the basics of the models, namely the discrimination- and naming game are very simple, the implementation on these simple robots has proven to be extremely difficult. Not all the designer's frustrations are made explicit in this book, but working with LEGO robots and "home-made" sensorimotor boards made life not easier. In order to concentrate on the grounding problem, some practical assumptions have been made leaving some unsolved technical problems.

1 Introduction

The two models that are proposed at the end of the experimental results show different interaction strategies that answer the second question. Both feedback and joint-attention are important types of extra-linguistic information necessary for agents to develop a lexicon, although not necessarily used simultaneously. How feedback and joint attention can be established is left as an open question. Technical limitations drove to leave this question open as one of the remaining frustrations. Some of these limitations are the same that introduced the assumptions that have been made.

Although more difficult to show, the quality of physical interactions have an important influence on the robots' ability to ground a lexicon. When the robots are not well adapted to their environment (or vice versa) no meaningful lexicon can emerge. In addition, when the robots can co-ordinate their actions well to accomplish a certain (sub)task, they will be better in grounding a lexicon than when the co-ordination is weak.

1.5 Contributions

How does this book contribute to the field of artificial intelligence and cognitive science? The main contributions made in this book that there is an autonomous system that is grounded in the real world of which no parts of the ontology or lexicon is pre-defined. The categorisation is organised hierarchically by prototypical categories. In addition, the book investigates different types of extra-linguistic information that the robots can use to develop a shared lexicon. No single aspect is more or less unique. However, the combination of some aspects is.

Table 1.1 shows the contributions of research that is most relevant to this work. The table lists some aspects that the various researchers have contributed in their work. The aspects that are listed are thought to be most relevant to this work. Note that with Steels' work the Talking Heads experiments are meant. In the discussion at the end of this book, a more detailed comparison with the Talking Heads is made.

Of the related work, the work of Cangelosi & Parisi (1998), de Jong (2000), and Oliphant (1997) is not grounded in the real world. The work of Cangelosi et al. and de Jong is grounded only in simulations. This makes the grounding process relatively easy, because it avoids the problems that come about when categorising the real world. Oliphant does not ground meaning at all. The work of this book is grounded in the real world.

Some researchers, notably Billard & Hayes (1997), Cangelosi & Parisi (1998), and Yanco & Stein (1993), pre-define the language. I.e. they define how a word-

1.5 Contributions

Table 1.1: Various aspects investigated by different researchers. Each column of the table is reserved for a particular research. The related work in this table is from (the group of): Billard (B), Cangelosi (C), de Jong (D), Oliphant (O), Rosenstein (R), Steels (S), Vogt (V), and Yanco & Stein (Y). The other symbols in the table stand for "yes" (+), "no" (−) and "not applicable" (·).

Aspect	B	C	D	O	R	S	V	Y
Grounded in real world	+	−	−	−	+	+	+	+
Language pre-defined	+	+	−	−	·	−	−	+
Meaning pre-defined	+/−	−	−	+	−	−	−	+
Prototypical categories	−	−	−	·	+	−	+	−
Hierarchical layering of categories	−	−	+	·	−	+	+	−
Nr. of meanings given	+/−	−	−	+	−	−	−	+
Nr. of forms given	+	+	−	+	·	−	−	+
Nr. of agents	2	≥ 2	≥ 2	≥ 2	1	≥ 2	2	≥ 2
Calibrated world	−	−	−	·	−	+	−	−
Mobile agents	+	+	+	·	+	−	+	+
Camera vision	−	·	·	·	−	+	−	−
Autonomous	+	+	+	+	+	+	+	−
Task oriented	+	+	+	−	−	−	−	+
Extra-linguistic	−	−	+	+	·	−	+	−

form relates to a behaviour or real world phenomenon. The pre-defined language in Billard and Hayes' experiments is only given to the teacher robot, the student robot has to learn the language. Although in the work of Yanco & Stein the robots learn the language, the researchers have pre-defined the language and they provide feedback whether the language is used successfully. Rosenstein & Cohen (1998a) do not model language yet. Hence the question if they pre-define the language is not applicable. In the work done at the VUB AI Lab no such relationships are given to the agents. This is also not given in the work of Mike Oliphant (1997). This means that the agents construct the language themselves.

Meaning is pre-defined if the agents have some representation of the meaning pre-programmed. This is done in the work of Billard & Hayes (1997), Oliphant (1997) and Yanco & Stein (1993). In the work of Billard & Hayes, the meaning is only given to the teacher robot. The student robot learns the representation of the meaning. Oliphant's agents only have abstract meanings that have no relation to the real world. In the work that is done in most of Steels' group the agents construct their own ontology of meanings.

Of the researchers that are compared with this work, only Rosenstein & Cohen (1998a) make use of prototypes as a way of defining categories. All other work makes use of some other definition. This does not mean that the use of prototypes is uncommon in artificial intelligence, but it is uncommon in the grounding of language community.

A hierarchical structuring of the categorisations is only done by the researchers of Steels' group, this book included. The advantage of hierarchical structuring of categories is that a distinction can be either more general or more specific.

Quite some researchers pre-define the number of meanings and/or forms that is, or should arise in the language (Billard & Hayes 1997; Cangelosi & Parisi 1998; Oliphant 1997; Yanco & Stein 1993). Naturally, language is not bound by the number of meanings and forms. Therefore, the number of meanings and forms is unbound in this book.

It may be useful if the position of the robot in relation to other robots and objects in their environment is known exactly. Especially for technical purposes, like pointing to an object. However, such information is not always known to the language users. In the Talking Heads experiment, the robots have calibrated knowledge about their own position (which is fixed) and the position of the other robot, and they can calculate the position of objects in their world. Such information is not available to the robots in this book. This is one of the main differences between the Talking Heads and the current experiments. Another difference with the Talking Heads is the use of camera vision, rather than low-level sensing. Still other differences are at the implementation of the model. These differences have been discussed above and will be discussed more in Chapter 7.

Not all experiments deal with robots that are mobile in their environment. In particular the Talking Heads are not mobile, at least not in the sense that they can move freely in their environment. The Talking Heads can only go from physical head to physical head. The locations of these heads are fixed.

Except the work of Yanco & Stein (1993), all experiments are autonomous, i.e. without the intervention of a human. Yanco & Stein give their robots feedback about the effect of their communication. This feedback is used to reinforce the connections between form and meaning. The system designed in this book is completely autonomous. The only intervention taken is to place the robots at a close distance rather than letting them find each other. This is done in order to speed up the experiments. In previous implementations, the robots did find each other themselves (Steels & Vogt 1997). There is no intervention at the grounding and learning level involved.

In most of the experiments mentioned, the agents have only one task: developing language. Some scientist argue that language should be developed in a task-oriented way, e.g. Billard & Hayes (1997), Cangelosi & Parisi (1998), de Jong (2000) and Yanco & Stein (1993). In particular, the task should have an ecological function. This seems natural and is probably true. However, in order to understand the mechanisms involved in lexicon development, it is useful to concentrate only on lexicon development. Besides, developing langauge is in some sense task-oriented.

As explained, one of the research goals is to investigate the importance of extra-linguistic information that guides the lexicon development. This has also been investigated by Oliphant (1997) and de Jong (2000).

So, in many respects the research that is presented in this book is unique. It takes on many aspects of a grounded language experiment that is not shared by other experiments. The experiment that comes closest is the Talking Heads experiment. The results of the experiments from this book will therefore be compared in more detail at the end of this book.

1.6 The book's outline

The book is basically divided in three parts. In the first part, the model by which the experiments are developed is introduced. Part two presents experimental results. And the final part is reserved for discussions and conclusions.

Chapter 2 introduces the experimental set-up. This includes the environment in which the robots behave and the technical set-up of the robots. This chapter explains the Process Description Language (PDL) in which the robots are programmed. PDL is for the purpose of these experiments extended from a behaviour-based architecture in a behaviour-based *cognitive* architecture. This is to enable better controllable planned behaviour. People not interested in the technical details of the robots may omit this chapter. For these people it is advisable to read Section 2.1 in which the environment is presented. In addition, the part on the white light sensors in Section 2.2.1 is important to follow some of the discussions.

The language game model is introduced in Chapter 3. It explains how the robots interact with each other and their environment. The interaction with their environment includes sensing the surroundings. The result of the sensing is pre-processed further to allow efficient categorisation. The discrimination game with which categorisation and ontological development is modelled is explained. After that, the naming game is presented, which models the naming part of the language game and the lexicon formation. The chapter ends with a presentation of how the discrimination game and the naming game are coupled to each other.

The experimental results are presented in Chapters 4, 5 and 6. Chapter 4 first introduces the measures by which the results are monitored. The first experiment that is presented is called the BASIC EXPERIMENT. A detailed analysis is made of what is going on during the experiment. As will become clear it still has a lot of discrepancies. These discrepancies are mostly identified in following chapters.

The experiments presented in Chapter 5 are all variants of the basic experiment. In each only one parameter or strategy has been changed. The experiments investigate the impact from various strategies for categorisation, physical interaction, joint attention and feedback. In addition, the influence of a few parameters that control adaptation are investigated. Each set of experiments is followed by a brief discussion.

The final series experiments are presented in Chapter 6. Two variants of the language games that have proven to be successful in previous chapters are investigated in more detail. Each of these experiments have a varying strategy of using extra-linguistic information and are additionally provided with parameter settings that appeared to yield the best results. The first experiment is the GUESSING GAME in which the hearer has to guess what light source the speaker tries to name, without previous knowledge about the topic. In the second experiment prior topic knowledge is provided by joint attention. No feedback on the outcome is provided in the second game, called the OBSERVATIONAL GAME.

Chapter 7 discusses the experimental results and presents the conclusions. The discussion is centred on the research questions posed in the previous section. Additional discussions centre on the similarities and differences with related work, in particular with the work done by other members of the VUB AI Lab and Sony CSL Paris. Finally some possible future directions are given.

2 The sensorimotor component

In this chapter the design and architecture of the robots is discussed. The experiments use two small LEGO vehicles, which are controlled by a small sensorimotor board. The robots, including their electronics, were designed at the VUB AI Lab. They were constructed such that the configuration of the robots can be changed easily. Sensors may be added or changed and the physical robustness of the robots has improved through time. In some experiments they *are* changed substantially, but in most experiments the robots remain the same.

The robots are controlled by a specialised sensorimotor board, the SMBII[1] (Vereertbrugghen 1996). The sensorimotor board connects the sensory equipment with the actuators in such a way that the actuators and sensor readings are updated 40 times per second. The actuators respond to sensory stimuli, where the response is calculated by a set of "parallel" processes. These processes are programmed in the *Process Description Language* (PDL), which has been developed at the VUB AI Lab as a software architecture to implement behaviour-oriented control (Steels 1994c).

The outline of the experiments is discussed in Chapter 3; this chapter is concentrated on the physical set-up of the robots and their environment in the different experiments. The robots' environment is presented in Section 2.1. Section 2.2 discusses the physical architecture of the robots. Section 2.3 discusses the Process Description Language.

2.1 The environment

The environment that has been used for the experiments in the past varied across some of the experiments. The environment in early experiments (Steels & Vogt 1997; Vogt 1998b,a) had different light sources than the current environment. Furthermore, the size of the environment shrinked from $5 \cdot 5 m^2$ to $2.5 \cdot 2.5 m^2$. In the current environment there are four different white light sources, each placed at a different height (Figure 2.1).

---

[1] Read as SMB-2.

2 The sensorimotor component

These white light (WL) sources (or light sources for short) all emit their light from black cylindrical boxes with small slits. The light sources are halogen lights and each box now has a height of 22 cm, a diameter of 16 cm and 3 horizontal slits. Each slit has its centre at a height of 13 cm (measured from the bottom of the box) and is 0.8 cm wide. Although the different slits are intersected by a bar, they can be approximated to be one slit.

The boxes are placed such that the height of the slit varied per light source. The four different heights are distributed with a vertical distance of 3.9 cm. In one experiment the difference in height was changed to 2.9 cm. The robots were adjusted to this environment (or vice versa) so that the light sensors were placed at the same height as the centre of the slits.

Figure 2.1: The robots in the environment as is used in the experiments.

2.2 The robots

In the experiments two LEGO robots as in Figure 2.2 are used. Each robot has a set of sensors to observe the world. These sensors are low-level. They can only detect the intensity of light in a particular frequency domain. Other low-level sensors are used to control the robots in their movement. The sensors are connected to a dedicated sensorimotor board, the so-called SMBII. On the SMBII all sensors are read at a rate of 40 Hz. The sensor readings are processed according to the software, written in PDL (see next section). After the sensors have been processed the SMBII outputs the actuator commands and sends its appropriate signals to the actuators. The robots are powered by a re-chargeable nickel–cadmium battery pack as used in portable computers.

2.2 The robots

In this section the set-up of the sensors and actuators of the robots are discussed first. Secondly the architecture of the SMBII is discussed briefly.

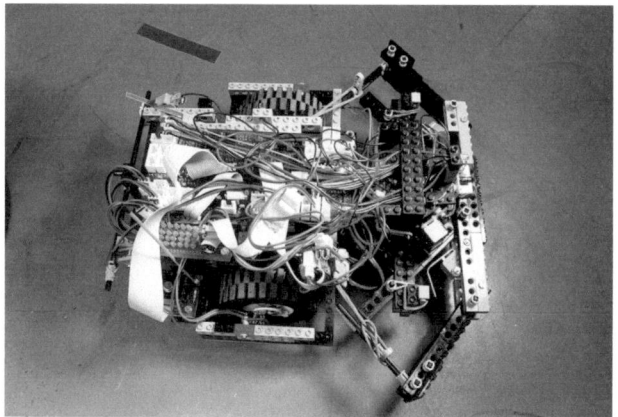

Figure 2.2: One of the LEGO robots used in the experiments.

2.2.1 The sensors and actuators

The robots in all experiments have a set-up like shown schematically in Figure 2.3. The sensory equipment consists of four binary bumpers, three infrared (IR) sensors and a radio link *receiver*. The radio link is a module that also has a radio link *transmitter*, which is classified as an actuator. The infrared sensors are part of the infrared module, which also consists of an actuator: the infrared transmitter. Two independent motors complete the actuator set-up. All sensors and actuators are connected to the SMBII, which is powered by a battery-pack. The battery-pack also powers the motor-controller. The motor-controller, controlled by the SMBII controls the motors. The motors are connected to the wheels via a set of gears. Finally there are four white light sensors that are responsible for the perception.

Below a more detailed description of the most important sensors and actuators are given.

The bumpers The robots have four bumpers that are used for touch based obstacle avoidance; two on the front and two on the back of the robot, both left and right. Each bumper is a binary switch: when it is pressed it returns 1, else it returns 0. The bumpers have a spanning construction of LEGO (see Figure 2.4(a) and 2.4(b)). If a robot bumps with this construction into an obstacle. The program can then react on the sensed collision.

2 The sensorimotor component

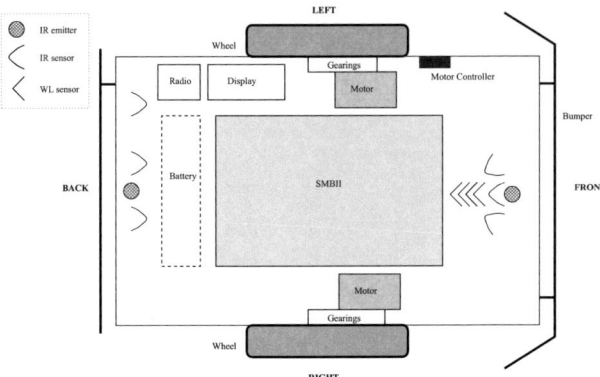

Figure 2.3: A schematic overview of the basic set-up of the robots that are used in the experiments.

The infrared module Whereas the bumpers are simple binary sensors, the infrared module Figure 2.4(a) is more complex. The infrared module consists of infrared emitters and sensors. The emitters are light emitting diodes emitting infrared. The infrared sensors themselves are sensors that can be found in e.g. television sets. They detect light at infrared wavelengths and send a signal to the SMBII that is proportional to the intensity of the infrared. The sensors are mounted such that they can discriminate infrared coming from the left, centre and right sides in front of the robot. The sensors are not calibrated in the sense that one can calculate the exact angle from where the infrared is coming or from what distance. Also the positions of the sensors are not exactly symmetric, due to some physical limitations of the sensors and the LEGO construction. Vogt (1997) discusses some practical problems concerning the modulation and characteristics of the infrared module in detail.

The radio link The radio link module is a transmitter/receiver device designed to connect with the SMBII (see Figure 2.4(b)). The module is a Radiometrix BM-433F module with RX (receive) and TX (transmission) connections. The module can send up to 40 Kbit/s, but is used at 9.6 Kbit/s.

Every clock cycle of the SMBII a packet of messages can be sent. A packet can consist of a maximum of 31 messages each up to 127 bytes long. A message has a transmission ID and an destination address, which define the sender and receiver(s) of the message. It also has a bit defining the reliability of the transmission; this bit has to be set to *unreliable*, i.e. to 0, because the reliability protocol has not been implemented in the radio link kernel. This has the consequence that if a message is sent, it is not sure if the message arrives at its destination. But *when* it arrives, the message arrives error-less. About 5 % of the messages sent do not arrive at their destination.

This unreliability has some technical impacts on the experiments. Since data logging, recording and communication passes through the radio link, not all information is received. Filters had to written to find out whether all data was logged and if not, part of the data would be unreliable and should therefore be discarded. It is beyond the scope of this dissertation to go into the details of such filters here. For the purpose of the book it is assumed that the radio transmission is reliable.

The motor controller and the motors The motor controller is a device that transforms and controls motor commands coming from the SMBII into signals that are sent to the standard LEGO DC motors. Each robot has two independent motors. So, in order to steer the robot, one has to send a (possibly different) signal to each motor.

Gearing The motors are not directly connected to the wheels. They are connected to the wheels with a set of gears (see Figure 2.4(c)). The wheels are placed such that they form an axis approximately through the centre of the robot so that it can rotate around this point. A third small caster-wheel is used to stabilise the robot.

The light sensors The white light sensors are the most crucial sensors in the experiments. This is because they are used for the perception of the analogue signals that the robots are supposed to ground. Each robot has four white light sensors stacked on top of each other. The sensors have a vertical distance of 3.9 cm between each other. Each sensor is at the same height as a light source (Figure 2.4(a)).

The light sensors were calibrated such that the characteristics of all sensors are roughly the same. Figure 2.5 shows the characteristics of the calibrated light sensors as empirically measured for the experimental set-up. On the x-axis of each plot the distance of the robot to the light source is given in centimetres; the y-axis shows the intensity of the light in PDL values. PDL scales the light sensors between 0 and 255, where 0 means no detection of light and 255 means maximum intensity. The calibration of each sensor is done while it was exposed to a corresponding light source. A sensor is said to *correspond* with a light source when it has the same height. The complete figure shows the characteristics of the two robots r0 and r1, each with four sensors (s0 ... s3).

It is notable that for light source L0 the characteristics of sensor s3 is high at the beginning (Figure 2.5 (a) and (e)). This is because for the lowest light source L0, sensor s3 is higher than the top of the box, which is open. At a larger distance the light coming from the top of this box cannot be seen.

It is clear that all characteristics are similar. The sensor that corresponds to a light source detects high intensities at short distances and low values at larger distances. From 0.6 m other sensors start detecting the light source as well. This is because the light coming from the slit does not propagate in a perpendicular beam, but is diverging slightly. It is important to note that corresponding light sensors are calibrated to read the highest intensities between 0 and 1.2 m. The shape of the plots are like they would have been expected from the physics rule that the intensity $I \sim \frac{1}{r^2}$, where r is the distance to the light source.

It is noteworthy that each sensor detects noise that comes mainly from ambient light.

The robots are also equipped with sensors and actuators that are used for interfacing the robot with the experimenter. It has for instance a serial port for connecting the robot to a PC, a display with 64 LEDs, a pause button, an on/off switch, etc. Since these sensors are not vital for the behaviour of the robots, they are not discussed in more detail here.

This subsection introduced the sensorimotor equipment that the robot carries in the experiments as discussed throughout this book. The next subsection discusses the sensorimotor board in some more detail.

2.2.2 Sensor-motor board II

The computing hardware of the robots is a sensorimotor board, called the SMBII, which is developed at the VUB AI Lab by Dany Vereertbrugghen (1996). It consists of an ADD-ON SMB-2 BOARD and a Vesta Technologies SBC332 micro controller board.

The Vesta board (see Figure 2.6(a)) contains a Motorola MC68332 microcontroller, 128 kB ROM and 1 MB RAM.[2] The board's micro-controller runs at 16.78 MHz

---

[2] In the original version of the SMBII there were only 256 kB RAM (Vereertbrugghen 1996).

2.2 The robots

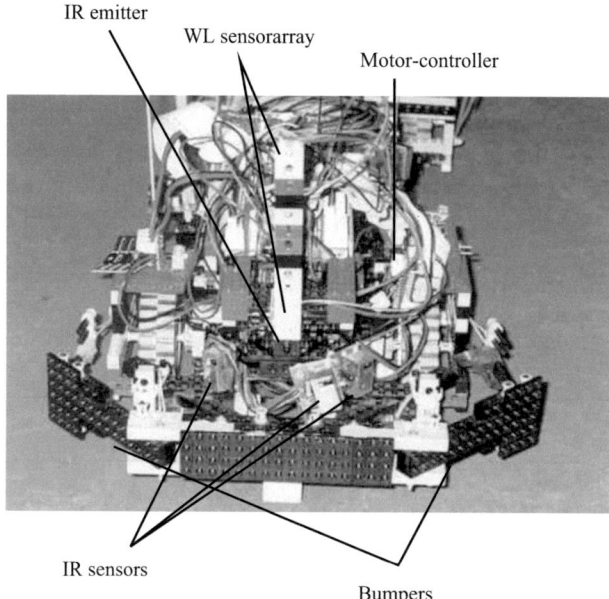

(a) Front

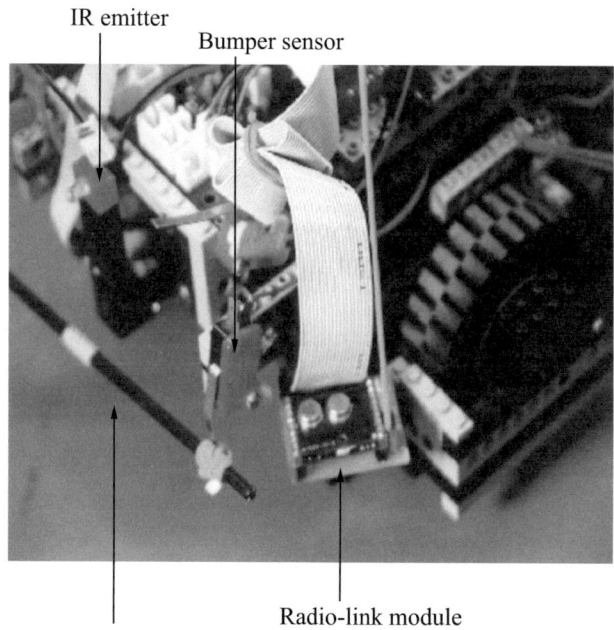

(b) Back

2 The sensorimotor component

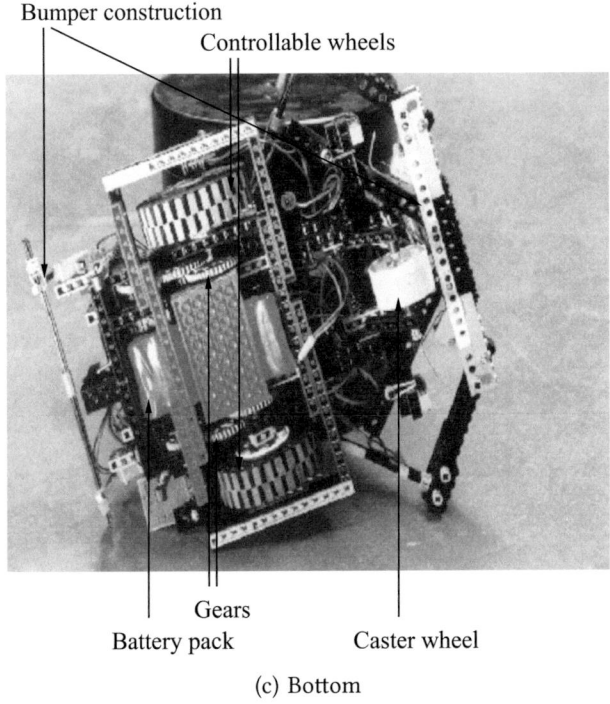

(c) Bottom

Figure 2.4: Several close ups of one of the robots. Figure (a) shows the front side of the robot. The bumper construction can be seen. The perceptual sensor array consisting of 4 light sensors, the infrared sensors and the infrared emitter are also visible. The radio link module can be seen in (b) as well as a part of the bumper construction on the back. Figure (c) shows the bottom of the robot. We see the wheels, gearing and the battery pack. Also a good view is seen of the bumper constructions.

at 5 Volt and everything is powered by a pack of rechargeable nickel–cadmium batteries.

The add-on SMB-2 board (Figure 2.6(b)) contains several I/O chips, bus controllers and connectors. The SMBII low-level program is run on the kernel and it can interface a user program written in any language as long a the kernel calls are written in C (Vereertbrugghen 1996). The program that is run on the SMBII for these experiments is written in the Process Description Language PDL.

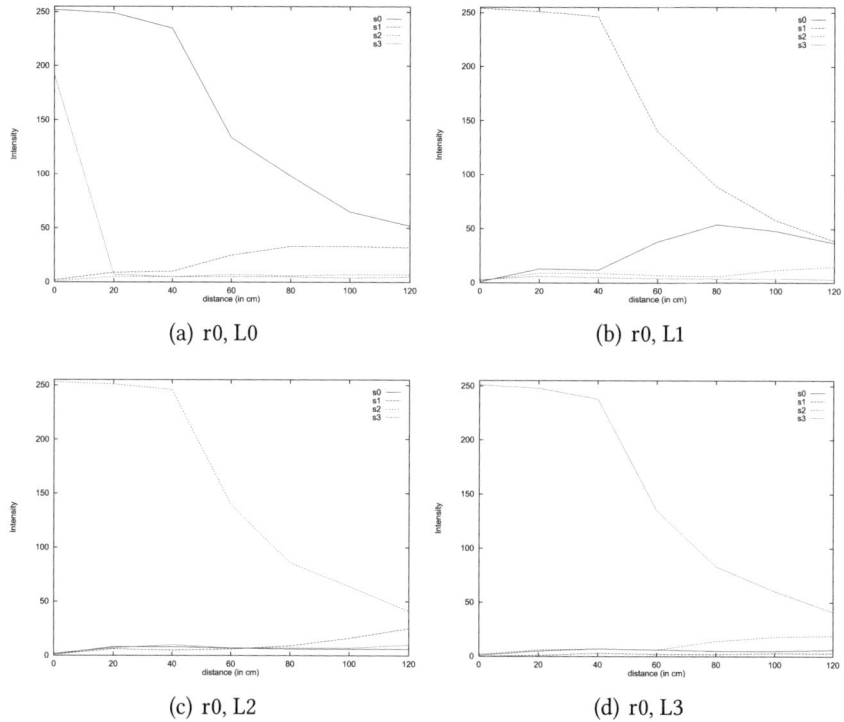

(a) r0, L0 (b) r0, L1

(c) r0, L2 (d) r0, L3

2.3 The Process Description Language

The robots are programmed in the so-called Process Description Language (Steels 1992; 1994b,c). PDL is designed as a framework for designing software for autonomous agents according to the behaviour-oriented control.

In PDL one can decompose a behaviour system in a set of dynamical processes. For instance, one can decompose the behaviour of PHOTOTAXIS (i.e. moving towards a light source) into two dynamical processes: (1) moving forward and (2) orienting towards the light. PDL is designed to implement parallel processes that are virtually evaluated simultaneously to output a summated response. So, suppose there are the two parallel processes (1) and (2) that are evaluated simultaneously. And suppose further that the output of the two processes are summated to give a motor response. Then the emergent behaviour is phototaxis.

PDL cycles the process of READING SENSORS, EVALUATE PROCESSES and CONTROL ACTUATORS (Figure 2.7). During a PDL cycle a robot reads the sensors to detect the current state of a robot in the world. These sensor readings are evaluated by processes that are defined in the software as explained below. The processes

2 The sensorimotor component

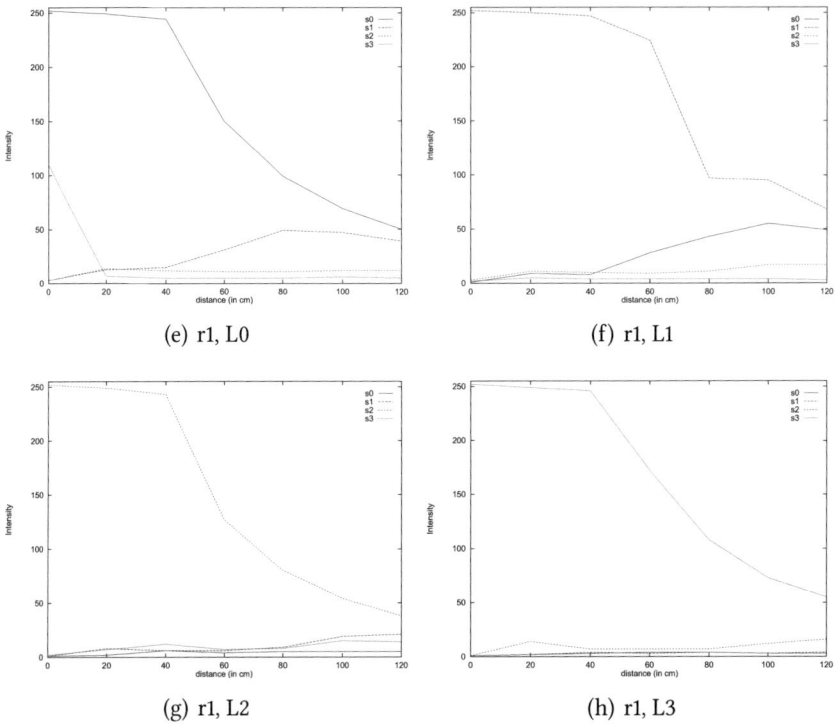

(e) r1, L0   (f) r1, L1

(g) r1, L2   (h) r1, L3

Figure 2.5: The characteristics of the calibrated light sensors as empirically measured for the experimental set-up when exposed to light sources $L0 - L3$. Plots (a) – (d) show the of robot $r0$ and plots (e) – (h) show them for $r1$. The distances are measured from the front of the robots to the boxes. Actual distances from source to sensor are 12 cm further.

output commands to activate the actuators. These actuators in turn change the state of the world. Such a cycle is processed at 40 Hz, so 40 PDL cycles take 1 second. Throughout the book the basic time unit is a PDL cycle ($\frac{1}{40}$ s).

The initial implementation of PDL was written in LISP, the currently used version is implemented in ANSI-C. It can compile both the specialised PDL syntax and ANSI-C commands within its architecture. The PDL architecture has as its basic symbolic units so-called quantities. A quantity is a struct type that has a NAME, a VALUE, an UPPER BOUND, a LOWER BOUND and an INITIAL VALUE. Each quantity can be connected to a serial port, interfacing the program with the physical sensors and actuators. Each type of sensor and actuator is defined within the operating system of the SMBII. The radio module has its own interface, but can be

2.3 The Process Description Language

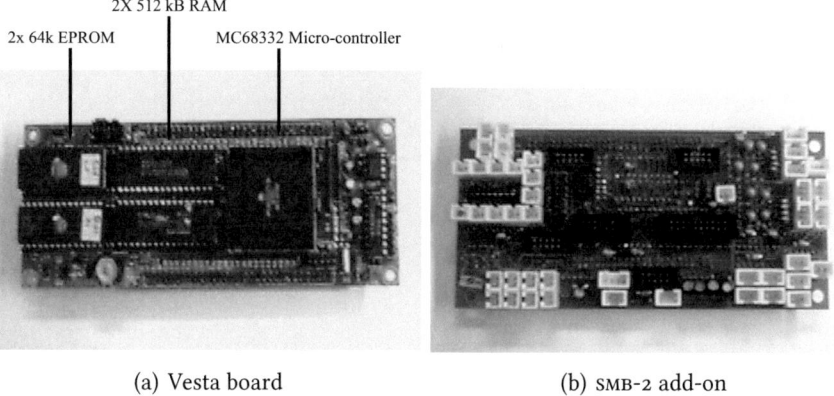

(a) Vesta board (b) SMB-2 add-on

Figure 2.6: The two components of the SMBII board: (a) the Vesta Technologies SBC332 micro controller board, and (b) the add-on SMB-2 sensorimotor board.

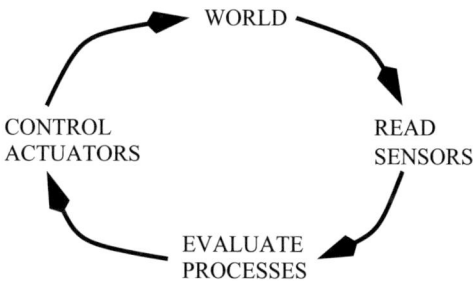

Figure 2.7: The way that PDL interacts with the world via a robot. Every $\frac{1}{40}$ s PDL is going through a cycle as shown in the figure.

called with a PDL command. The most important parts of a PDL program are the *processes*. Each time a PDL program is compiled, a network of processes is build up. The following example of phototaxis shows how this is done.

The example implements two behaviours: (1) INFRARED ORIENTATION and (2) INFRARED PHOTOTAXIS. In infrared orientation, the goal of the robot is to orient itself in the direction of an infrared source without approaching the source.[3] It is implemented using only one dynamic process called TAXIS. With infrared phototaxis the goal of a robot is to approach the infrared source. It is implemented with an additional process that causes a robot to try to move at a default speed.

After declaration, the quantities have to added to the system as follows:

---

[3] In the experiments the robots themselves are infrared sources.

2 The sensorimotor component

```
add_quantity(LeftFrontIR,''LeftFrontIR'',255.0f,0.0f,0.0f);
add_quantity(RightFrontIR,''RightFrontIR'',255.0f,0.0f,0.0f);
add_quantity(LeftMotor,''LeftMotor'',100.0f,-100.0f,0.0f);
add_quantity(RightMotor,''RightMotor'',100.0f,-100.0f,0.0f);
```

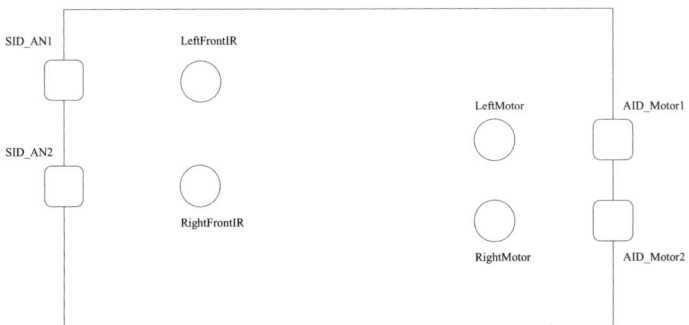

Figure 2.8: The construction of a PDL network. The program has serial ports SID_AN1 and SID_AN2 for analogue sensory input. Ports AID_MOTOR1 and AID_MOTOR2 are serial ports for the motors. The network consists of the quantities LeftFrontIR, RightFrontIR, LeftMotor and RightMotor.

The function add_q adds the quantity LeftFrontIR to the network, an upper bound of 255.0f (where f stands for "float"), a lower bound of 0.0f and an initial value of 0.0f. Likewise the quantities RightFrontIR, LeftMotor and RightMotor were added, see Figure 2.8. The upper and lower bound of the motors are 100.0 and −100.0, respectively. If, mathematically, an upper or lower bound would be exceeded, PDL sets the quantity-value to its upper or lower bound. The next step is to connect the quantities to the serial ports of the SMBII, which are connected to the sensors and actuators.

```
add_connection(SID_AN1,LeftFrontIR);
add_connection(SID_AN2,RightFrontIR);
add_connection(AID1_Motor,LeftMotor);
add_connection(AID2_Motor,RightMotor);
```

Now the network looks like in Figure 2.9. The above is part of the initialisation. Another step of the initialisation is to add processes to the network:

```
add_process(Taxis,''Taxis'');
add_process(TowardsDefault,''TowardsDefault'');
```

2.3 The Process Description Language

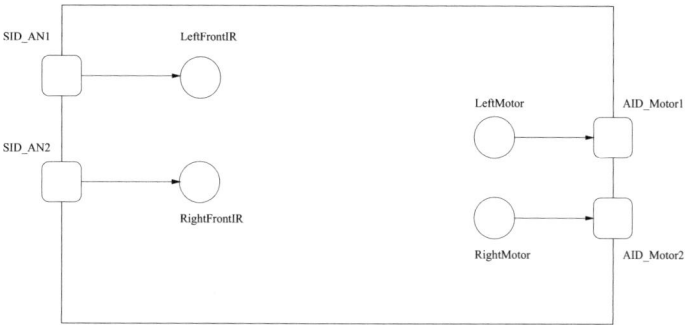

Figure 2.9: This is the PDL network after the quantities are connected with the serial ports.

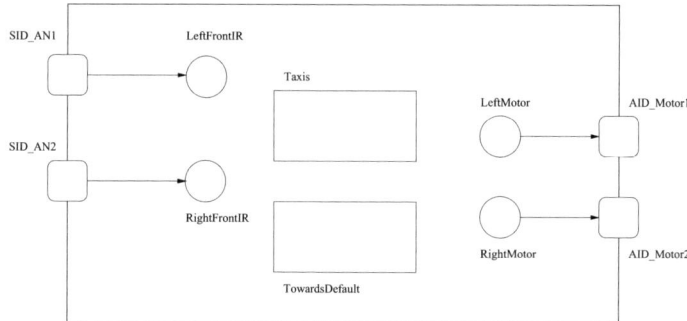

Figure 2.10: This is the PDL network after the processes Taxis and TowardsDefault are added.

This leads to the network as shown in Figure 2.10. To couple the sensors with the actuators, the processes have to be defined. The process Taxis causes the robot to orient towards an infrared light source.

```
void Taxis()
{
  D=value(RightFrontIR)-value(LeftFrontIR);
  add_value(LeftMotor,C*F(D)*D);
  add_value(RightMotor,-C*F(D)*D);
}
```

Here, value(Q) is a function that returns the value of quantity Q, add_value(Q,V) adds value V to the value of Q. The actual update of Q is done at the end of each PDL cycle. When more values are added to Q, these values are summed before they are added. C is a constant and F(D) is a scaling factor of difference

45

2 The sensorimotor component

(D) in infrared. $F(x)$ is implemented as an inverse sigmoid function.

$$F(x) = \frac{1}{1 + e^{\alpha \cdot (x - \beta)}}$$

$F(x) \cdot x$ dampens x strongly if x is large, it is less dampened if x is not large. If $F(x)$ is not applied, the robot would exaggerate its wiggling too much.

Taxis increases the LeftMotor and decreases the RightMotor by a value proportionate to D. If the infrared source is to the right of the robot, the difference D is positive. Hence the value of the LeftMotor increases and the value of the RightMotor decreases. This in effect causes the robot to turn to the right. When the infrared source is to the left of the robot, the opposite happens. So, the robot will rotate in the direction in which the intensity of infrared is detected the highest. If the robot passes the infrared source, the direction in which the infrared is detected (i.e. the sign of direction changes) and so the robot changes its direction of rotation. This will continue until D approaches zero or when the values become so small, that it there is no power left to move the robot.

Although the robot is rotating around its axis in varying directions, it does not move from its place. This is accomplished by introducing the following process:

```
void TowardsDefault()
{
  add_value(LeftMotor,(DefaultSpeed-value(LeftMotor))/Step);
  add_value(RightMotor,(DefaultSpeed-value(RightMotor))/Step);
}
```

This process causes the robot to change its speed towards a default speed with certain step size. The step size is introduced to let the robot accelerate smoothly. Note that this way the motor values do not reach the default speed; the values approach it asymptotically. When the processes are defined, the network looks like in Figure 2.12.

Taking the two processes together results in the emergent behaviour that the robot will move wiggling towards the infrared source (see Figure 2.11). Such phototaxis behaviour, although with a slightly different implementation, was introduced for a robot application by Valentino Braitenberg (1984) and has already been discussed extensively in the literature, see e.g. Steels 1994a.

Appendix B presents the structure of the implemented PDL program in more detail. In the next section the behaviour based architecture is expanded to incorporate planned behaviours as well.

2.4 Cognitive architecture in PDL

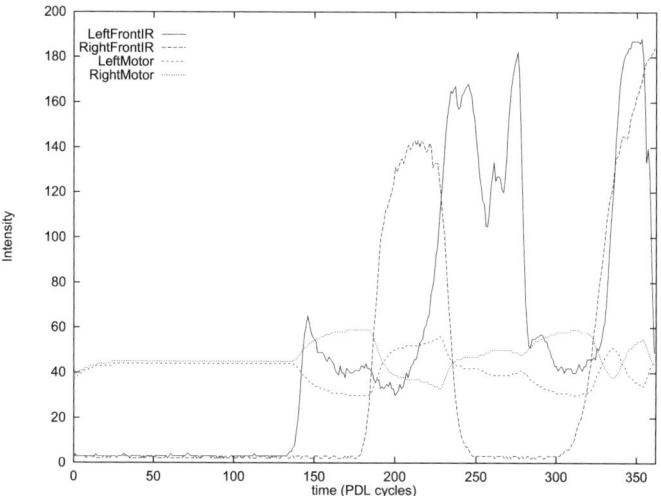

Figure 2.11: This figure shows the evolution of the infrared sensors and motor values in time during phototaxis, i.e. the emergent dynamics of combining the processes Taxis and TowardsDefault. On the x-axis the time is shown in the basic time unit of the robots, a PDL cycle ($=\frac{1}{40}$ s). The y-axis shows the intensity of the infrared sensors and motor signals. The data is taken from a robot that was driving using both processes Taxis and TowardsDefault. It drove straight forward until at time 140 the robot detected an infrared source after which it adjusted its motor signals to home in on the source.

2.4 Cognitive architecture in PDL

To accomplish a complex task like communication, a sequence of actions have to be planned. Reactive behaviours like phototaxis alone do not suffice. To allow the robots to execute planned behaviour a new architecture has been developed. This resulted in what could be called a BEHAVIOUR-BASED COGNITIVE ARCHITECTURE that is primarily based on the behaviour-based control architecture proposed by Luc Steels (1994c). This cognitive architecture could be applied as a general purpose architecture for complex and dynamic tasks like navigation. The architecture executes a script (or plan) through excitation and inhibition of processes that altogether result in some emergent behaviour. The scripts are implemented as finite state automata in which transitions are controlled by state-specific pre- and post-conditions. In each state of the finite state automaton (FSA) a particular set of processes are activated or inhibited. Figure 2.13 shows the basic principle.

2 The sensorimotor component

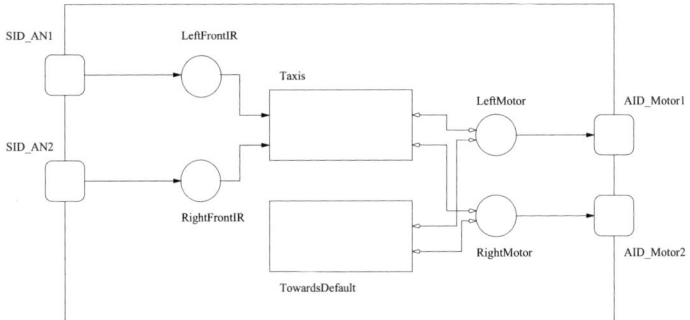

Figure 2.12: Finally the network of quantities and processes for the phototaxis example is complete. The `LeftFrontIR` and `RightFrontIR` are connected to input `Taxis`, which outputs to the motor quantities. The motor quantities are also used to calculate the output, hence this connection is bi-directional. The process TowardsDefault does not use any sensors; as in Taxis it only uses values of the quantities `LeftMotor` and `RightMotor` thus giving the bi-directional connection between `TowardsDefault` and the motors.

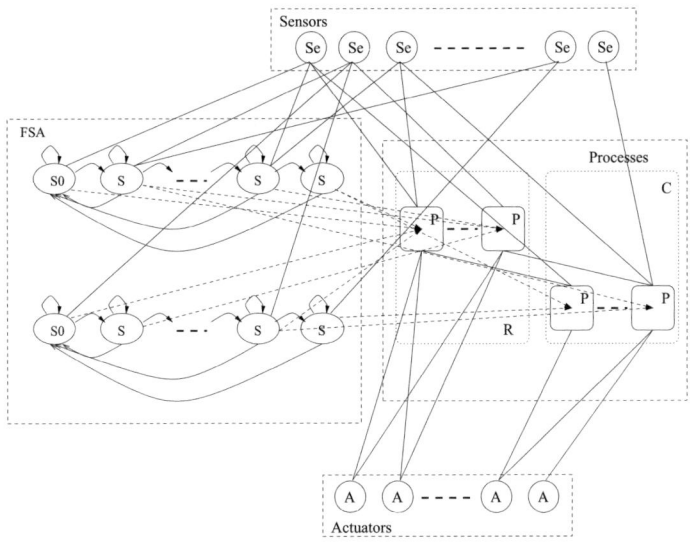

Figure 2.13: A schematic overview of the developed architecture. See the text for details.

2.4 Cognitive architecture in PDL

In the architecture the sensors *Se* and actuators *A* are coupled through a complex of connections. The agent consists of a set of scripts, which are implemented as finite state automata. The finite state automata are parallel processes where transitions are regulated by pre- and post-conditions. Usually the pre- and post-conditions are satisfied by some sensory stimuli. A state may also be fed with information coming from some internal process (not shown). Every state *S* has a post-condition that allows the system to enter the default state *S0* where nothing happens. Each state of the automaton has excitatory and inhibitory connections with dynamic sensorimotor processes *P*. The excitatory connections are drawn as dotted lines, the inhibitory have been left out for clarity of the picture. The processes are divided between reactive (R) and cognitive (C) processes. The reactive processes have more direct processing and can take usually only sensorimotor data as input. The cognitive processes are more complex, and may take also stimuli coming from other internal processes. Note that the finite state automaton could be considered as a cognitive process as well. The configuration of excitatory processes and the dynamics of the robot with its environment cause the robot to perform some emergent behaviour. Hence the system is consistent with the behaviour-based paradigm.

Activation of processes is modelled by invoking motivational factors (cf. Steels 1996a; Jaeger & Christaller 1998). For example if is a state that in which the motivation for doing infrared taxis is present, this state may be a motivational factor MotIRT that is set to 1. The process taxis can then look like this:

```
void Taxis()
{
  D=value(RightFrontIR)-value(LeftFrontIR);
  add_value(LeftMotor,MotIRT*C*F(D)*D));
  add_value(RightMotor,-MotIRT*C*F(D)*D));
}
```

A multi-agent system is a parallel process in which two robots cooperate autonomously. In order to synchronise these two parallel processes, the robots use pre-programmed radio communication. The robots playing a language game process dependent, but parallel operating finite state automata. A signal is broadcasted when both robots should transfer to another state simultaneously as the result of the transition of one of the robots.

Because the architecture uses finite state automata, readers may wrongly suggest it is the subsumption architecture proposed by Rodney Brooks (1990). In the subsumption architecture each process is viewed as a finite state automaton on its own with only one state that models a behaviour (Figure 2.14 (a)). The architec-

2 The sensorimotor component

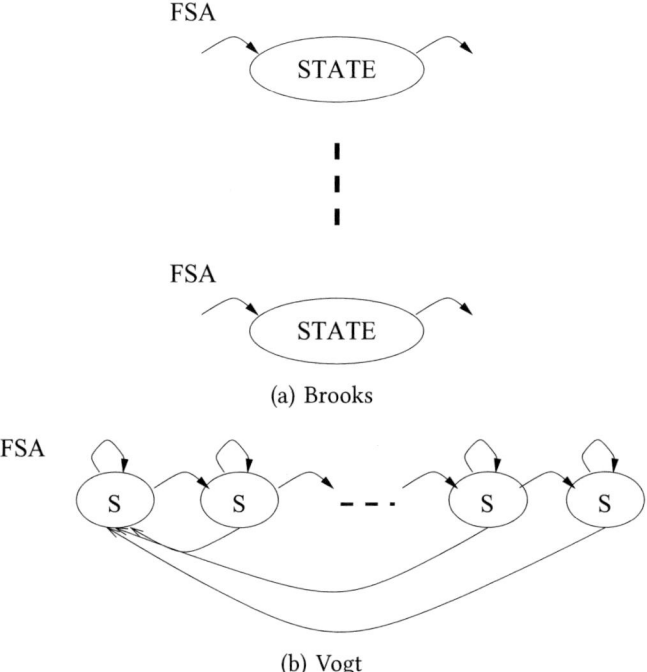

Figure 2.14: The finite state automata as used in the subsumption architecture (a) and in the cognitive architecture (b). In the subsumption architecture the finite state automata usually only has one state that models a particular behaviour. This behaviour can inhibit (or subsume) another behaviour. The cognitive architecture has some finite state automata each modelling a script-like behaviour. Each state excites or inhibits a number of dynamical processes. The finite state automata function independently as a parallel process.

ture proposed here uses possibly more finite state automata each with a sequence of states that can be entered (Figure 2.14 (b)). These finite state automata are used to control planning. A process in the cognitive architecture can be activated by several states, and a particular state can activate several processes. In addition the processes couple the sensors with the motors, like the behaviour-based architecture proposed by Luc Steels (1994c).

The behaviour-based cognitive architecture has strong similarities with the dual dynamics architecture (Jaeger & Christaller 1998). However, the in the dual dynamics the activation of processes is regulated internally of these processes. There is no explicit finite state automaton that regulates the activation.

The architecture proposed here is also similar to the architecture proposed by Barnes (1996) and Barnes et al. (1997), called the behaviour synthesis architecture (BSA), which synthesises a set of *behaviour patterns* with a certain utility (or strength) for accomplishing a task. A *behaviour script* controls a sequence of *behaviour packets*. Each behaviour packet consists of a set of behaviour patterns, a pre-condition and a post-condition. Comparing the behaviour patterns with the dynamical processes of PDL, the behaviour scripts with the finite state automata and the packets with a single state, then the BSA is very close to the architecture that has been incorporated here. Main differences with the work of Barnes (1996) is the use of utility functions as its synthesis mechanism. Although the architecture here is developed by a human programmer, Barnes et al. (1997) show that planning can be automated using the BSA.

2.5 Summary

In this chapter the basic set-up of the robots, their software and environment were introduced. The experiments use two small LEGO vehicles that are equipped with a set of sensors, actuators, a battery pack and a specialised sensorimotor board SMBII. The robots are programmed in a specialised programming language PDL, which is dedicated to process the dynamics of sensorimotor behaviours in the behaviour-oriented paradigm.

The principles of PDL have been extended to a behaviour-based cognitive architecture. In this new architecture robots can execute planned behaviour as cognitive processes.

The robots as introduced here are the physical bodies with which the agents try to develop their ontologies and lexicons. How they do that is explained in Chapter 3. As shall become clear some processing is done off-board. This is mainly done to experiment more efficiently and to be able to test different approaches

2 The sensorimotor component

on recorded data. In some specific experiments the architecture of the robots has been changed with respect to the description given in this chapter. Relevant changes will be reported when these experiments are discussed.

More detailed information on the PDL program can be found in Appendix B.

3 Language games

3.1 Introduction

In order to solve the symbol grounding problem the robots engage in a series of language games. Every language game can be thought of as a communication act in which the robots communicate about an object (in this case a light source). The goal of a language game is for the two robots to identify the same referent through the exchange of linguistic and possibly non-linguistic information. If this does not succeed they can adjust their set of meanings and/or lexicons so they may be successful in future games.

The notion of a language game was first introduced by Ludwig Wittgenstein (1958). Wittgenstein called every language use a language game. The meaning of the language game depends, according to Wittgenstein, on the *how* the game is used. Wittgenstein gave some examples of different types of language games Wittgenstein (1958: 11, §22):

- Giving orders, and obeying them
- Describing the appearances of an object, or giving its measurements
- Constructing an object from a description (a drawing)
- Reporting an event
- Speculating about an event
- ...

In the experiments done at the AI Lab different types of games are investigated. Besides the basic term of language game, the following games have been introduced NAMING GAMES (Steels 1996c), DISCRIMINATION GAMES (Steels 1996d), IMITATION GAMES (de Boer 1997), GUESSING GAMES (Steels & Kaplan 1999), IDENTIFICATION GAMES and FOLLOW ME GAMES (Vogt 1999; 2000b). All games model a communication act, except the discrimination and identification games which model categorisation. The types of games that will be used in this book are naming games, discrimination games, guessing games and two additional games that

3 Language games

will be explained further on in this chapter. The discrimination and naming game form a sub-part of what is called a language game here. The other games are a special type of language game.

In the context of this work, a language game is the complete process of performing a communication act. As mentioned in Chapter 1, grounding language is strongly influenced by an agent's interaction with its environment. Since it is assumed that language and meaning formation are complex dynamical adaptive systems, these systems can be defined by their mechanical processes and the systems boundary conditions (Prigogine & Strengers 1984). So, to develop a robot capable of constructing conceptual structures and language, one has to define such mechanisms and boundary conditions of the system. The mechanism has already been chosen, namely the SELECTIONIST APPROACH taken (Steels 1996c,d). The boundary conditions will be defined (for a great deal) by the PHYSICAL BODIES and INTERACTION of the robots with their ecological niche.

This chapter presents the physical interactions of the robots with their environment. It defines the language game scenario in detail, defining the physical interaction in which a context setting is acquired. This happens in the next section. Then Section 4.1.3 discusses the advantages of on-board vs. off-board processing as a methodology of experimenting with robots. Section 3.4.1 discusses the perception and segmentation during a language game. Sections 3.4.2 and 3.4.3 explain the higher cognitive functions of categorisation and naming. A final section of this chapter couples the different parts of the language game.

3.2 The language game scenario

The goal of a language game is to communicate a name for one of the light sources that the robots can detect in their environment. To do so, both robots first have to sense their surroundings. One of the robots takes the role of the speaker, the other takes the role of hearer. The speaker selects one sensation of a light source. This light source is the subject of the communication. The speaker looks for a category that relates to the sensation of this light source. When it did this, it searches a word-form that it has associated with this category in the past. This word-form is then communicated to the hearer.

The hearer, who has also sensed several light sources, tries to interpret the communicated word-form. It looks in its memory if it had stored an association of this word-form with one or more meanings that relate to the sensation of the light sources. If the hearer can find a link between the word-form and some light source, the language game is successful when both robots communicated about the same light source.

3.2 The language game scenario

In the beginning of the experiments, the robots have no categories or word-forms yet. These are the things that they need to develop. So, when the robots are not able to find a suitable category or a word-form, they may expand their memory in order to do so in the future. And if they were able to do so, they will increase the strength of the used association, which increases the chance that they will be successful in the future. How they do this will be explained in detail in this chapter. In this section, the sub-tasks of a language game will be identified and organised.

So, how is a language game organised? Table 3.1 shows the structure of the language game scenario. In a language game two robots – a SPEAKER and a HEARER – get together at close distance. In earlier experiments (Steels & Vogt 1997) the robots came together autonomously. When sensing each other's vicinity, the speaker approached the hearer by using infrared phototaxis. When both robots were close to each other, they aligned such that they faced each other prior to the sensing. This behaviour, however, took approximately 1.5 minutes for each language game. To speed up the current experiments the robots have been brought together manually. The PDL source code for finding each other is included in Appendix B. For more details on this part of the language games, consult Vogt 1997.

Table 3.1: The language game scenario. The "Get together and align" phase is done by the experimenter for practical reasons. "Pointing" and "Topic selection" may be omitted for methodological reasons. See the text for more details.

SPEAKER	HEARER
Get together and align	
Sensing, segmentation and feature extraction	
Topic choice	–
Pointing	Topic selection
Categorisation	
Production	–
–	Understanding
Feedback	
Adaptation	

55

3 Language games

When the robots are standing together at close distance, they acquire a spatial view of their surroundings by means of a specialised sensing task. This sensing task results in a spatial view of the robot's surroundings, which is then segmented resulting in a SET OF SEGMENTS (or CONTEXT for short). Each segment is supposed to refer to a light source as detected by the robot and is represented by a set of connected data points. These data points are sensory data that from which the noise is reduced. From these segments feature vectors are extracted that designate some properties of these segments.

The speaker chooses one segment from the context to be the topic of the language game and tries to categorise its relating feature vector by playing a discrimination game. The discrimination game results in one or more distinctive categories. The hearer identifies one or more segments from the context as a possible topic an tries to categorise its (their) related feature vector(s).

After the speaker has chosen a topic and categorised this segment, it produces an UTTERANCE. An utterance is the communication of a form. The hearer tries to understand this utterance by looking for matching associations of this form with a meaning in its lexicon. If one of these meanings is coherent with one of the distinctive categories of the topic, then the language game *may* be a success. The language game is SUCCESSFUL when the speaker and the hearer communicated about the same referent. The evaluation of the success is called the FEEDBACK.

If the language game was not a success, the lexicon has to be adapted either by creating a new form (if the speaker could not produce an utterance), by adopting the form (if the hearer could not understand the utterance) or by decreasing association scores. Association scores are increased when the language game is successful. The process that models naming and LEXICON ADAPTATION is called a naming game. Figure 3.1 illustrates the language game scenario schematically.

3.3 PDL implementation

To play a language game, a robot has to perform a sequence of actions. These actions need to be planned. The planning is pre-programmed as a script using finite state automata. There is a finite state automaton (FSA) for each role the robots can play: the speaker or hearer. Each finite state automaton is active all the time and when no language game is played, both robots are in state 0. A process called `DefaultBehavior` decides when an agent goes into state 1 of the speaker-FSA or hearer-FSA. In each state a set of dynamic processes is activated or inhibited.[1]

---

[1] See Chapter 2 for a general presentation of the behaviour-based cognitive architecture.

3.3 PDL implementation

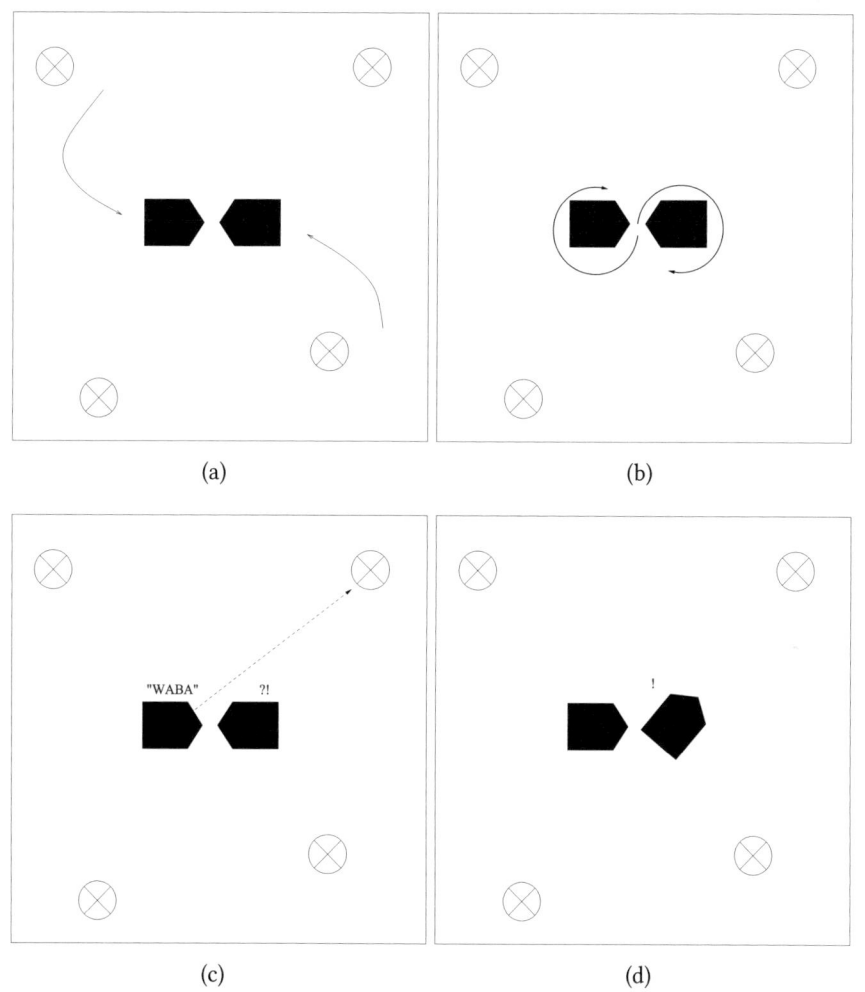

Figure 3.1: A temporal overview of the language game scenario. (a) The robots get together aligned and align. (b) The robots rotate in order to sense their surroundings. (c) The speaker produces an utterance and the hearer tries to understand the speaker. (d) When the hearer "thinks" it understood the speaker, feedback is established and the robots' memories are adapted.

3 Language games

How the physical behaviours of the robots are implemented in PDL is presented in Appendix B. Section 3.4 sketches the architecture as a general architecture for developing cognitive robots. After the introduction of the architecture sensing, segmentation and pointing is discussed in detail.

Table 3.2: A list of abbreviations as used in Figure 3.2.

	SENSORS
LFB	Left Front Bumper
RFB	Right Front Bumper
LBB	Left Back Bumper
RBB	Right Back Bumper
LIR	Left Infrared Sensor
FIR	Front Infrared Sensor
RIR	Right Infrared Sensor
WL	White Light Sensor
RX	Radio Receiver
	FINITE STATE AUTOMATA
0	Default State
Sx	Speaker's State x
Hx	Hearer's State x
	PROCESSES
TBOA	Touch-Based Obstacle Avoidance
	ACTUATORS
TX	Radio Transmitter
LM	Left Motor
RM	Right Motor
IR	Infrared Emitter

Figure 3.2 shows how the language games are implemented in the behaviour-based cognitive architecture. The architecture is built of a large set of parallel processes, which are continuously being processed. These processes, however, do model different types of behaviour and should not be viewed at one level of complexity. Rather, the processes are organised hierarchically.

3.3 PDL implementation

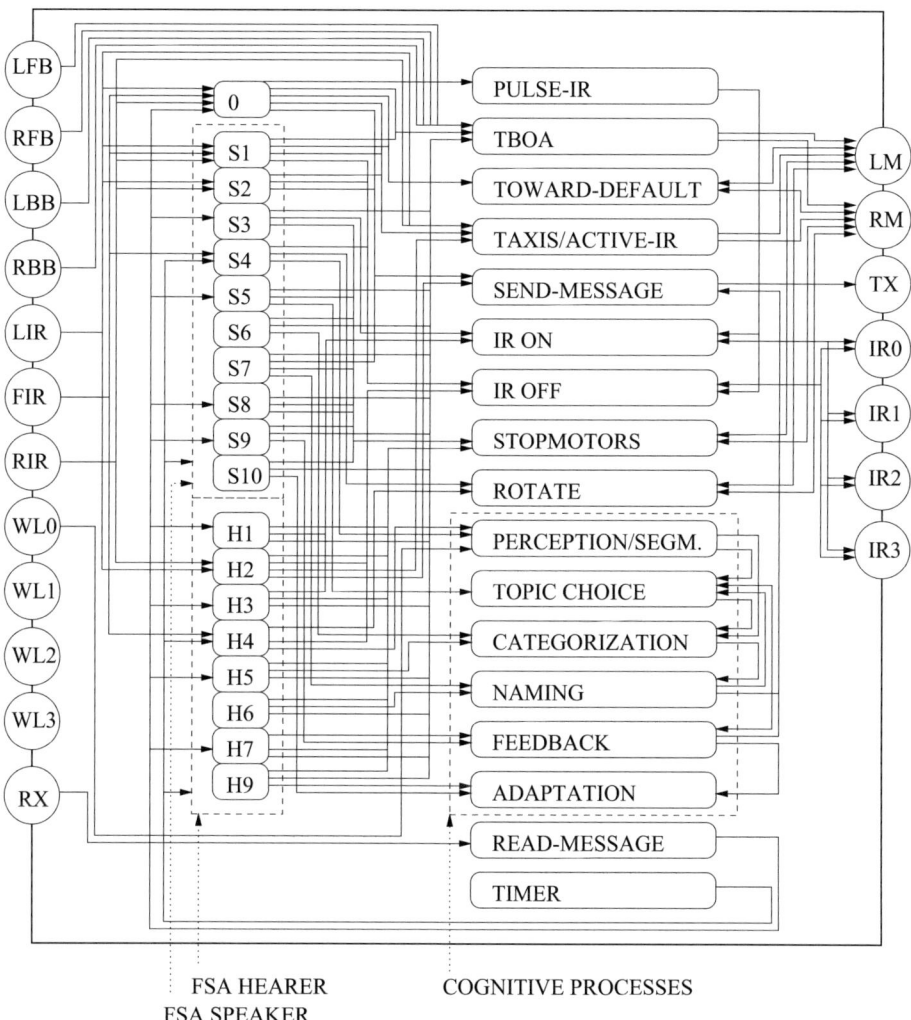

Figure 3.2: The behaviour-based cognitive architecture of the robotic system for processing language games. Note that the PDL-like network structure as introduced in Section 2.3. The flow of information follows each line in the direction of the arrow. If a cross-connection is found, the information follows the line straight. Only when a T-connection is encountered, the direction of the arrow is taken. Some lines are bi-directional, in such cases information flows in both directions. Basically, the information flows from the sensors on the left-hand side of the figure to the actuators on the right-hand side. In between, the information first flows in the finite state automata that controls the planning of the robots. Table 3.2 gives the translation of the abbreviations. Note that the term "perception" is used to designate the sensing.

3 Language games

There is a finite state automaton for the speaker role and one for the hearer. Each state of the finite state automaton activates a set of processes that are shown to the right of the finite state automaton. Those processes that are active respond to information that flows from connected sensors, actuators or other processes. All processes have been implemented in PDL on the real robots in previous versions (Steels & Vogt 1997). In the current experiments, the cognitive processes are implemented as software agents that are processed on a PC.

There are reactive processes like taxis, rotate and obstacle-avoidance. All these processes guide the physical behaviour of the robots.

The cognitive processes can be distinguished from the reactive processes in that they model more complex behaviour and need not directly influence actuators, but they can also influence the internal state of an agent.[2] Coincidentally all cognitive processes are implemented off-board, besides the sensing which is implemented on-board. The cognitive processes tend to work at different time scales then reactive ones. I.e. the time necessary to, e.g., categorise something takes computationally longer than reactive responses do. This has not only been observed in neuroscience,[3] but also during the implementation of so-called follow me games (Vogt 1999; 2000b). In the follow me games the hearer is following the speaker using phototaxis. When a change in direction is encountered the robot categorises a part of its movement. If both phototaxis and categorisation and naming are processed simultaneously on the SMBII, the robot fails to follow the speaker because the categorisation process takes more time than $0.025s$, which is the time of one PDL cycle. Although PDL normally cycles the read-process-execute cycle 40 times per second, it only does so when it finished all its processes.

The categorisation and naming are single processes that carry out a complex process of search, selection and adaptation, but these processes could in principle be modelled by a set of parallel processes as well. This has not been done for the sake of both simplicity and architectural requirements (the computers used are still serial machines).

Both the reactive and cognitive processes are activated or inhibited by the motivational factors which are set inside the states of the finite state automaton.

---

[2] Although the term "cognitive processes" is sometimes used to refer to reactive processes as well, the term is used here to indicate the distinction between reactive behaviours and behaviours that require more sophisticated cognitive processing. The cognitive processes refer to those processes that are fundamentally involved in categorisation and/or naming.

[3] There is a lot of evidence for fast and slow pathways in the central nervous system, where the fast pathways are reactive and the slow are considered to model higher cognition (see e.g. LeDoux 1996).

So, depending on the role an agent has, it will enter either the speaker-FSA or the hearer-FSA. Each finite state automaton models a script-like scheme that takes care of the plan. Note that of course, depending on the task, numerous finite state automata could be developed. Each state takes either direct sensory stimuli or indirect stimuli as read messages or a timer as their arguments. These stimuli are used to determine when the final condition of the state is reached. The final conditions of a state are immediately the initial conditions of the next state. If a robot is too long in one state, measured by the timer, a transition is made to the default state and consequently the language game fails. All other final conditions cause the robot to enter the subsequent state unless it is the final state of the automaton, then it also enters the default state. If no final condition is met, the robot remains in (or re-enters) the same state.

This section sketched how language games are implemented in the behaviour-based cognitive architecture. Of course, much more could be said about the architectural implementation, but this is beyond the scope of the dissertation, which is more concerned with grounding symbols.

3.4 Grounded language games

How are the different sub-parts of the language game scenario modelled? Up to now the physical set-up and implementation of the robots and their interactions have been explained. The only part of the implementation that still needs to be presented are the cognitive models that implement the sensing, segmentation, feature extraction, categorisation and lexicon formation. These models are the core of the present solution to the physical symbol grounding problem. The remainder of this chapter presents these processes.

Sensing, segmentation and feature extraction are important ingredients of the solution of the symbol grounding problem: they form the first step towards invariance. Invariance returns in the cognitive processes during the selection of elements. The three recognised problems in the symbol grounding problem iconisation, discrimination and identification (Harnad 1990) are cognitively modelled. Recall from Chapter 1 that iconisation is the construction of iconic representations that relate to the detection of some real world object. In these experiments, iconisation is more or less modelled by the sensing and segmentation. Harnad (1990) calls "discrimination" the process where it is determined how iconic representations differ. He uses discrimination at the sensing level. Here discrimination is used at the categorisation level. It is modelled by the discrimination games. Identification is the process where categories are identified that relate to

3 Language games

the iconic representations invariantly. This is modelled in this book by the naming game model. As will be explained soon, this classification is not so clear-cut.

As argued in Chapter 1, a symbol can be illustrated with a semiotic triangle. The semiotic triangle, a symbol or sign has three relations: (1) meaning – referent, (2) form – meaning, and (3) form – referent. So, how do robots that have no knowledge construct a meaningful ontology and lexicon for these three relations? Two models have been proposed to solve this problem. For relation (1), there are discrimination games (Steels 1996d). Relation (2) is modelled by the naming game (Steels 1996c). Coupling the two models in a grounded experiment provides relation (3). As argued in Chapter 1, this is because language and meaning co-evolve (Steels 1997b). Closing the semiotic triangle with success is then what Harnad (1990) called "identification" and the symbol grounding problem is solved for that particular symbol. This is so, because only if it is closed successfully, there is enough reason to assume that the symbol stands for the referent.

In the semiotic triangle there is a direct relation between meaning and the referent. However, in cognitive systems there is no such direct relation; the world has to be sensed first. So, to achieve a semiotic coupling, Steels (1999) proposes a semiotic square rather than a triangle (see Figure 3.3). Note that the square couples the semiotic relations in one robot with another. As argued, language dynamics is thought to give rise to the development of both the lexicon as the ontology. How the ontology and lexicon are developed is explained in Sections 3.4.2 and 3.4.3. Section 3.4.1 explains how the robots do their sensing, segmentation and feature extraction.

3.4.1 Sensing, segmentation and feature extraction

In the phase of sensing, the goal is that each robot observes its surroundings from its current physical position. To obtain a more or less identical view, the robots start close to each other. Sensing its surroundings means that the robots construct a spatial view of their environment. This spatial view is represented by the recorded sensory data. However the robots cannot obtain a spatial view directly with the sensors they have, because the sensors can only detect light intensity without spatial information. In order to get a spatial view of their environment, either the robots need to have a spatially distributed array of sensors or the robots need to move. Because of the robots' physical limitations (and the sensory-motor board in particular) it is opted to let the robots move. As a side-effect a higher resolution is obtained. To obtain a spatial view of their complete surroundings the robots rotate a full circle around their axis.

3.4 Grounded language games

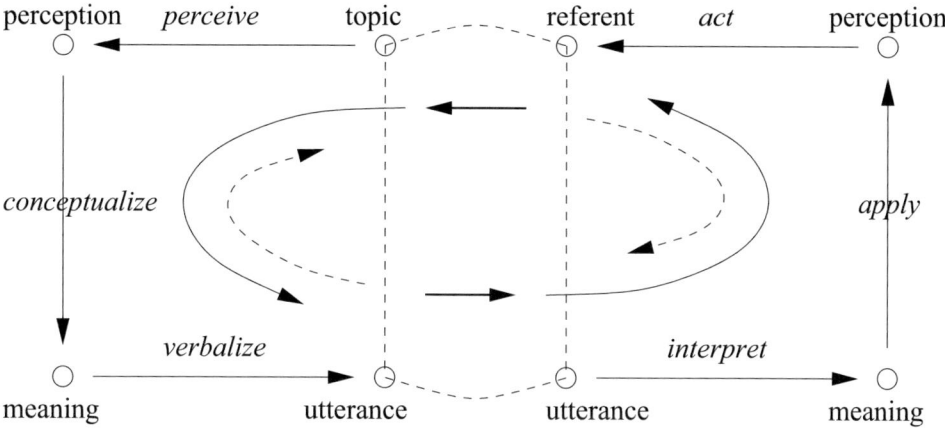

Figure 3.3: The semiotic landscape of a language game can be viewed as a structural coupling. In this landscape, there are two squares, representing the speaker (left) and the hearer (right). The speaker senses a topic, resulting in a perception. In the terminology of this book, this is called sensing. The perception is conceptualised (or categorised) yielding a meaning. This meaning is then verbalised by the speaker and when the hearer receives the utterance (or form), it tries to interpret this. The interpretation results in a meaning which can be applied to a perception. According to this perception, the hearer acts to identify the referent, which should be the same as the topic and thus completing the coupling. When at some point something goes wrong, the agent can adapt their memory. The errors are signalled by means of back propagation.

The robot's observation of its surroundings results in a set of raw sensory data that represents the scene. However, in order to identify the different light sources, the robots have to find connected regions of the sensory data that relate to the sensing of these light sources. This is done by the *segmentation* process. The segmentation can result in segments of varying length. To be able to identify a good category it is more efficient to have a description in a consistent manner that designates invariant and useful properties or features of the sensation of the light source. Extracting these features is done by means of what is called FEATURE EXTRACTION.

The detection of the raw sensory data is done completely on-board. This data is sent to a PC where it is processed further. So, the segmentation and feature extraction takes place on a PC. This is not necessary but convenient for reasons mentioned above.

3 Language games

3.4.1.1 Sensing

During the sensing, the robots construct a spatial view of their surroundings. But because the sensors cannot detect spatial information, sensing is done by letting the robots rotate (ideally) 360° and record their sensory information while doing so. While they rotate (one by one) they record the sensor data 40 times per second. Each sensor writes its data on a SENSORY CHANNEL. The data that enter the sensory channels is transmitted to the PC via the radio.

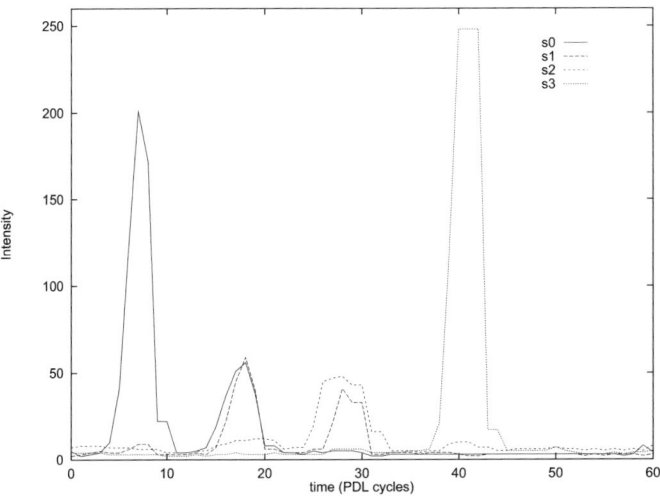

Figure 3.4: The sensing of a robot's surroundings as in the experiments. See the text for explanation.

Figure 3.4 shows a spatial view of a robot's sensing. The sensing took 60 PDL cycles ($= 1.5s$). Each peak *corresponds* to one of the four light sources in the environment. Remember that corresponding means that the sensor with the highest intensity at a peak detects the light source that is placed at the same height as the sensor itself. Recall that the environment consists of 4 light sources that are placed at different heights (Section 2.2).

Figure 3.4 shows that at time step 7 sensory channel $s0$ sensed a large peak, whereas the other sensory channels show low peak values. At time step 18 there is a main peak for sensory channel $s1$ with lower peaks for the other sensory channels. Sensory channel $s2$ shows a maximum at time 28 and sensory channel $s3$ sensed a maximum during time steps 40 to 43. Table 3.3 gives these peaks with their sensory channel values.

3.4 Grounded language games

Table 3.3: Peaks P observed in Figure 3.4. The table lists the highest intensity reached at time t with sensory channels $s0$, $s1$, $s2$ and $s3$.

P	t	s0	s1	s2	s3
1	7	201	9	7	3
2	18	56	59	11	3
3	28	5	41	48	6
4	42	3	3	10	248

These peaks can all be explained with the characteristics of the sensory channels seen in Figure 2.5, page 42. The intensity of each peak is dependent on the distance of the robot to the light source. The robot clearly detects light sources $L0$ and $L3$ from nearby; the corresponding sensory channels detect high values and almost all other sensory channels show low noise values. Light sources $L1$ and $L2$ are further away. The corresponding light sensors show relative low values and some adjacent sensory channels show values that are close to the corresponding sensory channels. Values lower than 10 between the peaks are noise values.

After the speaker finished its sensing, the hearer starts its sensing. That the hearer does not sense the same view as the speaker can clearly be seen in Fig-

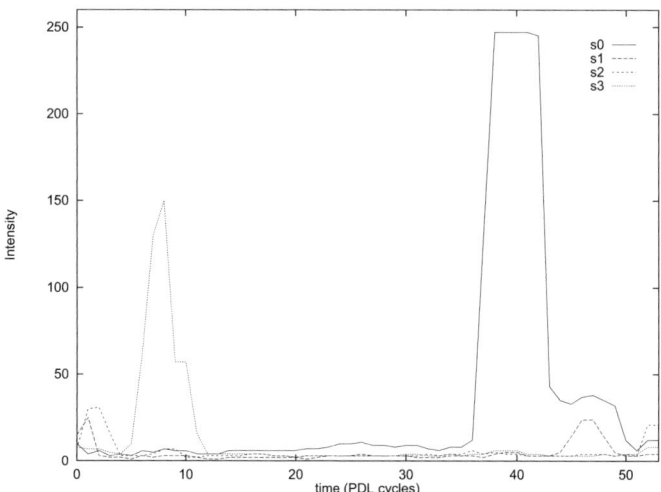

Figure 3.5: The sensing of the hearer in the same language game situation as in Figure 3.4.

65

3 Language games

ure 3.5, which shows the spatial view of the hearer during the same language game. If one looks carefully, one can see similarities, but there is no straightforward mapping. In this plot five interesting peaks can be identified (see Table 3.4).

Table 3.4: Peaks of Figure 3.5.

P	t	s0	s1	s2	s3
1	1	4	25	30	7
2	8	7	3	7	150
3	40	247	5	4	6
4	47	38	24	4	3
5	54	12	4	21	8

Peaks 1 and 5 (Table 3.4) both appear to correspond to $L2$. Although the times at which the peaks are observed lie far apart, these peaks are detected under almost the same orientation of the robot, namely in the front. This fits well with the sensing of $L2$ of the speaker as shown in Figure 3.4, where it is behind the speaker. Peaks 2 and 3 (corresponding to $L3$ and $L0$ resp.) can also be well related to the sensing of the speaker.

Peak 4, which is just observable after the largest peak (between time 55 and 60), does not clearly correspond to a light source. One would expect to detect $L1$, both intuitively as from the sensing of the speaker. Sensory channel $s1$ does indeed show a peak here, but $s0$ shows the highest peak. Peak 4 is also interesting from another point of view. As will be shown below, the segmentation will not recognise this segment. According to the definition just given, it is part of the same region of interest as peak 3 because the intensity does not drop below the noise value.

Usually, the sensing takes about 1.5 seconds, so the robots obtain approximately 60 subsequent data points. Since the robots have 4 sensory channels, they will have a spatial view of about $60 \cdot 4$ data points. Because the speed of rotation is not always constant and it also varies depending on the energy level of their batteries, the number of data points can vary per language game. During the sensing the sensory data is sent to the PC, where the data is processed further.

The onset and offset of the rotation induce two problems. They cause a warped signal on the sensory channels, which is a source of noise, and they do not guarantee a full $360°$ rotation. Therefore, the robots rotate approximately $720°$ while starting with their backs towards each other. The sensing, i.e. the data acquisition starts when the front of the robot faces the opponent robot. This is detected with infrared. It ends 360° later when the robot again detects a maximum in the infrared. The robot stops rotating approximately 180° later when the left back infrared sensor senses infrared. When a robot finished rotating, it sends a radio signal to the other robot. This way both robots can enter the next state in their finite state automaton that controls the planned behaviour of the robots. If the first robot finishes, the second robot can start its sensing, while the first robot waits.

So, during the sensing each robot records a spatial sensory data about its surroundings. To identify the regions of interest that correspond to the referents and to describe these regions consistently, the robots segment their data.

3.4.1.2 Segmentation

Sensing results in a set of approximately 60 observations for the 4 sensory channels for each robot. As shown above, the sensing yields a signal from which relevant information can be extracted concerning the observation of the light sources. The signal needs to be filtered for noise and the relevant regions of interest have to be recognised. The recognition of these regions is done by a process called segmentation.

The filtering of noise is modelled with the function $H(s_{i,j} - \Theta_i)$, where s_i is the sensory channel of sensor i at time step j,[4] Θ_i is the noise value of sensory channel i and $H(x)$ is the Hamilton function:

$$(3.1) \qquad H(x) = \begin{cases} x & \text{if } x \geq 0 \\ 0 & \text{if } x < 0 \end{cases}$$

Suppose that $\tau_{i,j}$ is the result of applying the Hamilton function to the sensory channel data of sensor i at time step j, i.e. $\tau_{i,j} = H(s_{i,j} - \Theta_i)$. The for noise reduced sensing data can be described by a series $(s_0, \ldots, s_{n-1})$ where n is the number of sensory channels and each $s_i = (\tau_{i,0}, \ldots, \tau_{i,M})$ for M data points.

The regions where one of the for noise reduced sensory channels is greater than 0 is supposed to relate to the sensing of a light source. Therefore, the segmentation should construct regions in which this is the case. Hence the segmentation in a set of segments $\{S_k\}$ where $S_k = \{s_{k,0}, \ldots, s_{k,n-1}\}$ consists of a series of sensory channel data. Each sensory channel $s_{k,i} = (\tau_{k,i,0}, \ldots, \tau_{k,i,m})$ where m is the length of the segment and for which $\tau_{k,i,j} > 0$ in at least one sensory channel at each time step j. The different sensory channels $s_{k,i}$ that have some

---
[4] Note that a time step designates at which angle the robot is sensing.

3 Language games

overlap will constitute one segment. For simplicity, the term sensory channel will also be used for the sensory data *after* noise reduction.

It is very common in perceptual systems that the amount of input needs to be reduced for, e.g., computational reasons. Usually the raw image contains one or more regions of interest. These regions of interest may be dependent on the task of the agent. To give an example: for a frog, only small moving spots on the visual field are interesting, since these may be edible flies. In the application described here, the regions of interest are indirectly defined by the goal of the experiments, namely categorising and naming the light sources.

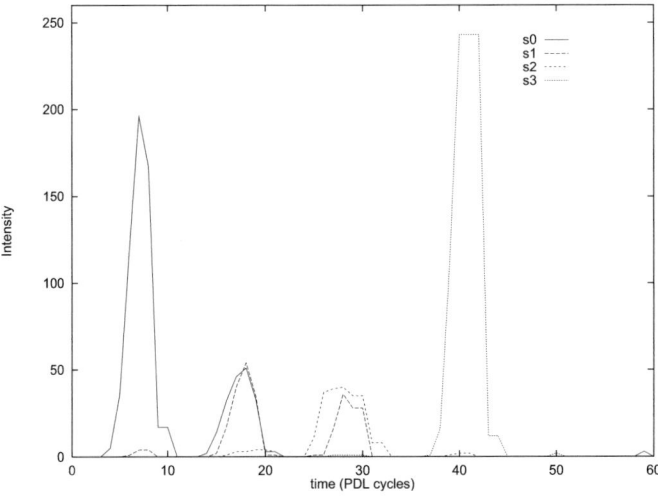

Figure 3.6: The for noise filtered sensed view of robot $r0$ as seen in Figure 3.4.

What does a robot detect of a light source? From Figures 3.4 and 3.5 it becomes clear that the robots detect peaks of intensity of the sensory stimuli in contrast to some background noise. Applying the Hamilton function to Figure 3.4 results in Figure 3.6. Each region where the response is greater than zero will from now on be called a segment. It is assumed that each segment corresponds to a light source. Although in the original figure only 4 regions of interest were identified, the above method identifies 6 segments. The two additional segments come from small perturbations in the landscape that exceed the noise values a little bit. This does not necessarily mean that these perturbations cannot be due to noise, but it can also be due to reflection.

To filter out these segments, an additional rule is applied that a segment should contain more than one data point. Nevertheless, this will not guarantee that all irrelevant regions are filtered out. Neither are all relevant regions segmented. If

3.4 Grounded language games

two peaks (partly) coincide, this segmentation fails to extract the relevant segments. Nevertheless, as will be shown in subsequent chapters, the segmentation makes it possible to ground the sensing of the light sources.

The segmentation of the spatial view of Figure 3.5 does not recognise peak 4 (Table 3.4), because the signal of sensory channel s_0 does not decrease the noise value between peaks 3 and 4. Hence these two peaks are recognised as one segment.

3.4.1.3 Feature extraction

The segments that result from the segmentation have different lengths and may still have a lot of data. Therefore, it is desirable to describe each segment with one vector of low and *equal* dimension. Low dimension benefits computational efficiency. Equal dimension is used for consistency in the data, which makes the computations easier.

In line with pattern recognition and computer vision such a vector representation will be called a FEATURE VECTOR (see e.g. Fu 1976). The elements of this feature vector will be called features. The extraction of the features is called feature extraction. The aim of the feature extraction is to extract features that bear *invariant* information about the light sources.

The feature extraction is applied to each segment S_k. It extracts for each sensory channel i the value $\tau_{k,i,j}$ that has the highest value in S_k. Or, in other words, it gives the highest intensity of a sensory channel in the segment. But the absolute intensities have information about the distance of the light source, which is not an invariant property. Therefore, this highest value is normalised to the absolute highest value of all sensory channels in the segment.

Formally the feature extraction of segment S_k for sensory channel i can be described by a function $\phi(s_{k,i}) : S \rightarrow S'$, where $S = [0, 255]$ is the sensory channel space of some sensory channel and $S' = [0, 1]$ is a one dimensional feature space.

$$(3.2) \quad \phi(s_{k,i}) = \frac{\max_{s_{k,i}}(\tau_{k,i,l})}{\max_{S_k}(\max_{s_{k,i}}(\tau_{k,i,l}))}$$

This function will yield a value 1 for the sensory channel on which the sensor reads the highest peak in a segment. For all other sensory channels the feature extraction yield a value between $[0, 1]$. Naturally, the values of these other features are irrelevant. However, this inference can easily be made by humans, but it should be unknown to the robots. This is so because in more complex environments this need not be an invariant property, and it is not the purpose to give

3 Language games

the robots much knowledge. In addition, the so constructed invariance helps a human observer to analyse the experiments easier.

The result of applying a feature extraction to the data of sensory channel i will be called feature f_i, so $f_i = \phi(\mathbf{s}_{k,i})$. A feature thus designates a property of the sensed segment. In this case, the property can be described as the maximum intensity of a sensory channel in the segment relative to the maximum intensity of this segment.

Segment S_k can now be related to a feature vector $\mathbf{f}_k = (f_0, \ldots, f_{n-1})$, where n is the total number of sensory channels. The space that spans all possible feature vectors $\mathbf{f}$ is called the n dimensional feature space $\mathcal{F} = \mathcal{S}'^n$, or feature space for short. Although this need not be so, in the current experiment the dimension of the feature space is equal to the number of sensory channels.

Applying the feature extraction of Equation 3.2 to the sensing of Figure 3.6 would result in the context given in Table 3.5. Consider for example segment 1 of Figure 3.6. In this segment the top of sensory channel s_0 has a value of 200, the top of s_1 has value 4 and the two other sensory channels have values 0. Normalising the tops of this segment to the highest value yields $f_0 = 1.00$, $f_1 = 0.02$, $f_2 = 0.00$ and $f_3 = 0.00$ (cf. Table 3.5).

Table 3.5: Feature vectors $\mathbf{f}$ after applying the feature extraction measuring the relative intensity of a sensory channel in a given segment.

f	t	f_0	f_1	f_2	f_3
1	7	1.00	0.02	0.00	0.00
2	18	0.94	1.00	0.07	0.00
3	28	0.00	0.90	1.00	0.03
4	40	0.00	0.00	0.01	1.00
5	50	0.00	0.00	0.00	1.00
6	59	1.00	0.00	0.00	0.00

The complete process of sensing and segmentation results in what is called the CONTEXT. This context Cxt is a set of segments S_i that relate to their feature vectors, so

$$Cxt = \{S_0, \ldots, S_m\} \rightarrow \{\mathbf{f}_0, \ldots, \mathbf{f}_m\} \qquad (3.3)$$

where m is the context size.

The feature extraction that calculates the relative intensities is the only transformation used in the experiments reported here. In Steels & Vogt 1997 and Vogt

1998b the feature extraction function calculates the absolute peak values. Other functions have been introduced for categorising spatial categories as in Steels 1996a. Still other functions have been designed for use in the Talking Heads experiments (Belpaeme, Steels & van Looveren 1998; Steels & Kaplan 1999). In the Talking Heads experiment as well as in this application, the functions were designed by hand. de Jong & Steels (1999) and Belpaeme (1999) have shown that such functions can be learned or evolved, respectively.[5]

3.4.2 Discrimination games

In a language game each robot is interested in categorising one or more segments from the context they constructed. The speaker is interested in the segment which it wants to communicate and the hearer is interested in the segment(s) that the speaker can possibly communicate. The segment that the speaker wants to communicate is called the TOPIC. For the hearer these segments are called the POTENTIAL TOPICS. For each (potential) topic the robots *individually* play a discrimination game.

As explained in Section 3.4.1, a segment is related to a feature vector. This feature vector is a point in the feature space. The first step of the discrimination game is to categorise this feature vector with one or more categories that the robot has stored in its memory and that resemble this point in the feature space. A category is defined as some region in the feature space. A feature vector is categorised with that category for which the feature vector falls within that region.

When the segments are categorised, the robots need to select the categories of the topic that are not used to categorise any other segment in the context. The process that does this is called DISCRIMINATION (cf. Steels 1996d). The discrimination can have different outcomes. If one or more categories are found, the discrimination is successful and hence the discrimination game is a success. In this case, the resulting categories can be used in the naming phase of the language game. If no distinctive category is found, this means that the repertoire of categories in the robot's memory is not sufficient to do the task. At the start of each experiment, the repertoire of categories (or ontology) is empty. So, no categorisation can be found and hence no discrimination game can be successful. To overcome this problem in the future, the robot can expand its repertoire of categories.

The complete task of categorisation, discrimination and adaptation is modelled by a discrimination game (Steels 1996d). The basis of the model has not changed

---

[5] Note that Belpaeme calls the feature extraction function "feature detectors".

3 Language games

since its first introduction in 1996, but the implementation and precise details have been adjusted ever since. The first robot implementation of the model can be found in Steels & Vogt 1997 and Vogt 1998a. The model exploits a selectionist mechanism of generation and selection of categories. This results in the self-organisation of categories and has the properties of a dynamical system.

Different types of methods for representation in the discrimination game have been developed: the binary tree method (Steels 1996d), the prototype method (de Jong & Vogt 1998; Vogt 1998b) and the adaptive subspace method (de Jong & Vogt 1998; de Jong 2000). The prototype method and a variant of the adaptive subspace method, which will be called the binary subspace method are investigated in this book and shall be explained in this section. Before doing so, a more general description of the discrimination game model is presented.

Following Steels (1996d), the discrimination game can be defined formally as follows: Assume that the robots can relate their feature vectors to categories and suppose that the robots have categorised a set of categories $C_k = \{c_0, \ldots, c_{n-1}\}$ for the feature vectors relating to segment S_k. Let S_t be the topic. The topic is the segment for which the robots try to find distinctive categories. A category is distinctive if it is related to the topic, but not to any other segment in the context Cxt. The distinctive categories are temporarily stored in a distinctive category set DC. If $DC \neq \emptyset$, the discrimination game is a success. DC is passed to the naming game model that the robots use to communicate. If $DC = \emptyset$, the discrimination game fails and one or more new categories should be created. Consequently, there are three parts in the discrimination game:

1. The distinctive category set DC is constructed according to the following relation:

   (3.4) $$DC = \{c_i \in C_t \mid \forall S_k \in Cxt\backslash\{S_t\} : \neg c_i \in C_k\}$$

2. If $DC \neq \emptyset$, the discrimination game is a success. Possibly adapt the scores of $c_i \in DC$ and pass the DC to the naming game model.

3. If $DC = \emptyset$, then create a new category as ill be explained below.

So, how are feature vectors categorised and how are categories created? The two models that do this are explained hereafter.

3.4.2.1 The prototype method

The prototype method is the main method investigated in this book. In this method the categories are defined in terms of prototypes. In the pattern recogni-

3.4 Grounded language games

tion literature, (see e.g. Banks 1990), a PROTOTYPE is defined as "a single representative sample" in the feature space, i.e. as a point in the feature space. However, a category is defined as a REGION in the feature space. For a prototype, this region can be defined by those points in the feature space that are nearest to this prototype. Therefore, a prototypical category can be defined as a region in the feature space that is represented by a prototype.

The prototypical categories are represented by prototypes and some scores: $c = \langle \mathbf{c}, v, \rho, \kappa \rangle$, where $\mathbf{c} = (x_0, \ldots, x_{n-1})$ is a prototype in the n dimensional feature space, and v, ρ and κ are some scores. As mentioned, categorisation is the process of finding categories for which the feature vector lies within the region that is defined by the category. The categorisation of this is done with the 1-nearest neighbour algorithm. The 1-nearest neighbour algorithm returns the prototype that is nearest to observed feature vector.

It can be useful to define categories at different levels of generality or specificity. If two segments are very distinctive, i.e. the distance between them in the feature space is large, then these segments can be categorised using general categories. However, if the two segments are relatively close to each other in the feature space, the categories may need to be more specific. This means that the regions should be smaller. When sensing a referent under different circumstances in different language games, the extracted feature vectors of the segmented segments differ as well. To select the categories as consistent as possible for various feature vectors relating to some referent in different language games, a general category is most useful. The region of a general category is larger, thus enhancing the chance that different segments of a referent from different language games is represented with the same categories. To enable discrimination under these different conditions and allowing both generality and specificity the categories are constructed in different versions of the feature space.[6] Each version has an increasing resolution of the feature space.

If the discrimination game is a failure, the ontology has to be expanded. Some new prototypes will be constructed and stored in the robot's memory. It is done by exploiting one arbitrary dimension (or feature) of the feature vector in one of the versions of the feature space. Suppose there are versions of the feature space $\mathcal{F}_\lambda$, where each λ designates the resolution of the feature space. In each dimension of the feature space $\mathcal{F}_\lambda$ there are a maximum of 3^λ exploitations, where $\lambda = 0, 1, 2, \ldots$. The choice of 3 is more or less arbitrary, but should not be too large.

---

[6] Note that the term "specificity" is defined differently in the next chapter. There it is defined as a measure that indicates how well a robot names a referent. Here "specificity" is used in the more intuitive and common sense.

3 Language games

Suppose that in the discrimination game the robot tried to categorise feature vector $\mathbf{f} = (f_0, \ldots, f_n)$. New categories are created now as follows:

1. Select an arbitrary feature $f_i > 0$.

2. Select the feature space $\mathcal{F}_\lambda$ that has not yet been exploited 3^λ times in dimension i for λ as low as possible.

3. Create new prototypes $\mathbf{c}_j = (x_0, \ldots, x_{n-1})$ where $x_i = f_i$ and the other x_r are made of already existing prototypes in $\mathcal{F}_\lambda$.

4. Add the new prototypical category $c_j = \langle \mathbf{c}_j, v_j, \rho_j, \kappa_j \rangle$ to the feature space $\mathcal{F}_\lambda$. v_j is a category score that indicates the effect of discrimination. ρ_j is the effectiveness score that indicates the use of the category in the language game. κ_j indicates how general the category is. The initial values of v_j and ρ_j are set to 0.01. κ_j is a constant, which is calculated as in equation 3.7.

The reason to exploit only one feature of the topic, rather than to exploit the complete feature vector of the topic is to speed up the construction of categories. The scores are introduced to enable a better selection in the naming game and are updated after a discrimination game (v) or a naming game (ρ) as follows:

- The categorisation score v is used to indicate how often the category is used to distinctively categorise a feature vector. It is calculated according to the following equation:

(3.5)
$$v = v + \eta \cdot X$$

where

$$X = \begin{cases} 1 & \text{if categorised distinctive} \\ 0 & \text{if categorised, but not distinctive} \end{cases}$$

where η is a learning rate. The default value of the learning rate is set to $\eta = 0.99$.

- The effectiveness score ρ is used to indicate the effective use in the language. I.e.

(3.6)
$$\rho = \rho + \eta \cdot Y$$

where

$$Y = \begin{cases} 1 & \text{if used in language game} \\ 0 & \text{if distinctive, but not used in language game} \end{cases}$$

where η is the learning rate.

- Another score that is calculated is the depth score κ. It indicates how general the category is. As mentioned, if possible it is preferable to use categories that are as general as possible. A category is as general as possible if it is in a feature space S'_λ with λ as small as possible. Because of the resolution of the sensors, the resolution cannot increase in a feature space with $\lambda = 5$, so that is the most specific feature space.

$$(3.7) \qquad \kappa_M = 1 - \frac{\lambda}{5}$$

This score implements a preference for the most general category, which is conform with Steels 1996d.

- In the naming game, the three scores are taken together to form a meaning score μ. Note that it is allowed to talk about meaning, since this score is only evaluated in relation to a form.

$$(3.8) \qquad \mu = \frac{1}{3} \cdot (\nu + \rho + \kappa)$$

The value of μ is averaged so that it can be scaled separately when using it in the naming phase as will be explained in the next section.

Because once the scores ν and ρ become greater than zero, they will never become zero again, they can by way of updating (equations 3.5 and 3.6) only approach zero asymptotically. In order to give new categories a chance to be selected, their initial values are not set to 0, but to 0.01.

There is another adaptation that is done with a prototypical category when it has been successfully discriminated. If the category is used as the meaning in a language game successfully, i.e. it has been the subject of a successful communication, the prototype of the category is shifted towards the feature vector that it categorises according to equation 3.9:

$$(3.9) \qquad \mathbf{c}'_3 = \mathbf{c}_3 + \varepsilon \cdot (\mathbf{f}_t - \mathbf{c}_3)$$

where $\mathbf{c}'_3$ is the new vector representation of $\mathbf{c}_3$ after shifting this category with a step size of ε towards $\mathbf{f}_t$. In the experiments $\varepsilon = 0.1$. This way the prototypical category becomes a more representative sample of the feature vector it categorised.

Because the resolution of a sensor is limited to six feature spaces, $\mathcal{F}_0$ to $\mathcal{F}_5$ are the only ones available. Another reason to keep the number of feature spaces

3 Language games

limited is to keep the computational efficiency within limits. Besides, as will become clear in the experiments, $\mathcal{F}_1$ will usually be sufficient to discriminate.

The prototype method is a variant of an instance-based learning technique (see e.g. Aha, Kibler & Albert 1991; Mitchell 1997). As mentioned, it uses the k-nearest neighbour algorithm, where $k = 1$. Instance-based learning assumes a set of training examples (prototypes) that consists of both positive and negative examples of some categorisation. However, in the prototype method training examples are added to the feature space when a categorisation failed. The validation of a positive or negative example is based on the discriminative power of the categorised prototype. The adaptation of scores that help to select the distinctive categories in the naming phase is very much like the update of Q values in reinforcement learning (see e.g. Sutton & Barto 1998).

3.4.2.2 An example

The prototype method can be illustrated with an example. Suppose there is an ontology of prototypes on $\mathcal{F}_0$ and $\mathcal{F}_1$ as displayed in Figure 3.7 (a) and (b). In Figure (a) there is one prototype $\mathbf{c}_0 = (0.20, 0.90)$. In Figure (b) there are two prototypes $\mathbf{c}_1 = (0.25, 0.75)$ and $\mathbf{c}_2 = (0.65, 0.75)$. Left of the division line in the space is category $\mathbf{c}_1$ and right is category $\mathbf{c}_2$. Suppose the robot has related topic t with a feature vector $\mathbf{f}_t = (0.30, 0.10)$ and it has another segment s in its context related with feature vector $\mathbf{f}_s = (0.15, 0.80)$.[7] Then both $\mathbf{f}_t$ and $\mathbf{f}_s$ are categorised with $\{\mathbf{c}_0, \mathbf{c}_1\}$. Hence the categorisation of topic t is not distinctive. So, the ontology has to be expanded.

The robot selects one dimension of the feature space to exploit. Suppose this is dimension WL1. In this dimension, the topic has a feature with value 0.10. The robot has to select a feature space on which there is still place in the selected dimension. In $\mathcal{F}_0$ each dimension can be exploited $3^0 = 1$ time. This has already happened, so the robot checks if it can exploit the next space, $\mathcal{F}_1$. In this space each dimension can be exploited $3^1 = 3$ times. Dimension WL1 has only been exploited once, so this dimension can still be exploited. New prototypes are constructed with the points $(x, 0.10)$, where x is filled in with the corresponding co-ordinates of the already existing prototypes. If some dimensions are not exploited yet, the new prototypes will not become active until all dimensions of the feature space are exploited. This yields two new prototypes $\mathbf{c}_3 = (0.25, 0.10)$ and $\mathbf{c}_4 = (0.65, 0.10)$, see Figure 3.7 (c). Since each dimension of $\mathcal{F}_1$ can be exploited up to 3 times, the robot can exploit each dimension of this space only once more.

---

[7] Note that these vectors are made up to illustrate the example.

3.4 Grounded language games

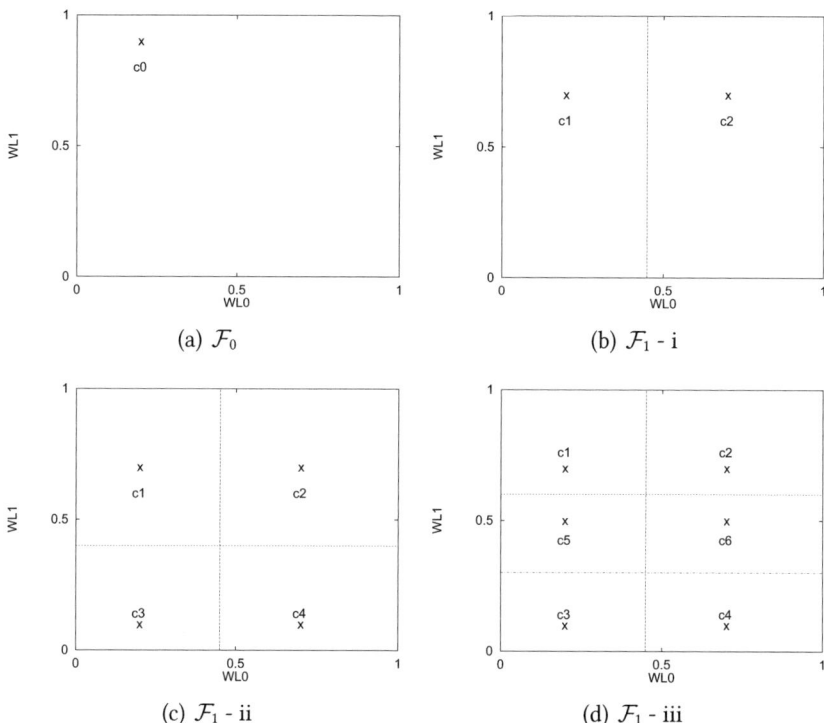

Figure 3.7: These figures show feature spaces $\mathcal{F}_0$ (a) and $\mathcal{F}_1$ (b), (c) and (d), each with their prototypes (x) as used in the example. The figures are displayed in two dimensions for illustrative purposes; in the actual implementation the spaces have 4 dimensions.

This has been done for one dimension in Figure 3.7 (d).

When the robot needs to find distinctive categories in this new ontology based on the same feature vectors as before, $\mathbf{f}_t$ will be categorised with $\{\mathbf{c}_0, \mathbf{c}_3\}$ and $\mathbf{f}_s$ with $\{\mathbf{c}_0, \mathbf{c}_1\}$. Yielding distinctive category set $DS = \{\mathbf{c}_3\}$. Now $\mathbf{c}_3$ may be used in the language game as the meaning of the symbol that is communicated. If this is done successfully, the category is shifted in the direction of the observation by using the following equation (see Equation 3.9):

$$\mathbf{c}_3' = \mathbf{c}_3 + \varepsilon \cdot (\mathbf{f}_t - \mathbf{c}_3)$$

so, in this case, $\mathbf{c}_3' = (0.255, 0.3)$.

Figure 3.8 shows a 2 dimensional version of a possible feature space $\mathcal{F}_2$. There are an increasing number of categories possible at each increasing "layer". In

3 Language games

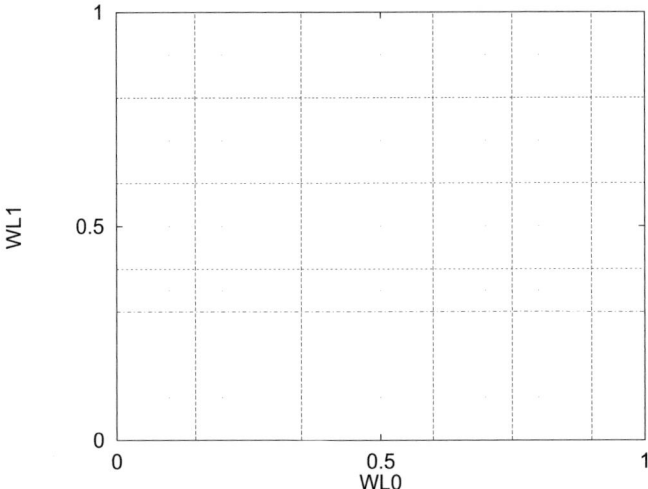

Figure 3.8: A possible feature space $\mathcal{F}_2$. In this space each dimension may be exploited up to 9 times. Again for illustrative purposes the space is shown in 2 dimensions. Note that the prototypes here are displayed as small points.

feature space $\mathcal{F}_0$ there is one place per dimension to be exploited, in $\mathcal{F}_1$ there are 3 places etc. So, $\mathcal{F}_0$ has a maximum of 1 prototype, $\mathcal{F}_1$ has a maximum of $3^4 = 81$ prototypes (recall there are 4 dimensions), in $\mathcal{F}_2$ there are $9^4 = 6561$ possible prototypes, etc.

3.4.2.3 Binary subspace method

The prototype method will be compared with the binary subspace method. The binary subspace method makes use of another way to make categorical distinctions. It is based on the original model introduced by Luc Steels (1996d) that has previously been implemented on the mobile robots (Steels & Vogt 1997; Vogt 1998a). In the original model categories are constructed from trees that make binary divisions of only one dimension of the feature space. The categories that are constructed may have one dimension, but can also be a conjunction of more dimensions. Hence they do not necessarily cover the *n* dimensions of the feature space. Figure 3.9 shows how the trees are constructed.

The binary subspace method combines the binary tree method with the adaptive subspace method (de Jong & Vogt 1998; de Jong 2000). In the adaptive subspace method, the categories (or subspaces) are always in the *n* dimensions of

3.4 Grounded language games

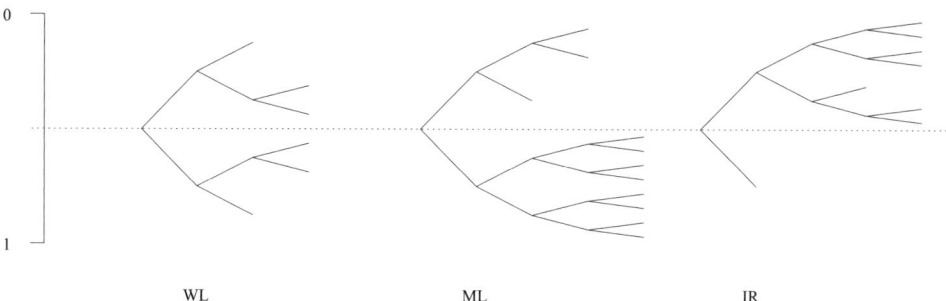

Figure 3.9: Categories represented as binary trees. Every sensory channel (like WL, ML and IR) is associated with a category tree. The root node of the tree is sensitive to whole range of the sensory channel. The tree is incrementally constructed during the evolution of discrimination games. Every time the discrimination game fails, two new nodes may be constructed by splitting one node.

the feature space. In the binary subspace method, the co-ordinates of a feature space $\mathcal{F}_\lambda$ are splitted in one dimension at a time. When all dimensions are thus exploited, the first categories at this space are born.

Categorisation in the subspace is done by relating feature vectors to those subspaces in which the feature vectors fall.

A subspace is defined as an n dimensional rectangle that is surrounded by their boundaries in each dimension of the feature space $\mathcal{F}_\lambda$. Note that this shape of a subspace differs from the one introduced by Oja (1983). Suppose there is a lower boundary x_i and an upper boundary y_i in dimension i of $\mathcal{F}_\lambda$. These boundaries do not necessarily coincide with the boundaries of $\mathcal{F}_\lambda$. A category c_j can be defined by these boundaries in each dimension of $\mathcal{F}_\lambda$: $c_j = \langle x_0, y_0, \ldots, x_{n-1}, y_{n-1}, v_j, \rho_j, \kappa_j \rangle$ for n dimensions. Like for the prototype method, v_j, ρ_j and κ_j are scores.

A feature vector $\mathbf{f} = (f_0, \ldots, f_{n-1})$ can be categorised with category c_j if $x_i < f_i \leq y_i$ for all dimensions of the feature space.

At the start of the experiment the category of $\mathcal{F}_0$ is given. This category spans the complete feature space. When a discrimination game fails, new categories should be formed. This is done by exploiting only one dimension every time the game fails. The following list describes how this is done step by step. Suppose that $\mathbf{f}$ is the feature vector that has been the topic of the discrimination game.

1. Select the category $c = \langle x_0, y_0, \ldots, x_{n-1}, y_{n-1}, v, \rho, \kappa \rangle$ that categorised $\mathbf{f}$ in the feature space $\mathcal{F}_\lambda$ for which λ is greatest. This means that no categorisation is made in $\mathcal{F}_{\lambda+1}$.

2. Select a dimension i of c that has not been exploited yet in feature space $\mathcal{F}_{\lambda+1}$ and for which $f_i > 0$.

3. Create the following lower and upper boundaries: $x'_i = x_i$, $y'_i = x_i + \frac{1}{2} \cdot (y_i - x_i)$, $x''_i = x_i + \frac{1}{2} \cdot (y_i - x_i)$ and $y''_i = y_i$.

4. If there are lower and upper boundaries x^r_p and y^r_p for some r in all other dimensions p of feature space $\mathcal{F}_{\lambda+1}$, then construct new categories by combining all these lower and upper boundaries and adding scores. This yields categories like $c_q = \langle x^r_0, y^r_0, \ldots, x^k_{n-1}, y^k_{n-1}, v_q, \rho_q, \kappa_q \rangle$.

5. If there are no lower and upper boundaries in all other dimensions, then add x'_i, y'_i, x''_i, y''_i to the set of lower and upper boundaries in $\mathcal{F}_{\lambda+1}$.

The binary subspace method differs from the binary tree method of Steels (1996d) in that a category covers all the n dimensions of the feature space. Steels defines categories in 1 to n dimensions, by taking conjunctions of the nodes in the binary trees. Conjunctions can have nodes at different hierarchical layers. Processing all these possible categories is computationally very costly. Suppose there are six hierarchical layers in the tree (as in the prototype method, the binary subspace method has six feature spaces) and 4 dimensions, which is completely filled. Then there are $6 \cdot 4 = 24$ one-dimensional categories. There are $6^2 \cdot 2! = 216$ two-dimensional categories. There are $6^3 \cdot 2! = 432$ three-dimensional categories and $6^4 = 1296$ four-dimensional categories. This makes a total of 1968 possible categories to be explored. The binary subspace method only considers n dimensional conjunctions of nodes each layered at the same layer in the tree. This yields a maximum of only 6 categories to be explored.

The adaptive subspace method developed by Edwin de Jong also differs from the binary subspace method (de Jong & Vogt 1998; de Jong 2000). Like in the binary subspace method, de Jong splits a category from feature space $\mathcal{F}_\lambda$ in $\mathcal{F}_\lambda$ very similar to the binary subspace. However, de Jong's agents directly create a new category, which is the former category splitted in one dimension. Every time this is done, only two new categories are made. In the binary subspace method, more categories may be made. Another difference is that de Jong lets his agents do not create new categories every time the discrimination game fails, but it is done after a fixed number of failures. The choice which subspace is splitted and in which dimension is calculated from some statistics of previous failures to find distinctions. For a detailed explanation of the adaptive subspace method see de Jong & Vogt 1998 and de Jong 2000.

3.4 Grounded language games

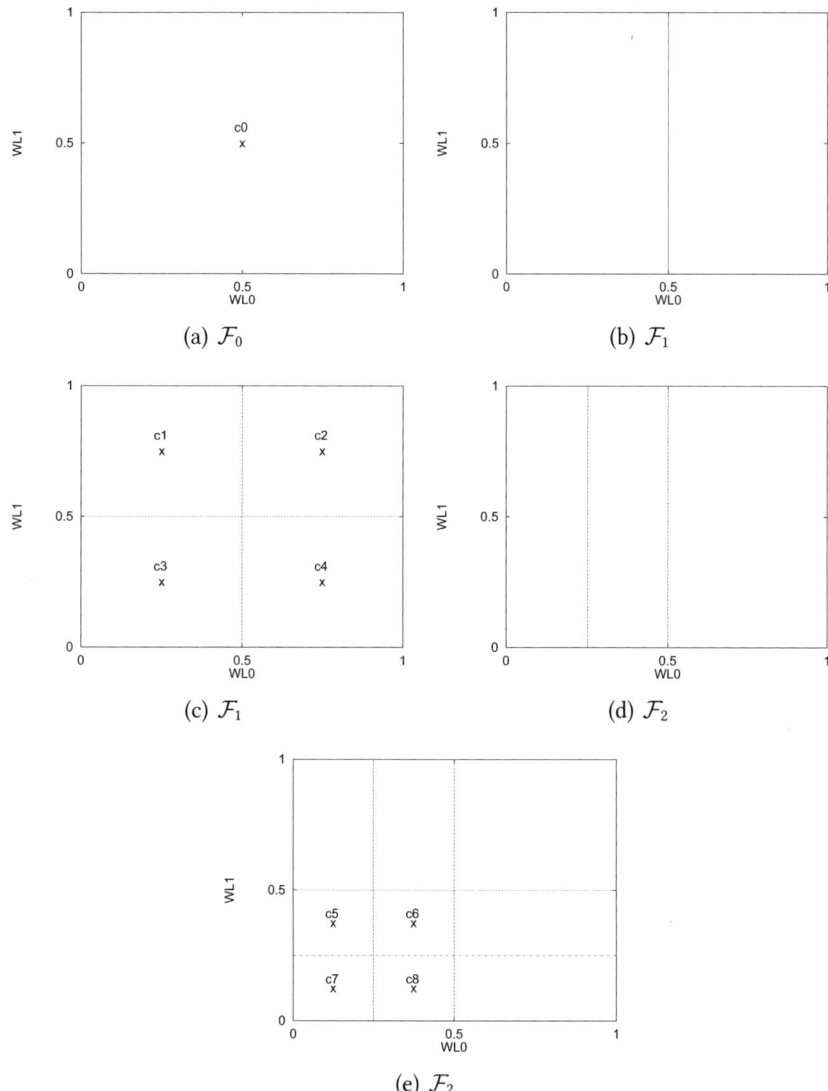

Figure 3.10: The binary subspace method splits the feature space at the lower layer (i.e. λ is smaller) in each dimension at a time. The split divides the former subspace in two equal halves in one dimension. As the plot in Figure (b) did for c_0 in Figure (a). A category is not formed until each dimension is exploited. If another split is made as in Figure (c), new categories are formed. Figures (d) and (e) are two subsequent splits of category c_3 from Figure (c). The last split results in four new categories on $\mathcal{F}_2$. If a split would be made on c_1 in dimension WL1 of Figure (c). Again four new categories are constructed.

Unlike in the prototype method, once a category is made, it is static, i.e. it does not shift in the feature space. Like the categories of the prototype method, the binary subspaces are associated with some scores. These scores are the same as for the prototype method.

One major difference of the binary tree, binary subspace and adaptive subspace with the prototype method is that there is not necessarily a categorisation in each feature space $\mathcal{F}_\lambda$ where there are categories. In the prototype method, the entire space is always covered once a category is there. This is not the case in the other methods.

A more fundamental difference with the prototype method is that the binary subspace method, like the binary tree method and the adaptive subspace method is biologically less plausible. Humans do not make binary distinctions of the world. The feature space of observations is usually not divided in binary distinctions.

The binary subspace method, like the adaptive subspace method (de Jong 2000) is a type of ADAPTIVE RESOLUTION generalisation. In these methods a multidimensional space is divided in subregions based on some criteria in order to solve some tasks. Examples of such learning techniques can be found in Chapman & Kaebling 1991 and Moore & Atkeson 1995.

3.4.2.4 Summary

In this section the discrimination game model has been introduced. The aim of a discrimination game is to find distinctive categories that categorise one or more segments. Categories can be defined differently. In this book two methods are compared. The prototype method defines a prototype as a point in the feature space and a category is then defined as the region in the space where the points are closest to the prototype. The binary subspace method defines a category as a subspace that is constructed by splitting another space in two equal halves at one dimension. Categories are structured in different versions of the feature space, where each version has a different resolution. This allows making distinctions that are more general or more specific.

The prototype method is used in almost all experiments. In one experiment the binary tree method is used, and in still another experiment a fuzzy approach of the prototype method is used. This latter method is explained in Chapter 5.

The feature vector that relates to the topic is categorised with a category that covers the feature vector. A category is distinctive if it is not related to any other feature vector in the context than to the topic. If distinctive categories can be found, the discrimination game is a success. In this case the distinctive categories may be adapted, e.g. by shifting them, and one of the categories can be used as the meaning in the naming phase. If the discrimination game is a failure, new categories can be constructed.

3.4.3 Lexicon formation

Now that each robot has categorised the (potential) topic(s) distinctively, they can communicate these distinctive categorisations. Communication is established by the speaker and hearer. The speaker names the category. The hearer tries to interpret this name, i.e. it tries to identify the uttered word-form so that it corresponds to the categorisation of the topic. The topic is supposed to relate to the referent that the speaker's utterance stands for.

In some experiments the hearer already knows which topic this is prior to the verbal communication. This means that there is some sort of joint attention on the topic. This knowledge is exchanged from the speaker by means of extra-linguistic communication. In other experiments the hearer does not know yet what the topic is. The hearer then only has the uttered word-form and the distinctive categories at its disposal. The availability of such information is a source of discussions in the psycholinguistic literature (see e.g. Barrett 1995) and the discussion in Chapter 1. Therefore it is interesting to investigate whether and under what circumstances the robots can deal with these different types of knowledge.

When the hearer interpreted the utterance, the language game is successful when both robots communicated about the same referent. In case where the hearer already had this knowledge at its disposal, this is the case. Otherwise, the robots may evaluate whether they did so. This evaluation is called FEEDBACK. The evaluation of feedback is, like joint attention, done by means of extra-linguistic communication. Again, the availability of feedback to a language learner is of much debate in the psycholinguistic literature (see e.g. Bowerman 1988). So, is this really necessary?

Both types of extra-linguistic information is subject of investigation of this book. For this reason different types of language games have been developed: the ostensive game, guessing game, observational game and XSL game.

When the experiments start, however, the robots have no language to their disposal yet. They have to construct this. In the experiments the question of how grammar is evolved is left aside and only a lexicon is developed. How are forms associated with meanings? And how can both robots acquire a shared lexicon? To model this, the robots can adapt their lexicons. This lexicon development is based on the three mechanisms that Luc Steels (1996c) proposed for lexicon formation: individual adaptation, cultural evolution and self-organisation.

3 Language games

The previous section presented the discrimination game model by which the first two steps (iconisation and discrimination) of the grounding problem is tackled. The model tries to find categories that relate to the topic, but not to any other segment that has been observed in that context. Such a category can be related to a form. If this is done, the category functions as the meaning of a semiotic sign in the Peircean sense. When this form is either arbitrary or conventionalised (e.g. through language) the sign becomes a symbol according to Peirce (see e.g. Chandler 1994). Since it is assumed that meaning co-evolves with language (Chapter 1), the symbol is grounded in language and hence the form will be conventionalised. The naming game model implements how the form is conventionalised.

The lexicon formation is based on the naming game model introduced by Luc Steels (1996c). The naming game implements the communication between two agents that try to name the meaning of the referents they sensed in their environment. One of the agents plays the role of the speaker and chooses a topic from the segments that constitute the context. It searches its lexicon for a form-meaning association of which the meaning matches the category of the topic. The associated form is "uttered" and in turn, the hearer tries to understand the utterance. The hearer does so by searching its own lexicon for a form-meaning association of which the form matches the utterance. If there exist such an element, the hearer compares the associated meaning(s) with the category of the topic. If there is a match and both the speaker and the hearer named the same topic, the naming game is successful. Otherwise there is a failure. According to the outcome of the game the lexicon will be adapted.

3.4.3.1 Different language games

One of the issues that will be investigated in this book is what type of extra-linguistic information is necessary to guide a meaningful lexicon formation. As mentioned above and in Chapter 1, it is not clear what extra-linguistic information infants have at their disposal when learning language. Do they establish joint attention prior to the verbal communication? Or do they receive feedback on the effect of a linguistic interaction? Or is neither at their disposal?

To investigate whether robots can develop a shared lexicon under these different circumstances, four types of language games have been implemented. In these language games different configurations of the availability of joint attention and feedback have been implemented as shown in Table 3.6. The different games can be summarised as follows:

Ostensive game This game is conform with the original naming game model (Steels 1996c). The speaker informs the hearer prior to the linguistic communication what the topic is, e.g. by means of pointing at the referent. Hence joint attention is established. It then produces a (linguistic) utterance, which the hearer tries to understand. Feedback is evaluated to check if both robots finally identified the same topic. This game has also been implemented in Steels & Vogt 1997.

Guessing game In the guessing game (Steels & Kaplan 1999), the speaker does not provide the hearer with topic information. It produces an utterance and the hearer has to *guess* which referent the speaker is naming. As in the ostensive game feedback is evaluated to check if both robots finally identified the same topic. The guessing game has first been implemented in Vogt 1998c and will be the model of most experiments in this book.

Observational game This game is influenced by the work of Mike Oliphant (1997). First joint attention is established, so the hearer knows in advance which segment is the topic. Access to this kind of information is what Oliphant calls "observation". The speaker produces an utterance, which the hearer tries to interpret. No feedback on the game's effect is evaluated, so the lexicon is adapted independent of the effectiveness of the game.

XSL game The XSL game is to check if either joint attention or feedback is really necessary. It is to show that lexicon formation does not work without joint attention of feedback. So, without providing topic information, the speaker produces an utterance. The hearer tries to interpret the utterance. The robots adapt their lexicons despite the fact that they have no idea what the other has been communicating. Note that XSL stands for "cross-situational learning" (Pinker 1984; Siskind 1996), which is the learning mechanisms on which this model is based. (As noted in the preface, this was not noted at the time of writing this book, so no further reference to the literature of cross-situational learning is made.)

The four games differ in the availability of joint attention and feedback as illustrated in Table 3.6. In most of the experiments reported in this book the guessing game is applied. The remainder of this section explains the different subparts of the naming: joint attention, production, understanding, feedback and adaptation.

3.4.3.2 The lexicon

Each agent constructs a lexicon. How does the lexicon look like? A lexicon is a set of form-meaning associations that an individual robot stores in its memory. The

3 Language games

Table 3.6: A schematic overview of the extra-linguistic information that is available in the different language games.

Game	Joint attention	Feedback
ostensive	Yes	Yes
guessing	No	Yes
observational	Yes	No
XSL	No	No

lexicons of the two robots in the experiments can differ and are shared when the lexical entries are used such that both robots can communicate a referent successfully. So, the lexicon consists of elements of form-meaning associations. Each form-meaning association *FM* is a tuple of a form *F*, a meaning *M* and an association score σ. So, the lexicon *L* can be defined as:

$$(3.10) \qquad L = \{FM_0, \ldots, FM_N\}$$

where *N* is the size of *L* and form-meaning $FM_i = \langle W_i, M_i, \sigma_i \rangle$. At the beginning of an experiment, $L = \emptyset$. It is constructed during the experiment. The form *F* is an arbitrary string of characters from the alphabet. The shape of a form is given as a "CVCV" string where C is a consonant and V a vowel.

Note that there may be more entries with the same form or with the same meaning. So, there may be a many-to-many relation between form and meaning. The adaptation of the lexicon is done by form-invention, form-adoption (both in which new *FM* associations are constructed) and the adaptation of scores. During the experiments, where thousands of games are being played, the form-meaning associations that have been effective in the past (i.e. their scores are high) tend to be used more often than ineffective form-meaning associations. This way a more or less coherent communication system emerges.

3.4.3.3 Joint attention

As mentioned, the robots establish joint attention in two types of language games: the ostensive game and the observational game. Joint attention means that the two robots participating in a language focus their attention on the same topic. To be more concrete, both robots know what the topic is. In the experiments it is established *prior* to the verbal communication. To establish joint attention the robots use what is called extra-linguistic communication. In human cultures, it can be established by means of pointing, following eye-gaze and other means that humans have at their disposal to communicate extra-linguistically.

Joint attention is modelled by comparing the feature vectors of the speaker's topic with the feature vectors of the segments in the hearer's context. To allow a single algorithm for the hearer's understanding, the cases where there is no joint attention is modelled as if there would be joint attention.

More formally, the availability of joint attention is modelled by calculating a *topic score* ϵ_S for each segment $S \in Cxt$. The idea of the topic score is to estimate the likelihood that segment S is the topic. There are different ways to calculate ϵ_S (e.g. Vogt 1998c). Here two methods are implemented: a *correspondence* method and one simulating *no* joint attention. The methods are defined as follows:

Correspondence

$$(3.11) \qquad \epsilon_S = \begin{cases} 1 & \text{if } S \text{ corresponds to } t_s \\ 0 & \text{otherwise} \end{cases}$$

where t_s is the speaker's topic. This information is drawn from the topic that the speaker observed.

Of course this method for calculating the topic score is very unlikely to exist in nature. Agents usually are not capable inspecting the internal state of other agents. However, to increase the reliability of the topic information, establishing joint attention here is simulated by INTERNAL INSPECTION.

No joint attention

$$(3.12) \qquad \forall S \in Cxt : \epsilon_S = \text{Constant} > 0$$

The first method is used in the ostensive and observational games. The latter is used in the guessing and XSL games. Both joint attention (by means of correspondence) and no joint attention are modelled by the topic score. This has the advantage that the understanding phase of the naming game can be modelled with one algorithm. As will be explained, for this ϵ must be greater than zero. In Vogt (1998b) ϵ was calculated using cross-correlations and using information about the angle under which the topic was observed. Both methods work less well than the correspondence method used in this book, because there was too much stochasticity in the system.

In the experiments the hearer has to identify the topic of the speaker without using verbal communication. Attempts to implement joint attention physically

3 Language games

on the mobile robots failed. A form of pointing has been implemented, but this led to unsatisfactory results (Steels & Vogt 1997; Vogt 1998a). The simplistic LEGO robots have no sophisticated means to establish joint attention without using language. It is beyond the scope of this book to discuss why this is the case. For more discussions on this technical issue, see Vogt 1998b,c.

To overcome this technical problem in the current implementation, it is assumed that the robots can establish joint attention and it is simulated using a trick. The robots inspect the feature vectors of each other, so that they can compare them. The hearer compares the feature vector of the speaker with the feature vectors of its own context. If a feature vector corresponds, the segment that relates to this feature vector is assumed to be the topic. Two feature vectors correspond when they have a feature with value 1 in the same dimension. This is conform the fact that the sensor at the same height as a light source reads the highest intensity and hence this sensor *corresponds* to the light source.

3.4.3.4 The speaker's production

Whether or not joint attention is established, the speaker will try to name the topic. From the discrimination game, it has found a set of distinctive categories. If the discrimination game failed, the speaker cannot name the topic. Otherwise, it will select one of the categories and searches its lexicon if there is an entry that is consistent with this category. If such an entry exists, the speaker can name the topic. Otherwise, it has to invent a new form. This form will be associated with the category and a new lexical entry is born. This form is then uttered, so that the hearer can do its part of the naming phase.

So, when the speaker categorised the topic, which yielded a nonempty set of distinctive categories, the speaker will try to name one of these categories. Which category is selected may depend on several criteria and the selection method used. One method has been implemented that could be called a "lazy search method". In this method the speaker orders the categories in linear order of decreasing representation score μ. Then it tries to match these categories with a lexical entry one by one until a matching association has been found.

Suppose that $DC' = DC$ is the ordered set of distinctive categories, $L = \{\langle F_i, M_i, \sigma_i \rangle\}$ is the lexicon, $U = $ nil is the utterance ("nil" means that the utterance has no value yet) and $\sigma_{\max} = 0$ is the maximum score. The algorithm, based on Steels (1996c) for finding a matching entry can be described as follows:

1. Set $L' = L$.

2. If $DC' \neq \emptyset$ and $U = $ nil, take out the first category c_i from DC', set DC' to the remainder of this set and goto 3, else goto 5.

3. If $L' \neq \emptyset$, take out the first element $\langle F_j, M_j, \sigma_j \rangle$, set L' to the remainder of this set and goto 4, else goto 1.

4. If $M_j = c_i$ and $\sigma_j \geq \sigma_{max}$, then $U := F_j$ and $\sigma_{max} := \sigma_j$. Goto 2.

5. If $U =$ nil, goto 6, else goto 7.

6. Create new form F as an arbitrary string of consonant-vowel-consonant-vowel with a certain probability, set $U := F$, $M := c$ (where c is the first element of DC) and $\sigma := 0.01$. Add the new entry $\langle F, M, \sigma \rangle$ to L. Goto 7.

7. Send U to the hearer. Stop.

In natural language: As long as there are distinctive categories, the speaker tries to name the first (and best) distinctive category. It searches its lexicon for a form-meaning association for which the meaning matches the distinctive category. If there are more such associations, it selects the entry for which the association score is highest. If there are no such associations the speaker takes the next distinctive category and repeats the above, else it continues as follows. If no lexical entry is found, a new form may be invented with a certain probability (this is discussed in more detail when the adaptation is discussed). If a new form is invented, a new lexical entry is added to the lexicon and this entry is selected. The form of the selected entry is uttered.

Note that as soon a distinctive category will be used in a language game where it relates a form with a referent, this distinctive category is called the *meaning*.

3.4.3.5 The hearer's understanding

In the understanding phase, the hearer tries to select a lexical entry that fits the utterance best. This way it is able to select which topic it "thinks" the speaker meant. When the hearer receives an utterance that is relevant (i.e. not nil), it tries to interpret the utterance. It does so by searching its lexicon for associations that fit the utterance. From the associations found and that are consistent with the distinctive categories of the potential topic(s) the most effective one is selected. The effectiveness is based on information about the likelihood of the potential topic, the effectiveness of the meaning in the past and the effectiveness of the association in the past. The most effective entry determines the hearer's selection. If no such entry exists, a new entry must be made. This is done in the adaptation phase as will be explained below.

The hearer's understanding is a little bit more complex than the production. It first of all depends on what knowledge the hearer receives about the topic

3 Language games

other than the linguistic exchange. Secondly, it may depend on how effective a distinctive category has been in the past. And finally, it depends on how effective a certain form-meaning association has been.

Suppose that $D = DC_p$ is the set of distinctive category sets of potential topics p. Each potential topic p has a non-zero topic score ϵ_p. And suppose that $U = $ nil is the utterance received from the speaker, $t = $ nil is the topic, $L' = L$ is the lexicon and $P = $ nil is the best selection so far. The hearer's understanding algorithm is based on the stochastic naming game model (Steels & Kaplan 1998) and can be described as follows[8]:

1. If $L' \neq \emptyset$, then select first element $\langle F_i, M_i, \sigma_i \rangle$. Else goto 8.

2. If $F_i = U$, then goto 3, else goto 1.

3. Set $D' = D$. Goto 4.

4. If $D' \neq \emptyset$, then select first element DC_p from D' and goto 5, else goto 1.

5. If $DC_p \neq \emptyset$, then select first element c_j from DC_p and goto 6, else goto 4.

6. If $c_j = M_i$, then calculate $\Sigma = w_1 \cdot \epsilon_p + w_2 \cdot \mu_j + w_3 \cdot \sigma_i$, where the w_k are weights. Goto 7.

7. If $\Sigma > \Sigma_{max}$, then set $P := \langle F_i, M_i, \sigma_i, p \rangle$ and $\Sigma_{max} := \Sigma$. Goto 5.

8. If $P \neq $ nil, then $t := p$ where p is part of P. Stop.

In the experiments the weights are set to $w_1 = 1$, $w_2 = 0.1$ and $w_3 = 1$. This way the meaning score μ has little influence on the selection process. Only when either μ is very large, or when there is a conflict between the topic scores and association scores of different elements, the meaning scores influence the selection process.

So, the hearer looks for the topic that can be related with a form-meaning association that best fits the expressed form and a distinctive categorisation of a potential topic. The language game may be evaluated by means of feedback. Whether or not feedback is actually incorporated depends on the type of language game being played. To have a consistent implementation, however, there is always a feedback model as explained hereafter.

---

[8] Note that Steels & Kaplan (1998) lets the hearer construct a matrix from which similar decisions are made.

3.4.3.6 Feedback

It might seem obvious that an agent has to know whether the language game it is participating is effective in order to learn a language: it needs *feedback*. What type of feedback is present is an important issue in the psycholinguistics, (see e.g. Bowerman 1988). Is the feedback of a language game about its effectiveness or not? Is it only positive or is it negative as well? In the experiments reported here, the feedback gives information on the language game's effectiveness, both positive and negative. Since the robots should be able to determine this feedback themselves (possibly with each other's help), some mechanism has to be developed to achieve this.

Feedback has been implemented by means of correspondence. Both these methods work similar to the methods explained used for joint attention. Both methods are used to provide feedback in the ostensive and guessing games, provided that both robots activated a form-meaning association. The observational and XSL games do not use such feedback. However, for consistency in the implementation, no feedback is implemented similarly. Instead of a topic score ϵ, a success score ε is computed. This success score indicates the likelihood that both agents have identified the same topic.

Correspondence The language game is successful when the confidential factor $\varepsilon = 1$.

$$\varepsilon = \begin{cases} 1 & \text{if the two topics corresponds} \\ 0 & \text{otherwise} \end{cases} \quad (3.13)$$

No feedback

$$\varepsilon = \begin{cases} 1 & \text{if both robots have selected a lexical entry} \\ 0 & \text{otherwise} \end{cases} \quad (3.14)$$

The above methods implement feedback in terms of success. In the case of no feedback, the success is based on the ability to select a form-meaning association. This could be called feedback, but the feedback meant in this book is in terms of the actual success of a language game, i.e. both robots should have identified a symbol that has the same form and that stands for the same referent. So, what are the outcomes of the feedback using the correspondence criterion? If the topic is related to the same referent that the speaker intended, the language game is successful and $\varepsilon = 1$. If it is not, there is a misunderstanding (or "mismatch in referent") and $\varepsilon = 0$. The outcome of the evaluation will be available to both robots.

Besides the evaluation of the success, there are other types of "feedback" in the system. First, if the speaker cannot produce an utterance, the hearer need not to do anything, except skip the current language game. The speaker can easily determine its own shortcomings. Second, sometimes the hearer cannot understand the speaker. This is because it does not recognise the uttered form in the current context. Either it does not have the form in its lexicon, or its meaning does not match one of the distinctive categories. In this case, the speaker must be informed that the language game is a failure. The third and most common-practice is that the hearer did interpret the form in the context. However, it may have misinterpreted to what referent the speaker's utterance referred. So, both agents have to find out that they both identified the same topic. Attentive readers will recognise that this is technically the same problem as when the hearer when the speaker and hearer need to establish joint attention on the topic.

Why not use language as a means of providing feedback? Since language is the issue of learning, it does not seem to be the most reliable source of attention mechanism. If the robots do not know the language yet, how can they use language as a source of feedback? Therefore a non-linguistic means is preferable. Such means have already been defined for joint attention.

Like was the case with joint attention, one attempt has been made to implement this by means of physical pointing (Vogt 1998b). Since this method did not work well, the technical problems have been set aside and providing feedback has been simulated assuming the robots can do it properly. The methods used are the same as in the case of joint attention. The lexicon is adapted according to the outcome of the game as will be explained hereafter.

3.4.3.7 Adaptation

The naming game may fail in various ways. Both at the production level as at the understanding level. Especially in the beginning when there are no or few lexical entries. In these cases the robots have to adapt their lexicons. They may have to invent new word-forms or they may need to adopt a word-form from the other robot. In order to increase the chance that effective lexical entries will be selected more often than ineffective ones, the association scores have to be adapted. This can happen when the language game is a failure, but it should also happen when the language game is a success. It is important to realise that the robots adapt their lexicons individually.

As made clear before, there are several possible outcomes of a language game. First, the game can already fail during categorisation. This will put pressure to the agent to increase its repertoire of categories as explained in Section 3.4.2.

3.4 Grounded language games

Another failure could be due to the fact that the speaker does not have a form association matched to category to be named. In this case the agent can invent a new form to associate with the category. If the hearer does not understand the speaker, this can mean that it does not have a proper form-meaning association. The expressed form can be adopted and associated with one or more categories. When there is a mismatch in reference and when the language game was a success, the association scores are updated. When all this is not the case, the language game is a success. The adaptation is based on (Steels 1996c), although the updates of the association scores is a little bit different.

No lexical entry speaker The speaker has no form associated with the categories it tried to name. In this case, the speaker may invent a new form as an arbitrary string of characters. It does so with a creation probability P_s that is kept low to slow down the form creation rate. In most experiments $P_s = 0.02$. This way the lexicon will become less ambiguous. The invented form is associated with the category that has the highest meaning score μ. The new lexical entry is related with an association score σ that is set to 0.01. (Not to 0.0, because then it may never be selected, as explained in Section 3.4.2.)

No lexical entry hearer The hearer has no association in its lexicon where the form is associated with a meaning that is consistent in the current context. The hearer now may adopt the form from the hearer to associate it with a segment of which it has a non-zero topic score ($\epsilon_t > 0$). In this case the most likely segment is chosen, i.e.

$$\epsilon_t = \max_S(\epsilon) \tag{3.15}$$

If there are more than one segments for which equation 3.15 holds, then one segment is selected at random. This is e.g. the case in the guessing game, where all segments have equal topic score. The meaning of the selected segment is then associated with the word-form and the lexical entry is related to an association score $\sigma = 0.01$.

Mismatch in reference The hearer misinterpreted the speaker's utterance. I.e. the topic's of both robots do not coincide. In the case that both robots selected a form-meaning association, but when the topics did not coincide, at least according to their own evaluation, the robots decrease the ASSOCIATION SCORE σ of the used association:

$$\sigma := \eta \cdot \sigma \tag{3.16}$$

3 Language games

where η is the LEARNING RATE. In some experiments the hearer also adopts the form with another segment.

Communicative success Both robots communicated the same referent and hence the language game was a success. The used association is strengthened while association scores of other form-meaning associations are laterally inhibited. Let $FM' = (F', M', \sigma') \in L$ and $FM = (F, M, \sigma) \in L$ be form-meaning associations. Here FM' are the form-meanings to be adapted and FM is the association used in the communication. The scores are updated as a walking average:

$$(3.17) \qquad \sigma := \eta \cdot \sigma + (1 - \eta) \cdot X$$

where

$$X = \begin{cases} 1 & \text{if } FM' = FM \\ 0 & \text{if } (FM' \neq FM) \wedge ((F' = F) \vee (M' = M)) \end{cases}$$

In all other cases, i.e. when $((F' \neq F) \wedge (M' \neq M))$, nothing happens.

The adaptation scheme thus implements generation, cultural evolution and selection. Generation is part of the adaptation through invention. Cultural evolution is implemented by form adoption. Whereas the selection is influenced by the excitation and inhibition of the association scores. The seemingly effective associations are excited and the ineffective ones are inhibited.

The learning of the lexicon for each individual is based on REINFORCEMENT LEARNING (see e.g. Sutton & Barto 1998). In reinforcement learning, a task is learned according to the reward that is evaluated from the effect of some action. In the naming game, the action is the communication, the reward is based on the effect of the communication and it is evaluated with the feedback.

3.5 Coupling categorisation and naming

This chapter presented the language game model. It explained sensing, segmentation, feature extraction, categorisation, discrimination and lexicon formation in detail. The different processes that make up the language game are, together with the data flow illustrated in Figure 3.11. This section explains how the coupling of the different aspects of the language game model work together in order to develop a shared and grounded lexicon.

3.5 Coupling categorisation and naming

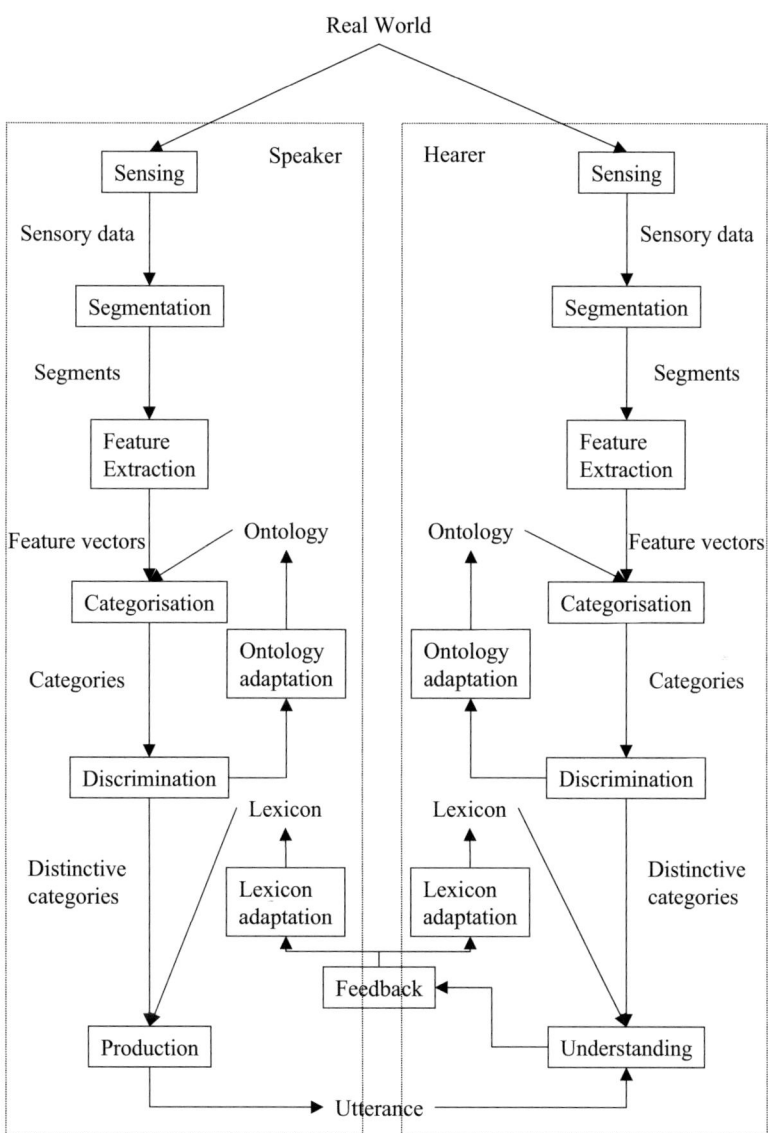

Figure 3.11: A schematic overview of the processes and data flow in the language game.

3 Language games

It is important to realise that in an experiment the robots play a series of language games. Typically there are thousands of language games played in one experiment. The robots play language games at different locations in their environment under different conditions. The different conditions are caused by changing light conditions, different energy levels and wear. Under these different conditions, the robots acquire a different sensing of the light sources. Although different sensations of a light source can be categorised with one category, the different sensations induces different categorisations. The number of different (distinctive) categorisations in an experiment can be very high.

In order to have an efficient communication system, the number of forms that are used should not be too large. Ideally, there is a one-to-one mapping between referent and form. As explained, the categories that are used in the language games make up the meaning of the symbols. They interpret the sensing of the referent and are associated with a form. Since there are many meanings used in the language games, while there are only four referents (light sources) in the environment, there are one-to-many mappings between referent and meaning. So, to come to an ideal one-to-one mapping between referent and form, there should be a many-to-one mapping between meaning and form.

The way the lexicon formation is modelled, the many-to-one relations between meaning and form are allowed. Although the speaker invents a one-to-one mapping between meaning and form, the hearer may adopt a (possibly already known) form with more than one categories it has related to the sensing of a referent. This way the many-to-one relations are made. However, there may also emerge one-to-many mappings between meaning and form.

In different language games, one meaning can be associated with different forms. The two robots have different categorisations of the world. Partly because they create different categories and associations, but also because in a language game, they view their world from different locations. Suppose that one robot in a language game is at a different location than in previous language games, and suppose that the other robot is in a location it has visited before. The first robot is likely to have a different categorisation of a light source than before, so it may use a different form than in other language games. But if the other robot views the light source from more or less the same location as before, it would prefer the form used in the other language games. It may not know the new form yet and might associate this one with the meaning it already had. Another reason for this one-to-many mapping is that the hearer adopts a word-form with a categorisation of an arbitrary selected segment. It may well be that this category is already associated with another word-form. Logically, if there may be both

3.5 Coupling categorisation and naming

one-to-many and many-to-one mappings between meaning and form, it is likely there exist many-to-many mappings.

The many-to-many mappings makes the system more complex, especially when one realises that the mappings differ per robot. The reinforcement type of learning (selection and adaptations depending on the rewards) allows the robots to converge a system where the effective associations are used more often. The robots have mechanisms to select associations that have been most effective in the past. This selection is based on the scores which are adapted according to the rewards that are given to the agents. The rewards are based on successful language games. Since a language game is successful when both robots communicate the same referent, the forms that are exchanged will be selected more and more to relate to the same referent. This is so, because in the different language games, the robots have different but returning locations. Once a language game has been successful, the used associations for the robots are reinforced. In another language game, where one robot is at the same location, while the other is not, the latter can learn that the form that is communicated relates to this new situation. If this newly learned association is applicable in a later language game, this game may be successful. Hence this association is reinforced. The more these associations are reinforced, the better the robots can deal with the different categorisations in different locations.

When an association is used successfully this association is reinforced, whereas lateral associations are inhibited. So, there will be a competition between the different form-meaning associations. This appears to antagonise the force of the dynamics explained above. The adaptations are mainly made at the form-meaning layer. Nevertheless, it will be shown that the robots are capable to deal with this. Because hearer processes the data in different directions (cf. Figure 3.11), the selection it can make often depends on the availability of a distinctive category rather than on the selection preference in its lexicon. This is especially a strong principle when the robots use joint attention. The selection based on the scores is more important when it is not available. In this case the robots are depending on the rewards (feedback) given. Since both joint attention and feedback is provides information about the topic of the language games, the tendency to use a minimal set of forms to name a referent emerges.

As will be shown in the experimental results, the robots do not develop a one-to-one relationship between the referents and the forms, but the results are pretty good nevertheless. In the most successful experiments (see Chapter 6) there is almost a one-to-few relationship between referent and form.

So, there is a strong level of co-evolution of meaning and form. Since there is

3 Language games

a one-to-many relation between referent and meaning, it is necessary to have a damping mechanism between meaning and form. The dynamics of the cultural interactions between the robots and the joint attention or feedback mechanisms (actually a part of the cultural interactions) are the damping mechanisms that allows the "self-organisation" of a shared and grounded lexicon.

4 Experimental results

Now that the model has been described, it is time to present experimental results. The results will be presented in three forthcoming chapters including this one. The current chapter presents the complete outline of one experiment that will form the basis with which the results of most other experiments will be compared. This experiment will be called the basic experiment and implements the guessing game.

Chapter 5 will show how some parameters and methods influence the language game. Some experiments will be discussed in which the quality of the communication completely breaks down, but most experiments will show which parameter settings and methods improve the language game.

Before the experiments are discussed some methodology and measures have to be defined. This is done in the next section. The physical recording of the sensory data is discussed in Section 4.2. Section 4.3 presents the basic experiment. Both the effectiveness and evolution will be discussed. A summary is given in Section 4.4.

4.1 Measures and methodology

4.1.1 Measures

As in any empirical investigation, measures are needed to monitor the effectiveness of the system. For the experiments presented here seven measures have been proposed, each measuring a certain aspect of the system. Three measures monitor the categorisation: DISCRIMINATIVE SUCCESS, DISTINCTIVENESS and PARSIMONY. The other four measures are involved with the quality of the communication system: COMMUNICATION SUCCESS, ACTUAL SUCCESS, SPECIFICITY and CONSISTENCY. All measures are values between 0 and 1; 0 means complete failure and 1 complete success.

The measures distinctiveness, parsimony, specificity and consistency were introduced by Edwin de Jong (2000). These measures are based on the entropy measure taken from information theory (Shannon 1948). Entropy measures the

4 Experimental results

uncertainty about a set of elements. The higher the entropy, the higher the uncertainty introducing chaos. Low entropy means order and less uncertainty. Information theory defines entropy as follows:

Let X be a random variable with a set of possible outcomes $A_X = \{a_1, \ldots, a_n\}$, having probabilities $P_X = \{p_1, \ldots, p_n\}$ with $P(x = a_i) = p_i$, $0 \leq p_i \leq 1$ and $\sum_{i=1}^{n} P_i = 1$. Then according to Shannon (1948), the entropy H of X is defined by:

$$(4.1) \qquad H \equiv -\sum_{i=1}^{n} P_i \cdot \log P_i$$

with the convention for $P_i = 0$ that $-0 \cdot \log 0 = 0$. The information theoretic entropy used here should not be confused with entropy in physical systems, as in the second law of thermodynamics, although there is a relation in that both forms of entropy measure disorder (de Jong 2000: 76).

All measures that are used can now be described as follows:

Discriminative success To monitor the ability of the robots to discriminate a segment from other segments in the context, discriminative success (DS) has been introduced (Steels 1996d). At each instance, the discriminative success measures the average success of an agent to discriminate over the past 100 language games. Although a robot may play more discrimination games than language games, it is opted to measure the success over 100 language games for simplicity. So, if during 100 language games a robot played 120 discrimination games, the discriminative success measures the average success of those 120 discrimination games. On the other hand, if there are only 80 discrimination games played, the discriminative success monitors the success of these 80 games as a function of the 100 language games. So, the discriminative success monitors the evolution of categorisation, although its information is not always equally reliable. Note that the discriminative success is calculated for each individual robot.

Distinctiveness "Intuitively, distinctiveness expresses to what degree a meaning identifies the referent." (de Jong 2000) For this we can measure how the entropy of a meaning in relation to a certain referent $H(\rho|\mu_i)$ decreases the uncertainty about the referent $H(\rho)$. For this we can calculate the difference between $H(\rho)$ and $H(\rho|\mu_i)$. Here ρ are the referents $\rho_1, \ldots, \rho_n$ and μ_i

relates to one of the meanings $\mu_1, \ldots, \mu_m$ for robot R. The distinctiveness D_R can now be defined as follows:

$$H(\rho|\mu_i) = \sum_{j=1}^{n} -P(\rho_j|\mu_i) \cdot \log P(\rho_j|\mu_i) \tag{4.2}$$

$$\text{dist}(\mu_i) = \frac{H(\rho) - H(r|\mu_i)}{H(\rho)} = 1 - \frac{H(\rho|\mu_i)}{H(\rho)} \tag{4.3}$$

$$D_R = \frac{\sum_{i=1}^{m} P_o(\mu_i) \cdot \text{dist}(\mu_i)}{m} \tag{4.4}$$

where $H(\rho) = \log n$ and $P_o(\mu_i)$ is the occurrence probability of meaning μ_i. The use of $P_o(\mu_i)$ as a weighting factor is to scale the importance of such a meaning to its occurrence. In de Jong (2000) this has only been done for specificity and consistency, because there the occurrence of meanings and referents was a normal distribution.

Parsimony The parsimony P_R is calculated similar to the distinctiveness:

$$H(\mu|\rho_i) = \sum_{j=1}^{m} -P(\mu_j|\rho_i) \cdot \log P(\mu_j|\rho_i) \tag{4.5}$$

$$\text{pars}(\rho_i) = 1 - \frac{H(\mu|\rho_i)}{H(\mu)} \tag{4.6}$$

$$P_R = \frac{\sum_{i=1}^{n} P_o(\rho_i) \cdot \text{pars}(\rho_i)}{n} \tag{4.7}$$

with $H(\mu) = \log m$. Parsimony thus calculates to what degree a referent gives rise to a unique meaning.

Communicative Success The communication success (cs) is calculated similar to the discrimination success. communicative success is the average success in communication over the past 100 games. It must be noted that when a language game ends in communicative success, the robots not necessarily communicated the same topic. The robots considered the language game successful as a result from the feedback. Since the feedback is not always sound, the communicative success does not always say anything about the robots ability to communicate about a certain referent.

4 Experimental results

Actual success In order to say more about the actual success of a language game, when the communicative success is not the ideal measure, the measure actual success (AS) has been introduced (Vogt 1998b). The actual success measures the success of a language game as if it were observed by an objective observer. The objective observer may regard the language game successful when it is so according to the correspondence criterion, i.e., when the topic of both robots correspond to the same light source. This method is not completely sound, because at larger distances to a light source the correspondence criterion is not sound. But in most cases it suffices. The actual success measures the average success over the past 100 language games. When feedback is provided by the correspondence criterion, the actual success is the same as the communicative success.

Specificity "The specificity of a word[-form] is [...] defined as the relative decrease of uncertainty in determining the referent given a word that was received." (de Jong 2000) It thus is a measure to indicate how well a word-form can identify a referent. It is calculated analogous to the distinctiveness and parsimony. For a set of word-forms $\sigma_1, \ldots, \sigma_q$, the specificity is defined as follows:

$$(4.8) \qquad H(\rho|\sigma_i) = \sum_{j=1}^{n} -P(\rho_j|\sigma_i) \cdot \log P(\rho_j|\sigma_i)$$

$$(4.9) \qquad \mathrm{spec}(\sigma_i) = 1 - \frac{H(\rho|\sigma_i)}{H(\rho)}$$

$$(4.10) \qquad S_R = \frac{\sum_{i=1}^{q} P_o(\sigma_i) \cdot \mathrm{spec}(\sigma_i)}{q}$$

where $H(\rho) = \log n$ is defined as before and P_o is the occurrence probability of encountering word-form σ_i.

Consistency Consistency measures how consistent a referent is named by a certain word-form. It is calculated as follows:

$$(4.11) \qquad H(\sigma|\rho_i) = \sum_{j=1}^{q} -P(\sigma_j|\rho_i) \cdot \log P(\sigma_j|\rho_i)$$

$$\text{(4.12)} \qquad \text{cons}(\rho_i) = 1 - \frac{H(\sigma|\rho_i)}{H(\sigma)}$$

$$\text{(4.13)} \qquad C_R = \frac{\sum_{i=1}^{n} P_o(\rho_i) \cdot \text{cons}(\rho_i)}{n}$$

where $H(\sigma) = \log q$ and $P_o(\rho_i)$ is defined as before.

Distinctiveness, parsimony, specificity and consistency are all calculated every 200 language games. Obviously calculations can only take place when the pairs referent – meaning or referent – word-form are used. This happens either when the discrimination game is successful (influencing distinctiveness and parsimony) or when a robot produced or understood a communication act (influencing specificity and consistency).[1]

4.1.2 Statistical testing

Every experiment (unless otherwise mentioned) consists of 10 runs in which either 5,000 or 10,000 language games are played. When appropriate, the results are presented in a plot that displays the average evolution of the experiment. However, to save space, most results are presented in a table where the global averages of an experiment are given. Using global averages means that the average measure of each complete run (5,000 or 10,000 games) is averaged over 10 runs. This average is given with its standard deviation of the population. When comparing to other experiments, the results are usually displayed in a bar chart. In addition, statistical significance testing is done by these comparisons.

All statistical significance testing is done using the two-tailed Mann–Whitney U test, also known as the Wilcoxon rank-sum test. Applying the Mann–Whitney U test requires that the population does not show a normal distribution. Investigations of the distributions revealed that the populations were not normally distributed.

The null-hypothesis of the test may be rejected when $p < \alpha$ for some low α. In all testing, the null-hypothesis states that two populations of measurements are the same, with the alternative hypothesis that they are not the same. For stating that one result is significantly better than another, the distributions of the two populations of measurements need to be similar. This has not been observed, so the only inference one can make of a low p-value is that the two populations are

---

[1] Note that this does not necessarily mean that the language game was successful.

not the same. However, if one measurement is higher than another, the assumption will be made that this is the case if a *p*-value is low. The value α will not be filled in as the reader may decide whether or not the difference is significant. For readers unfamiliar with statistical testing, the literature usually takes $\alpha = 0.05$, which becomes $\alpha = 0.025$ for a two-tailed test. The used method and tables are taken from Aczel (1989).

Other methods will be used to evaluate an experiment's success. These methods include semiotic landscapes, competition diagrams and others, and will be introduced with their initial appearance.

4.1.3 On-board versus off-board

In the original experiments all the processing, including the meaning and language formation, was done on-board the robots (Steels & Vogt 1997). But, since the robots failed to enhance the lexicon due to the lack of on-board memory and because the robots' batteries only work for one hour while the experiments take much more time, a large part of the processing is done off-board on a personal computer. The sensory information that the robots detect during sensing is sent to the PC by the radio link. After the robots recorded the sensory information of a language game, segmentation, categorisation and naming are further processes on the PC. There are many advantages for off-board processing:

1. Larger internal memory
2. No loss of data during change of batteries
3. Faster processing
4. Repeatable experiments to compare parameter settings and methods more reliably
5. Debugging

After approximately one hour of experimenting, the robot's batteries die. The robots have no persistent data storage on-board. So, when the batteries are empty and the robot shuts down, the memory built up disappears unless it is saved off-board first. Of course, the robots may be powered by a cable, but in practice this proves to be rather cumbersome. The advantage would be that a serial cable can be attached to monitor the internal dynamics of the robots during a game, but this could also be done using radio communication.

The recording of one language game when the robots need to look for each other takes approximately 1.5 min. Recording a minimum of 5,000 language games takes therefore 125 hours, which takes 25 days or 5 weeks assuming that there are 5 effective experimental hours a day.[2] *If nothing goes wrong, naturally!* This period can be reduced to 5 days if the researcher manually brings the robots together after which the robots play a series of, say, 10 games in a row.

Now suppose that one wants to tune a parameter by varying this parameter 5 or 10 times. Or that one wants to change a method, or what if the researcher finds a bug in its program. For all these reasons off-board processing is the outcome. Another important advantage is that one can use the same recordings over and over again across different experiments, so comparing different experiments is more reliable.

Debugging is a good reason to process data as much as possible off-board as well, it saves huge amounts of time. Many more advantages can be found, but the biggest have been stated. However, if one divides a system in on-board vs. off-board processing, then one should be careful to define the division line. The experiment should not loose its embodied and situated character, otherwise one is better off using simulations.

4.2 Sensory data

As mentioned in Chapter 3 the sensory data of the sensing during a language game is recorded to further process the game off-board. For convenience the sensing is segmented in advance, using the method described in Chapter 3. The same is done for the feature extraction. The data set thus consists of the contexts described by the feature vectors of the two robots participating in the experiment. The two contexts that relate to one language game will be called a SITUATION.

For obvious reasons of time, a few data sets of only 1,000 situations have been recorded. One of these sets is used for the experiments of this chapter, the others will be presented in Chapter 5. As will become clear soon, an experiment requires approximately 3,000 language games before the communication system becomes more or less stable. In most experiments 5,000 games are played. In these experiments the 1,000 recorded situations will be used over and over again. Some people may ask if the reuse of situations will bias the system. But it is unlikely that two language games in the experiment are the same. Every language game one situation is selected. One of the robots is then randomly assigned to

---

[2] Perhaps some robotics researchers laugh at this positive estimation, but in good days this is manageable.

4 Experimental results

play the role of the speaker. The speaker then randomly selects one of the segments to be the topic. Since, on average, each context consists of approximately 3–4 segments (1017 in the first data set to be precise), a situation can be used in, say, 7 different ways. Assuming perfect randomness of the system, each possible setting (situation, role assignment and topic choice) has been explored only once after approximately 7,000 games, which justifies this method.

The data set is first run through linearly, i.e. the system that runs the experiment reads the data set in recording sequence. The situations are stored in a list and each situation is then selected in random order.

The 1,000 situations have been recorded as described in Chapter 3. The recording of each data set took approximately 8 hours of work, spread over two days.

Before the results of the cognitive processing is presented, it is useful to look at some statistics of the basic data set. Some additional statistics of the basic data set are presented in Appendix C. This appendix shows the distribution of the feature values measured by the robots. This distribution shows one reason why it seems impossible that a real-world environment can be simulated.

Table 4.1 shows the average context size $\langle |Cxt| \rangle$ of each robot together with its standard deviation. In addition, this table shows the POTENTIAL UNDERSTANDABILITY U_r of each robot. The potential understandability of a robot is a measure that indicates how well a robot can be understood by another robot according to their context sharing. Suppose that robot r has segmented context $Cxt_{r,l} = \{S_{1,r,l}, \ldots, S_{n,r,l}\}$ for situation l, then the understandability U_r for n situations is calculated as follows:

$$(4.14) \qquad U_{r,l} = \frac{\sum_{i=1}^{n} u_{i,l}}{n}$$

where

$$(4.15) \qquad u_{i,l} = \begin{cases} 1 & \text{if} S_{i,r,l} \sqsubseteq Cxt_{r',l} \ (r \neq r') \\ 0 & \text{otherwise} \end{cases}$$

$$(4.16) \qquad U_r = \frac{\sum_{l=1}^{L} U_{r,l}}{L}$$

where the symbol $\sqsubseteq$ is used to denote the relation whether the segment on the left hand side of $\sqsubseteq$ corresponds to one of the segments in the context of the other robot. L is the total number of situations recorded. So, the global potential understandability U_r is the average of the average potential understandability per situation. In Table 4.1 this average is given with its standard deviation.

Table 4.1: The average context size $\langle|Cxt|\rangle$ and average potential understandability U_r of the recorded data set.

	r0	r1
$\langle|Cxt|\rangle$	3.33 ± 1.07	3.54 ± 1.21
U_r	0.81 ± 0.27	0.78 ± 0.27

The potential understandability is lower than 1, because the two robots do not always share a similar context. That this happens has already been discussed in the preceding Chapter 3.

What can be expected in the experiments when observing the statistics of this data set? The first thing that can be said is that the a priori probabilities that both robots select the same topic based on the average context size is:

$$P = \frac{\langle|Cxt_{r0}|\rangle + \langle|Cxt_{r1}|\rangle}{2} \cdot \frac{1}{\langle|Cxt_{r0}|\rangle} \cdot \frac{1}{\langle|Cxt_{r1}|\rangle} = 0.29$$

So, if the robots perform better than 30 % in their communicative success, they are actually learning a meaningful language. The second observation that can be made is that it is impossible to reach a communicative success of 100 % since the robots are in principle not capable of understanding each utterance given the current context setting. They are not likely to perform better than approximately 80 %, as has been calculated from the potential understandability. Third, it is likely that the robots will learn to name L0 better than others, since this light source is detected most often. Given these expectations and conclusions it is time to see how the robots do in the language formation.

4.3 The basic experiment

This first experiment will be referred to as the basic experiment. It is called so because this experiment will serve as the basic experiment from which parameters and methods are changed to investigate their influence. That it is not the best experiment will be shown in subsequent chapters.

The experiment is a guessing game with feedback obtained by means of CORRESPONDENCE (see Section 3.4.3.6).

4 Experimental results

Table 4.2: Parameters of the system. The parameters include the step-size δ by which the categories shift towards an observation, the learning rate η controlling the adaptation of scores, the creation probability P_s by which the speaker may invent new word-forms, the adoption probability P_h by which the hearer may adopt a new word-form when it does not find a matching word-form with an associated meaning it also categorised, and the success threshold Θ_F by which the success of a language game may be accepted.

Par	Value
δ	0.10
η	0.99
P_s	0.02
P_h	1.00

Table 4.2 shows the parameter settings of the most important variables that have been introduced in Chapter 3. Unless otherwise mentioned, the parameters are not changed in the different experiments.

4.3.1 The global evolution

The results of the experiment are shown in Figure 4.1. Note that the actual success is not shown. This is because the actual success is calculated under the same criteria as the feedback of the language games, namely the correspondence criterion. Therefore the actual success is equal to the communicative success. In the experiments where the feedback is provided using the correspondence criterion, the plot of the actual success will not be provided.

In Figure 4.1 (a) the evolution of the communicative success is shown. The communicative success first increases rapidly towards a value of 0.2 after 500 language games, then the communicative success slowly grows to a value of 0.45 after approximately 5,000 language games. The low success is partly due to the relatively poor performance the robots' physical behaviour. This poor behaviour causes the robots to acquire an incoherent context, so a completely successful system cannot emerge. However, the potential understandability predicts a maximum success 80 %. So this cannot explain why the success stays around 40 % in the last 3,000 games. Note however that the success is still increasing, but the success stabilises around 55 % after approximately 8,000 games, as will be shown

4.3 *The basic experiment*

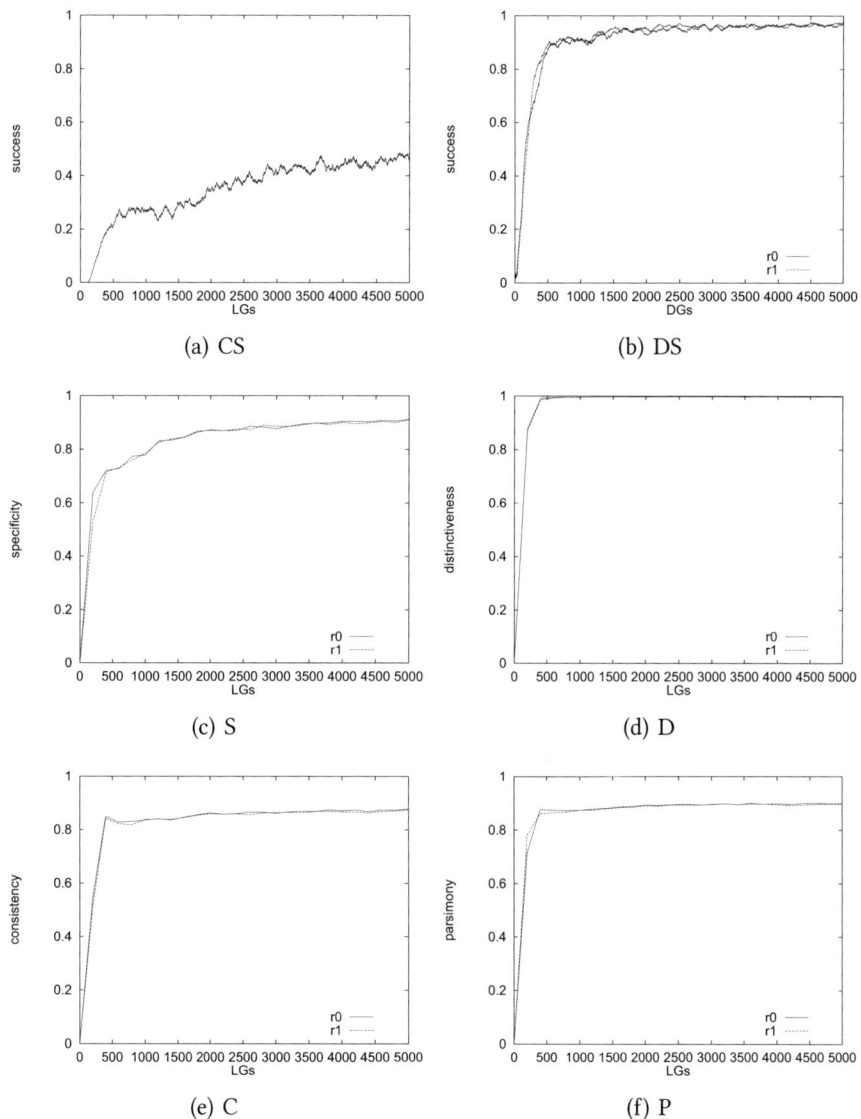

Figure 4.1: The results of the basic experiment showing (a) the communicative success, (b) discriminative success, (c) specificity, (d) distinctiveness, (e) consistency and (f) parsimony. Objective success is not shown, because in this experiment it holds no value (see text).

4 Experimental results

in Section 4.3.5. Although the communicative success is low, some important observations can be made when a closer look is taken at the evolution of the communication system. This is done from Section 4.3.3.

Figure 4.1 (b) plots the discriminative success of the two robots $r0$ and $r1$. As can be seen, the discriminative success grows to a value around 95 %. This success rate is reached quite rapidly. Already after approximately 500 language games a success larger than 90 % is achieved. That the discriminative success does not converge to 100 % is due to (1) the hearer does not play a discrimination game in all language games and the discriminative success is a function of the language games, and, (2) a success-rate of 100 % can never be reached. This latter finding is due to the fact that on the average about 0.5 % of the segments in one context are the same.

Figure 4.3 shows the discriminative success of an experiment where all possible configurations are used in the discrimination games. The robots interacted as if they were playing language games, only they did not communicate. The speaker only categorised its selected topic, the hearer categorised all its detected segments. Note that more discrimination games are played than when the robots also communicate, since the hearer only plays a discrimination game when it receives an uttered word-form. Furthermore, since each agent plays a discrimination game every language game, the discriminative success is independent of the language games. The average distinctive success over 10 runs of 5,000 language games is 0.984 ± 0.001 for robot $r0$ and 0.987 ± 0.000 for $r1$. Due to limitations of the implementation it is difficult to extract all possible configurations, so these experiments are not used for language formation.

Figures 4.1 (c) and (e) show that the specificity and consistency is rather good. When a communication act establishes, whether or not it is successful,[3] the robots' utterances specify the referents pretty well and they are also pretty consistent in naming the referent. So, in principle they mastered a good communication system.

The meanings that are used almost uniquely identify a particular referent. This can be seen in Figure 4.1 (d), which shows the distinctiveness of the two robots. When the robots are able to discriminate a segment corresponding to some referent, they do so rather parsimonious (i.e. they tend to use the same meanings), but not very well. The parsimony (Figure 4.1 (f)) is around 0.85.

So, when the robots are successful in communicating and categorisation, they do so with high accuracy and invariance. Table 4.3 shows the average (Avg)

---

[3] A communication act is established when the speaker produced an utterance and when the hearer found a matching WM association. This is independent of successful communication.

4.3 The basic experiment

scores of the different measures over 10 runs of the complete experiments. All scores given with their standard deviation of the averages over the *population* of 10 runs. In forthcoming experiments tables and bar charts with the average scores will be the main comparison source. Plots like in Figure 4.1 will only be used when it is useful to make a certain point.

In Figure 4.2 the communicative success of one run is shown. It is obvious that this run shows a different evolution than the averaged evolution, as has been shown in Figure 4.1. The next section will discuss the evolution of the run for which the communicative success has just been shown.

Table 4.3: The table listing the average scores for the different measures. The suffix 0 or 1 indicates from which robot the score is (r0 or r1). The second column gives the global average of the experiment, together with its standard deviation over the population of 10 runs.

Score	Avg
CS	0.351 ± 0.010
DS0	0.916 ± 0.004
DS1	0.920 ± 0.004
D0	0.956 ± 0.002
D1	0.955 ± 0.002
P0	0.852 ± 0.004
P1	0.851 ± 0.002
S0	0.822 ± 0.017
S1	0.817 ± 0.011
C0	0.816 ± 0.008
C1	0.811 ± 0.007

4 Experimental results

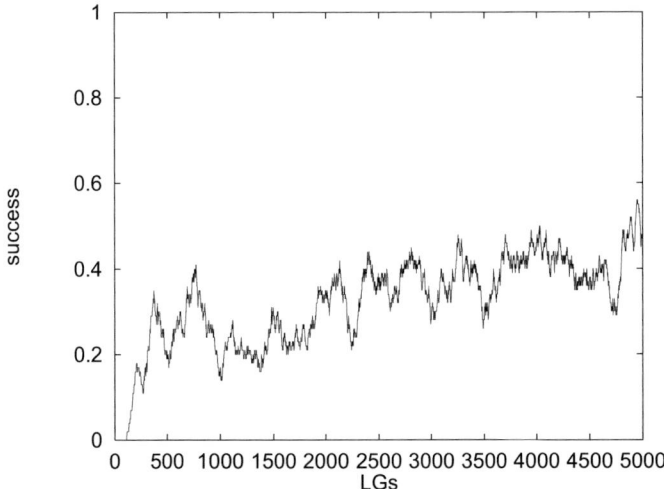

Figure 4.2: The communicative success of one run. The evolution shows a fast increase towards 30 %, after which it slowly grows to 50 % at the end. The evolution further shows a lot of fluctuations. Apparently the robots learn to communicate with ups and downs. A lot of these fluctuations are caused by polysemy and synonymy in the system as will become clear hereafter.

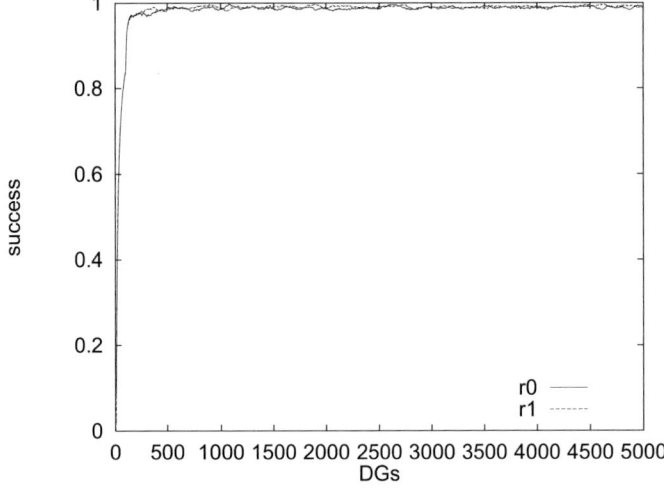

Figure 4.3: The discriminative success of 10 runs of 5,000 language games in which only discrimination games were played (i.e. without communication). The discrimination games here considered all possible configurations of categories in their contexts.

4.3.2 The ontological development

It is interesting to see how the ontology of prototypical categories develop and evolve in time.

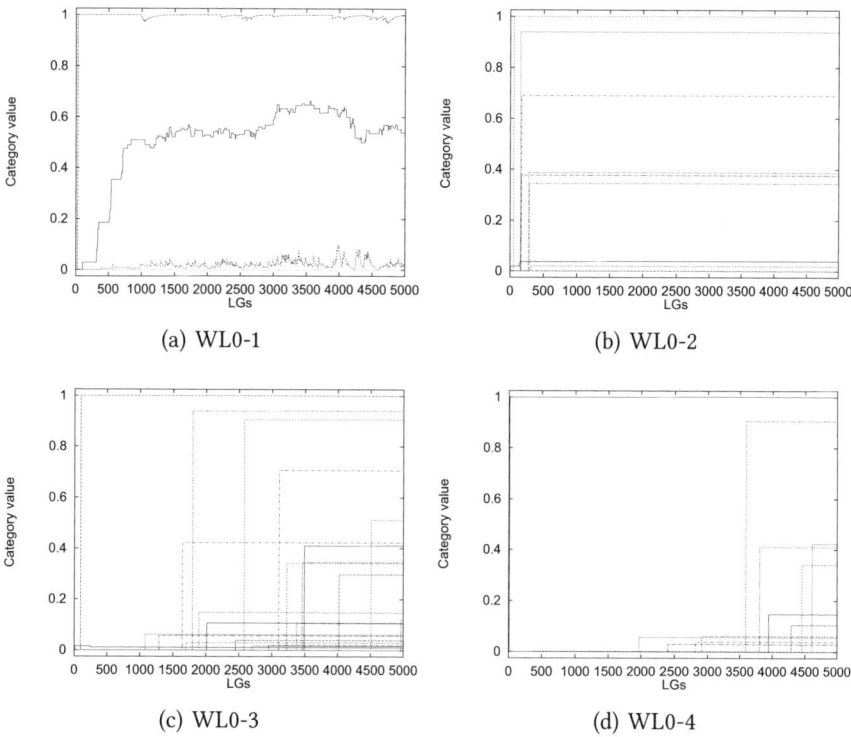

Figure 4.4: The development of prototypes in dimension WL0 of feature spaces $\mathcal{F}_1$ to $\mathcal{F}_4$. Note that the x-axis shows the number of language games and the y-axis shows the value of the prototype in dimension WL0. Similar evolutions are observed in the other dimensions of the feature spaces.

Figure 4.4 shows the evolution of prototypes in dimension WL0 of feature spaces $\mathcal{F}_1$ to $\mathcal{F}_4$. Similar development is observed for the other dimensions. Recall that each feature space $\mathcal{F}_\lambda$ allows a maximum of 3^λ exploitations in each dimension. The first exploitations in the different feature spaces are constructed quite rapidly. It is interesting to note that only the prototypes of feature space $\mathcal{F}_1$ are continuously changing (Figure 4.4 (a)). This means that they are used successfully to name a segment and shift towards the feature they categorised.

4 Experimental results

The lower and upper exploitations remain close to 0 and 1, respectively, the middle values shift toward values somewhere in the middle between 0 and 1. The categories have the tendency to move towards what could be called the central tendency of the features for which the prototypical categories have been used successfully in the language games.

At the other feature spaces from Figure 4.4, an increasing amount of prototypes are constructed, but once they are introduced they hardly change. Apparently, these prototypical categories are not often used successfully in the language games. So, the robots appear to be sufficiently effective with the categories constructed in feature space $\mathcal{F}_1$. This does not mean that in a more complex environment, the further refinements would not be effective.

Table 4.4: The legend of some of the meanings represented by their prototypes. The subscript indicates the feature space $\mathcal{F}_\lambda$ at which the prototypes are stored. The given meanings are taken from the ontology after 5,000 language games.

M5	$(0.02, 0.01, 1.00, 0.02)_1$
M6	$(0.04, 0.00, 0.00, 0.00)_2$
M18	$(0.56, 0.99, 0.02, 0.02)_1$
M20	$(0.02, 0.01, 1.00, 0.44)_1$
M27	$(0.02, 0.31, 1.00, 0.44)_1$
M30	$(0.02, 0.99, 0.02, 0.02)_1$
M37	$(0.00, 0.00, 0.00, 0.00)_3$
M53	$(1.00, 0.01, 0.02, 0.02)_1$
M55	$(1.00, 0.31, 0.02, 0.02)_1$
M58	$(0.02, 0.01, 0.30, 0.99)_1$
M61	$(0.02, 0.01, 0.02, 0.99)_1$
M67	$(1.00, 0.99, 0.02, 0.02)_1$
M90	$(0.00, 0.00, 0.01, 0.00)_5$
M393	$(0.00, 0.00, 0.00, 0.01)_4$
M394	$(0.00, 0.00, 0.00, 0.01)_5$

Table 4.4 gives a sample of some meanings that are present in the competition diagrams. An additional legend can be found in Appendix D. Each meaning is a set of categories of which the values are given in a vector notation. So, the category is a 4 dimensional prototype of the (4 dimensional) segment. The first dimension corresponds with sensory channel WLO (the lowest light sensor), etc.

4.3 The basic experiment

The subscript index indicates feature space at which the categories are stored. Most prototypes have a value of 1 (or 0.99) at the dimension that corresponds to the referent for which they are mostly used.

There are some exceptions, like for M6, M37, M90, M393 and M394, which have all values of (almost) 0. These meanings are used in the beginning of the experiment in which a certain feature space is explored. The relating categories were distinctive, despite the low values in each dimension, because the other segments in the context were categorised with other categories at sensory channels that had higher values in another dimension.

An interesting meaning is M67, which has low distinctiveness. This meaning is used both in relation to light sources L0 and L1. Table 4.4 explains why. The prototype has high values for both dimension wL0 and wL1. If a light source is sensed from a large distance, the sensory channel adjacent to the corresponding sensory channel, both sensory channels may detect intensities close to each other, conform the characteristics shown in Chapter 2. After feature extraction, the feature vector has high values in these dimensions. Hence meaning M67 might be activated.

Meanings M53, M55 (both L0), M18, M30 (L1), M5, M20, M27 (L2), M58 and M61 (L3) all have values of 0.99 or 1.00 in the corresponding dimensions. So, the discrimination process clearly selects the invariant property of correspondence. The meanings that have values of 0.99 in one dimension of their prototypes are used successfully to categorise a feature vector that has a value lower than 1 in this dimension. In such cases the prototypes evolve to a value lower than 1 since it shifts towards the feature vector. If this prototype would be used only to categorise feature vectors with value 1 in some dimension, this dimension will end up with value of 1.

4.3.3 Competition diagrams

Up to now only superficial measures have been presented, which already gave useful information on the quality of the emerged communication system. Although the communicative success is low, the system is performing better than chance and a reasonable system seems to have emerged. There is another way of looking at the system that emerged, namely by inspecting so called COMPETITION DIAGRAMS. A competition diagram takes one entity at its basis (e.g. a referent) and shows which elements of another entity (e.g. meanings or word-forms) compete to mean or name this basis.

Figure 4.5 shows the competition diagram with the referents at the basis and the meanings as the competitors, or in short the referent-meaning (RM) diagram.

4 Experimental results

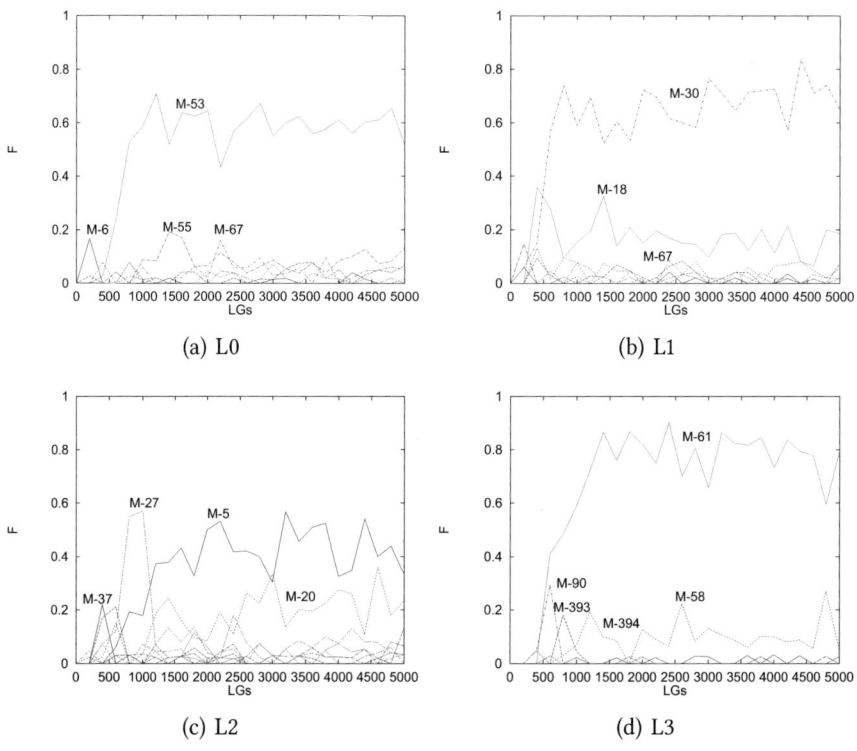

Figure 4.5: Competition diagrams referent-meaning (or RM diagram).

All plots in this figure show the competition diagrams of robot $r0$ for each referent L0, L1, L2 and L3. Each plot shows the relative frequency of the co-occurrence of the meaning with the referent, where the referent is taken as the basis to which the frequencies are compared. These relative frequencies are calculated every 200 language games. A co-occurrence of meanings and referents does not imply they were successfully used. It is obvious that each referent has been categorised by different meanings, although each referent has a clear winning meaning. Hence there is a one-to-many relation between referent and meaning.

All frequently used meanings are active at feature space $\mathcal{F}_1$ (see also Table 4.4). It appears that, mostly the discrimination is successful using meanings from this feature space.[4] Although this is not shown here, meanings from a feature space with $\lambda > 1$ tend not to be used much. Obviously they may just as well be distinc-

---
[4] Note that categories from feature space $\mathcal{F}_0$ cannot be distinctive unless there is only one segment in the context.

tive, but they are not used in the communication, otherwise they would move in the feature space. That this is not the case is observed in Figure 4.4. So, at higher feature spaces, there are more prototypes, but those are selected less frequently. This makes their competition for the referent harder and less successful.

The occurrence frequency of meanings M53, M30, M5 and M61 constitute the parsimony of the system. It can be inferred that referents L0, L1 and L3 have a relative high parsimony, whereas L2 has relative low parsimony. The higher the parsimony the better a referent is categorised by a single category.

Figures 4.6 (a)–(d) show the meaning-form competition diagrams (MF diagrams) of the winning meanings in the referent-meaning competitions. Figure (a) shows the competition of meaning M53. The word-form *huma* clearly wins the competition right from the beginning. Little competition is given by *xomu*, *poma*, *lyzu* and *kyga*. Similar competitions can be seen with meanings M30 and M5 (Figures 4.6 b and c). So, every meaning shows one-to-many relations between meaning and form. This is highest in for M30 and M61. Such one-to-many relations are fed by mismatches that arise in the communication. The mismatches cause word-form adoption, so that a meaning can be associated with several word-forms. The mismatches are mainly due to the rather high level of one-to-many relations between referent and meaning as shown in the referent-meaning diagram.

The dynamics on the association scores allow the different other lexical elements a chance to compete. Lateral inhibition of competing associations is a main ingredient of the self-organising effect that one element wins the competition. Note again that occurrence in the competition diagram does not equal a language game's success.

Meaning M61 (Figure 4.6 d) shows a different competition than M53, M30 and M5. Initially word-form *kyga* wins the competition. This word-form is also the winning competitor for M5, so there is representational polysemy in the system. After game 1750 or so, word-form *lyzu* starts to win the competition for M61 and *kyga* is then solely used for M5. Thus the lexicon is somewhat disambiguated. Disambiguation is established by excitation of scores of successful association and the lateral inhibition of competing associations.

Figure 4.6 (e) shows the opposite competition of form *huma* with its associated meanings, i.e., it shows the form-meaning competition for *huma*. Again there is a clear winner, namely M53 as would be expected. Furthermore some small competition is observed from other meanings. Notably is meaning M30, which is 'the best of the rest'. M30 is winning competitor referring to L1 (see Figures 4.5 b and 4.6 b). In Figure 4.6 (b) *huma* also wins the competition of the meanings that are not used for L1, compare Figure 4.5. The form *huma* is also used for

4 Experimental results

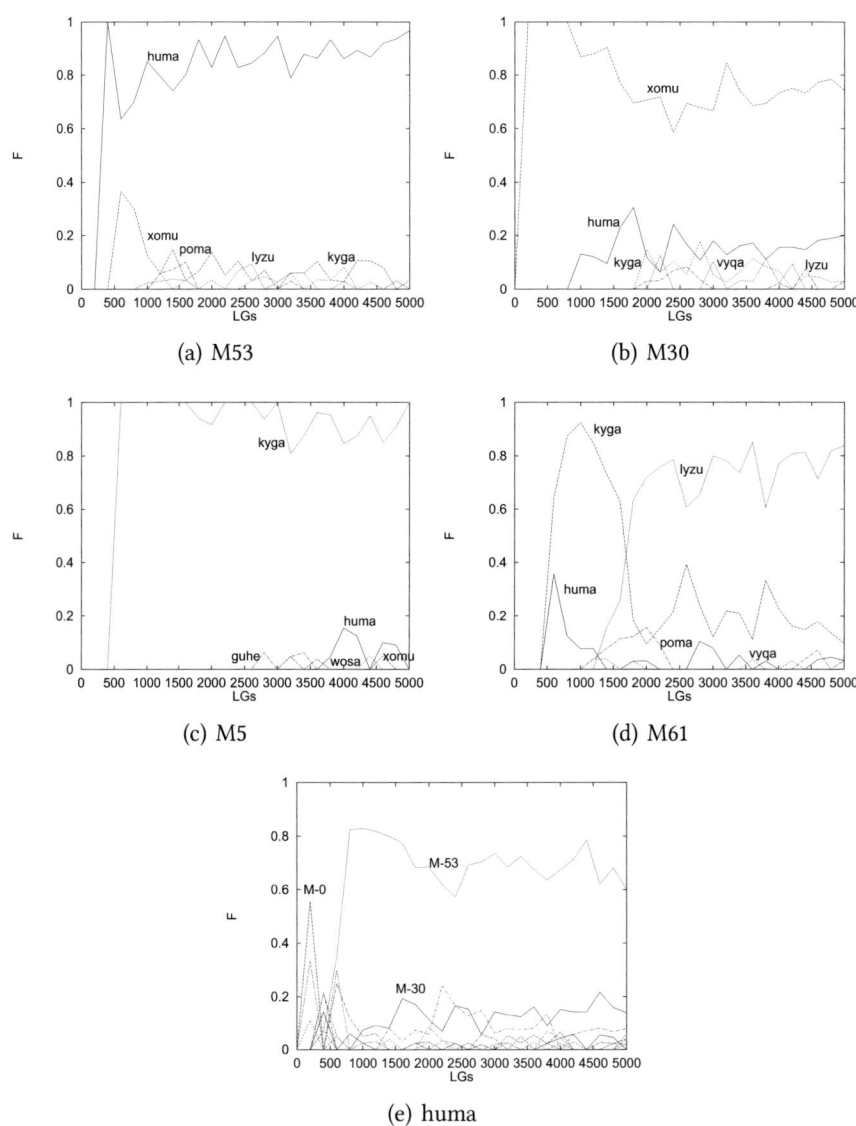

Figure 4.6: Competition diagrams (a) to (d) meaning-form (MF), and (e) form-meaning (FM).

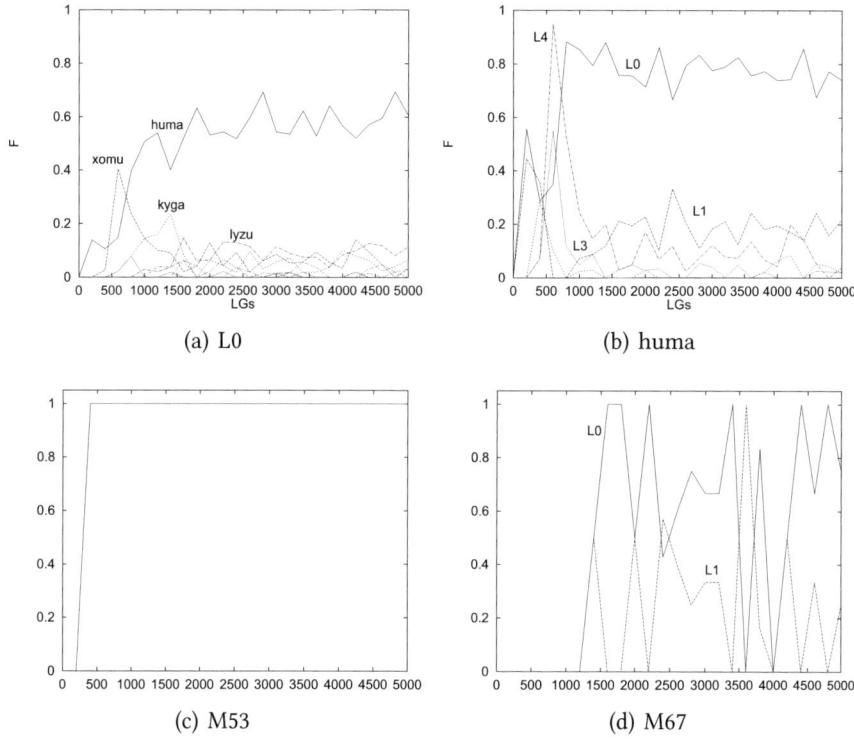

Figure 4.7: Competition diagrams (a) referent-form, (b) form-referent, (c) and (d) meaning-referent. Meaning M53 (c) uniquely refers to referent L0.

naming M5, M30 and M61, although in a lesser extend. So, there is a one-to-many relation between *huma* and some meanings, and there is polysemy is present for *huma*. Polysemy means that there are one-to-many relations between the form and referent. Polysemy is one of the causes why the communicative success is lower than the potential communicative success.

In Figure 4.7 some different competition diagrams are shown. Figure (a) shows the referent-form competition for L0. The synonymy (one-to-many relation between referent and form) is high, as can be inferred from the low relative frequency of winning word-form *huma* and the competing elements at the bottom of the plot. Note that not all competitors are shown in this plot. There are quite some more, but these have lower frequencies than the ones that are shown. The synonymy is a result of the relatively low parsimony (i.e. one-to-many relations between referent and meaning) combined with the one-to-many relations between meaning and form. Naturally, synonymy is an antagonising force against the communicative success.

4 Experimental results

Polysemy of the word-form *huma* is also shown in Figure 4.7 (b). At first there is competition between all referents. After 1,000 language games, the tendency to use *huma* for naming LO wins the competition. Thus influencing the specificity positively. However, the polysemy antagonises the communicative success. Polysemy is caused by a combination of one-to-many relations between form and meaning and one-to-one relations between meaning and referent, cf. Figure 4.7 (c).

Distinctiveness is high, as can be seen in the meaning-referent diagram for M53 (Figure 4.7 c). The relative frequency in using M53 for referring to LO goes to 1 where it remains. Some meanings have lower distinctiveness like M61 (Figure 4.7 d), which after its introduction around language game 1,200 keeps on competing between LO and L1. That this competition has little influence in the global distinctiveness of robot $r0$ is seen in Figure 4.1 (d). This is so because the occurrence frequency of M67 is relatively low.

4.3.4 The lexicon

One way of inspecting the resulting lexicon is looking at the competition diagrams. Another way of presenting the lexicon is a table. In such tables word-meaning associations of the two robots are given. Although such tables give good information about an individual's lexicon, it provides difficult to read and incomplete information about its structure in the language using society. Similar tables can display the ontology of the robots in relation to their use for referents. The tables of the lexicon and ontology are given in Appendix D.

4.3.4.1 Semiotic landscape

Still another way the lexicon can be presented is by a semiotic landscape as in Figure 4.8. In a semiotic landscape the semiotic relations between referent, meaning and form are displayed for the two robots. The connections are weighted by their co-occurrence frequencies, like given in the tables (see Appendix D). Entries with very low frequencies are left out for clarity. When no connections are drawn, these associations have frequencies lower than 0.01.

Figure 4.8 clearly shows that winning associations (bold connections) always make closed couplings, thus constituting the successfully grounded and shared symbols. The associations also show coherent connections of referent and form between both robots. This way the sign can be said to be conventionalised. Hence it becomes a symbol. Another interesting observation that can be made is that word-forms like *huma*, *kyga* and *xomu* (only for $r0$) show one-to-many relations

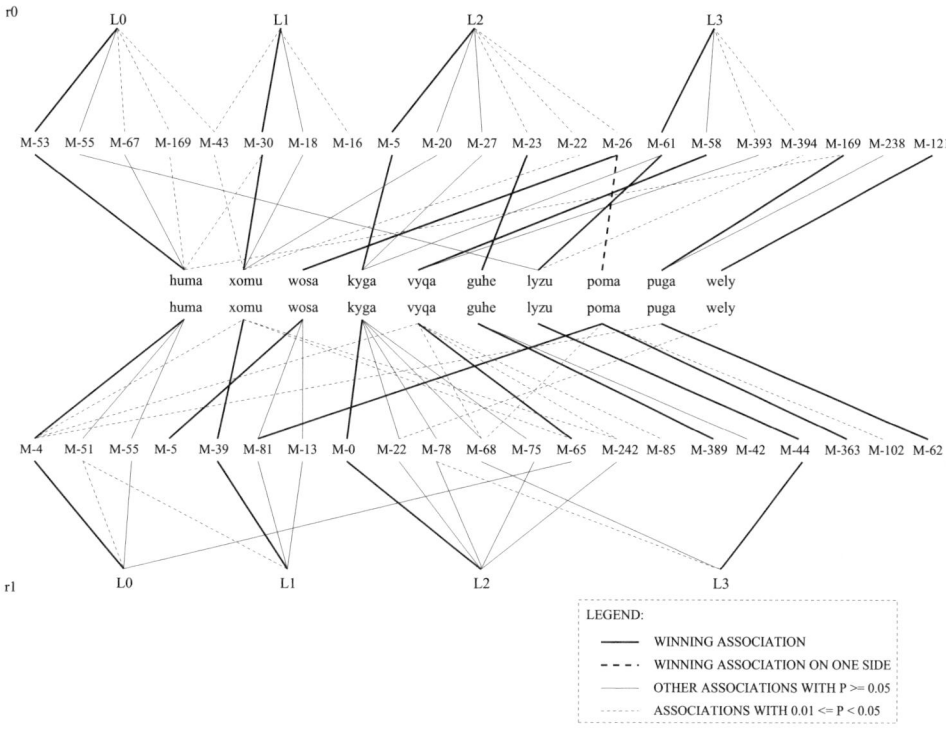

Figure 4.8: The semiotic landscape of one of the experiments.

between form and meaning, but they show hardly any polysemy. Ideally a figure should emerge where for each referent there is a closed graph where no polysemy or synonymy is shown. In such a graph the referents are orthogonal to each other.

Most word-forms that show one-to-many relations between form and meaning also show some polysemy and INCOHERENCE. A word-form is incoherent when one robot uses it to name another referent than the other robot. Incoherence can be seen for the word-forms *wosa* and *vyqa*. Such incoherence can be caused by language games that are evaluated to be successful inappropriately or that the meanings have no other associations.[5]

4.3.4.2 Lexical and ontological growth

How does the lexicon and ontology grow through time? Is the growth incremental as has been observed in studies on language acquisition and as is likely to

---

[5] Recall that co-occurrence does not imply a successful language game.

4 Experimental results

have happened in language evolution (Aitchison 1996)? Incremental growth is typically illustrated with an S-shaped logistics curve as shown in Figure 4.9.

Figure 4.10 shows a similar evolution of growth. These figures show the growth of elements that have been used successfully in the language games averaged over the ten runs. After a short while the number elements start to grow rapidly until the growth seems to stabilise a bit. It is shown that the lexicon growth of successfully used forms ends up with a lower amount of elements than is shown in the previous section. Some of the elements of the lexicon discussed in the previous section have not been used successfully.

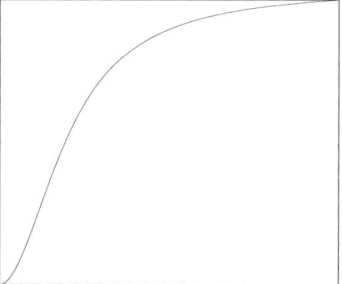

Figure 4.9: The course of knowledge development as observed in psychological and evolutionary data.

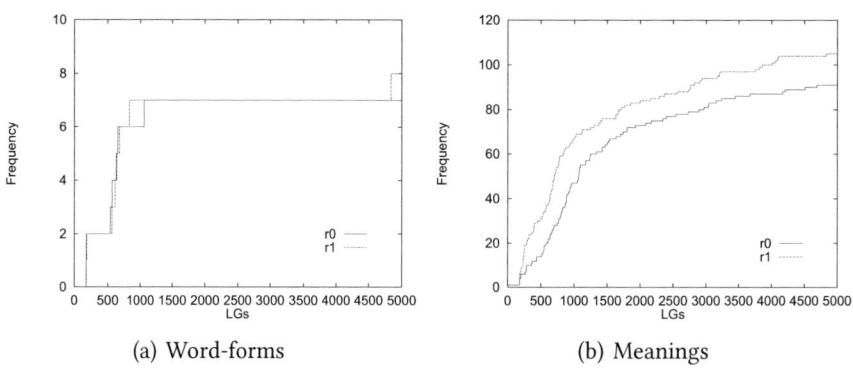

Figure 4.10: The average growth of the word-forms (a) and meanings (b) from the experiments. The growth is taken over elements that are used successfully in the language games.

4.3 The basic experiment

The number of meanings that are used keep on growing, although slower than in the beginning. Figure 4.10 (b) actually shows that the 8 word-forms that have been used successfully are associated with approximately 100 meanings. So, every word-form is associated with on the average 12.5 meanings. The semiotic landscape shown in above shows that this need not be a big problem.

4.3.5 More language games

The experiment introduced was done with 10 runs of 5,000 language games. Most experiments that are discussed have 10 runs of 5,000 language games, but what happens when the experiment is run for a longer time. Figure 4.11 shows the results when the robots play 10,000 games each run (again for 10 runs). As is clear the system keeps on improving slightly. The communicative success for instance increases towards a value of 0.5. Also the specificity is increasing continuously. So, the communication system seems to keep on learning, but slowly.

It is unknown exactly when the slight growth stops, but the system does seem to stabilise towards the end. As will be shown in later chapters, some experiments will stabilise before 10,000 games are played.

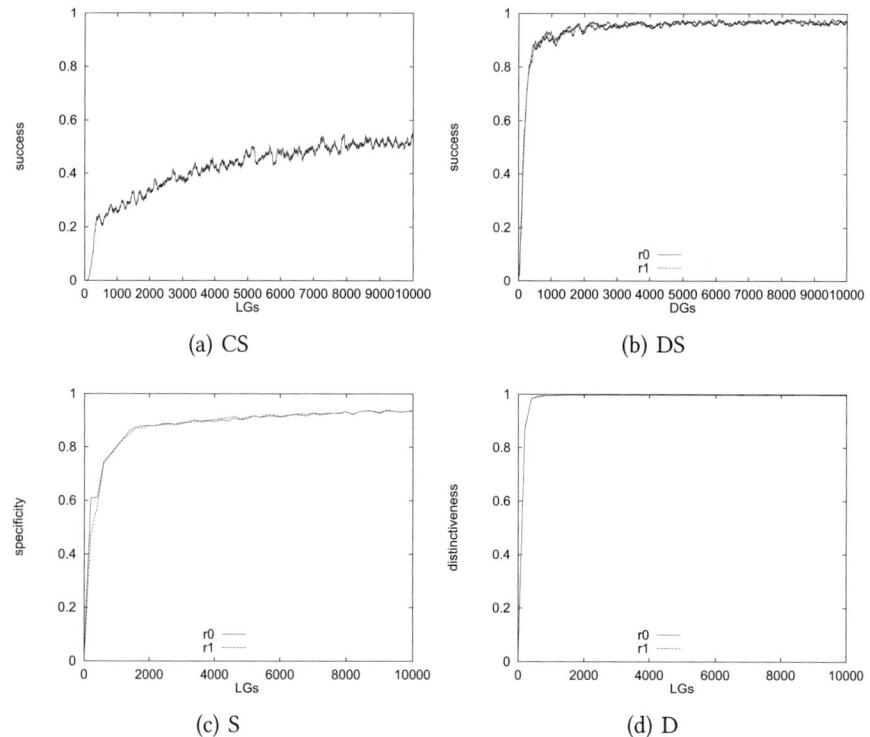

4 Experimental results

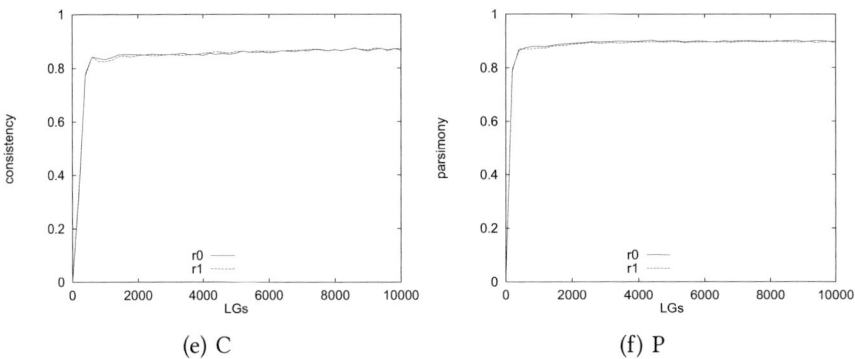

Figure 4.11: The evolution of the basic experiment with runs of 10,000 language games.

4.4 Summary

This chapter introduced the first experimental results in detail. The experiment that has been presented here in detail will be used as the basic experiment from which parameters and methods are varied and with which the results of other experiments shall be compared. The experimental results of the forthcoming experiments will not be presented at the same level of detail. For most experiments only the global averages will be given. When appropriate, however, the results will be presented in more detail.

The basic experiment used a data set that has been recorded in advanced and that is used to process in different runs under different random seeds. The results have been presented with several measures, notably the communicative success, discriminative success, distinctiveness, specificity, parsimony and consistency. Although the communicative success is rather low, it is higher than the a priori communicative success. Furthermore, inspecting the other measures, it appeared that the robots did learn a reasonable communication system. Competition diagrams showed how the robots evolve to select preferred elements of their ontology and lexicon to name the referents. The semiotic landscape showed that one-to-many relations between referent and meaning need not be a problem as long as the polysemy is low. However, the system still carries quite some polysemy and synonymy.

The next chapters will show if and how a better communication system may emerge. First the impact from different methods and parameter settings Chapter 5. Chapter 6 reports some optimised systems.

5 Varying methods and parameters

Chapter 4 extensively presented the basic experiment. The results were not very satisfying, although closer investigation revealed not so bad results. In this chapter, variants of the basic experiment are investigated and compared with this experiment.

What is the impact on categorisation and lexicon formation when a different categorisation mechanisms is used? What influence has the physical conditions on the symbol grounding? What is the impact from applying joint attention and/or feedback? How do various parameter settings of the word-form creation probability and learning rate influence the experiments? And what if the robots also adopt word-forms when there is a mismatch in referent? These questions will be addressed in this chapter.

To answer these questions, a set of experiments have been carried out. Each experiment is done with 10 runs of 5,000 language games, as in the basic experiment. Unless otherwise mentioned, the basic data set is used in these experiments. Each section of this chapter relates to one of the questions and it presents some of the experiments. The sections introduce the problem addressed. They describe the difference(s) of the experiments, usually in relation to the basic experiment. Then the experimental results are given, which is followed by a short discussion of these results.

The next section investigates three variants of categorisation in the discrimination games. In Section 5.2, the physical conditions are varied. The four different types of language games introduced in Chapter 3, the guessing, ostensive, observational and xsl game, will be investigated in Section 5.3. Section 5.4 investigates the observational game in more detail. In Section 5.5, the creation probability is varied. The learning rate is varied in Section 5.6. Additional word-form adoption is investigated in Section 5.7. The chapter finishes with a summary.

5.1 Impact from categorisation

In the basic experiment the categories are prototypical as introduced in Section 3.4.2.1. When a category is used as a meaning that a robot successfully uses

5 Varying methods and parameters

in a language game, the value of the category shifts towards the feature value of the relevant sensory channel. What happens if the categories do not shift towards these feature values?

Categorisation is implemented such that a feature vector is always categorised with the prototypes that are closest in each feature space. It has been argued that categorisation is not so clear-cut, but that there may be fuzzy boundaries between adjacent categories (see e.g. Aitchison 1987 and Lakoff 1987). Especially around the boundaries of a category's sensitivity, the certainty of whether a feature vector belongs to one category or another becomes smaller. For instance, something that looks like a *cup* might be categorised by another person as a *vase* or *bowl* as has been shown by Labov (1973). FAMILY RESEMBLANCE (Wittgenstein 1958) is another example of such fuzziness. These are examples at a higher level of categorisation, but the same may hold at the lower level of categorisation.

These two questions are investigated in this section, together with the binary subspace method (see Section 3.4.2.3). The results are compared with the basic experiment.

5.1.1 The experiments

There are the following experiments (all are variants of the basic experiment, and thus implement the guessing game):

No shifting categories (NS) Once a prototypical category is introduced, its value does not change through time. Hence the categories are static.

Fuzzy sets (FS) Categories may overlap each other at their boundaries. In this experiment, a feature is categorised with those categories that are closer than a certain minimal distance, and if no such category exists, the feature is categorised with the category that is closest to the feature value.

More formally, a category c_k can be defined by region in a feature space $\mathcal{F}_\lambda$. The category c_k can be described as $c_k = \langle \mathbf{c}_k, d_k, v_k, \rho_k, \kappa_k \rangle$, where $\mathbf{c}_k = x_0, \ldots, x_{n-1}$ is a prototype in the n dimensional feature space $\mathcal{F}_\lambda$, $d_k = \frac{1}{2} \cdot 3^{-\lambda}$ is a distance based on the feature space in which the prototype is stored and v_k, ρ_k and κ_k are scores as described in Chapter 3. The distance d_k is based on an equal subdivision of the number of exploitations that are done in the feature space $\mathcal{F}_\lambda$.

A feature vector is $\mathbf{f}$ is categorised with c_k if its distance to c_k is shortest, or if in each dimension i the distance between f_i and $x_{k,i}$ is smaller than d_k, i.e. $|f_i - x_i| < d_k$.

5.1 Impact from categorisation

Note that in this way a feature vector may be categorised with more than one category in each feature space. If the vector is closest to the prototype of one category, but if it falls inside the region of another category as defined by d_k, it is categorised in two or more ways. It is also important to realise that, like in the prototype method, whenever there exists a prototype in some feature space $\mathcal{F}_\lambda$, a feature vector can be categorised in this space.

So, instead of one possible categorisation in each feature space, a feature vector may have several. This increases the chance that a referent is categorised more parsimoniously and thus increasing the communicative success. Note that the discrimination game is unaltered.

Binary subspace method (BIN) See Section 3.4.2.3.

5.1.2 The results

The results compared with the basic experiment are given in Figure 5.1 and Table 5.1. These results give the global averaged results of the communicative success, discriminative success, distinctiveness, parsimony, specificity and consistency.

Table 5.1: The results of the experiments on categorisations. The columns give the averaged results with their standard deviation of the basic experiment (B) compared with experiments NS, FS and BIN.

	B	NS	FS	BIN
CS	0.351 ± 0.010	0.349 ± 0.017	0.357 ± 0.024	0.264 ± 0.041
DS0	0.916 ± 0.004	0.933 ± 0.007	0.875 ± 0.014	0.893 ± 0.005
DS1	0.920 ± 0.004	0.935 ± 0.006	0.894 ± 0.013	0.895 ± 0.003
D0	0.956 ± 0.002	0.959 ± 0.000	0.956 ± 0.001	0.922 ± 0.005
D1	0.955 ± 0.002	0.959 ± 0.000	0.956 ± 0.001	0.933 ± 0.003
P0	0.852 ± 0.004	0.841 ± 0.005	0.875 ± 0.003	0.856 ± 0.004
P1	0.851 ± 0.002	0.835 ± 0.006	0.875 ± 0.002	0.858 ± 0.007
S0	0.822 ± 0.017	0.813 ± 0.022	0.843 ± 0.022	0.841 ± 0.045
S1	0.817 ± 0.011	0.810 ± 0.015	0.846 ± 0.024	0.852 ± 0.040
C0	0.816 ± 0.008	0.793 ± 0.007	0.835 ± 0.011	0.791 ± 0.016
C1	0.811 ± 0.007	0.793 ± 0.007	0.832 ± 0.008	0.789 ± 0.023

5 Varying methods and parameters

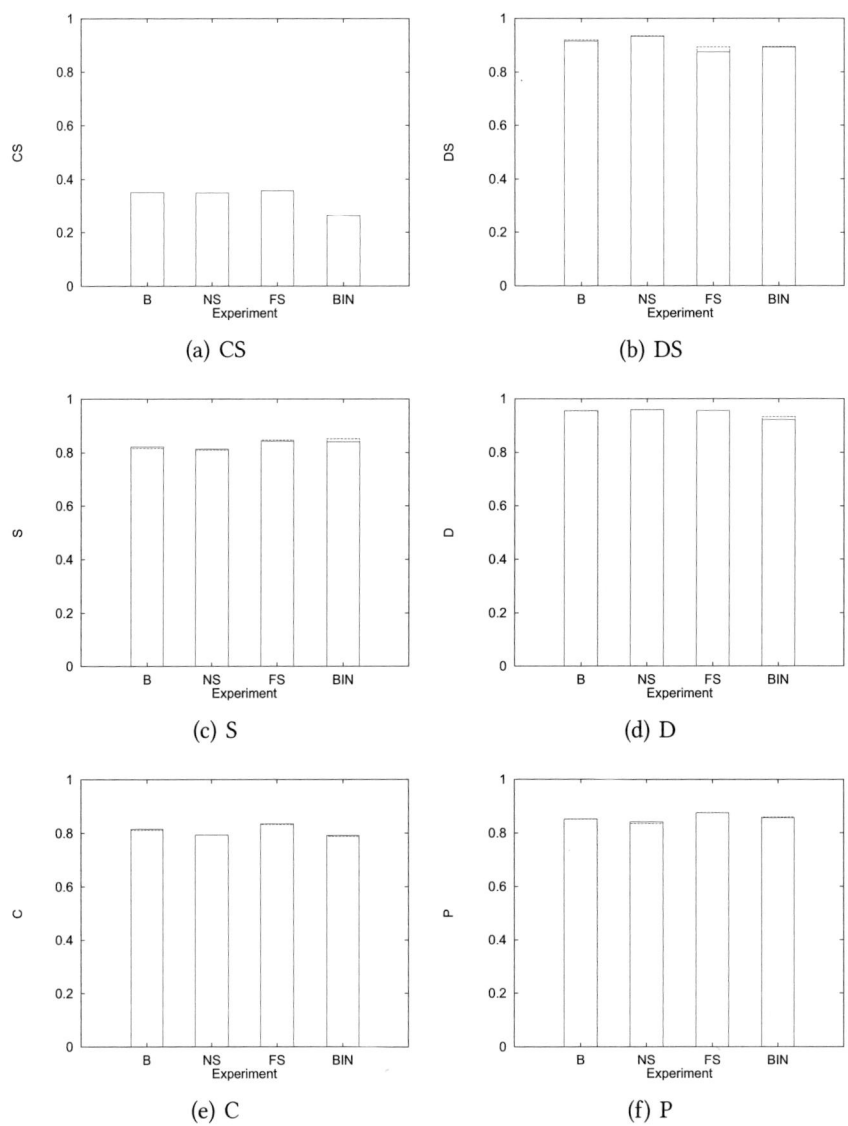

Figure 5.1: The average scores of the experiments discussed in this chapter: static categories (NS), fuzzy sets (FS) and binary subspaces (BIN) compared with the basic experiment (B).

5.1 Impact from categorisation

NS Experiment NS shows that there are hardly any *significant* differences compared to the basic experiment. The discriminative success is about 1.5 % higher with a significance of $p = 0.0052$. The parsimony and consistency appears to be lower with a *p*-value of $p = 0.0432$ and $p = 0.0354$, respectively. All other differences have no significance at all. So, although one might expect larger differences they have not been observed. If there is a function for shifting the categories it will be for increasing parsimony and consistency, but this has not been observed with much certainty.

FS The results of the FS experiments show that, although there are more possible meanings, the discriminative success is lower than in the basic experiment ($p = 0.0000$). The communicative success shows an insignificance difference ($p = 0.1230$). However, one run showed an exceptional small communicative success, namely 0.23. When throwing away this run (which is statistically valid) the average communicative success becomes 0.371 ± 0.025 which is different with a *p*-value of $p = 0.0504$. So, although this looks better, it is hard to say whether the communicative success of this experiment is better.

The distinctiveness is equal to the basic experiment. The specificity seems to be higher than in the basic experiment and the consistency seems to be lower, but these differences are insignificant ($p = 0.2176$ and $p = 0.1230$, respectively). The parsimony however is slightly higher (0.02) with a significance of $p = 0.0008$.

So, although the discriminative success is lower than in the basic experiment, the fuzzy set approach does not appear to influence the quality of the communication system that emerges.

BIN When examining the BIN experiment, a first thing that strikes is the lower discriminative success ($p = 0.0004$). This lower discriminative success is because it increases slower (Figure 5.2 b). It finally increases to the same level as in the basic experiment (see Figure 4.1 at page 109).

The communicative success stays well behind the communicative success of the basic experiment ($p = 0.0016$). It is not directly clear why the communicative success is about 8.5 % lower. The communicative success appears to stop learning after 1,000 language games, although it seems to increase slowly again after 4,000 games (Figure 5.2 a). The consistency is about 0.025 lower than in the basic experiment ($p = 0.0354$), but parsimony is ± 0.005 higher ($p = 0.0524$). Because the *p*-values are relatively high, it is difficult to assign meaning to these differences.

5 Varying methods and parameters

Most significant difference is the distinctiveness, which is ±0.03 lower with a significance of $p = 0.0002$. In contrast to previous plots that have been shown the distinctiveness does not grow towards a value of 1, but it stabilises around 0.97 (Figure 5.2 c). So, it seems that the meanings less reliably refer to the corresponding referents, thus indicating more one-to-many relations between a meaning and the referents. Specificity is higher than in the basic experiment, indicating that polysemy is less. This observation, however, has a low significance: $p = 0.1904$. Hence lower distinctiveness might explain a lower communicative success, since a word-meaning no longer refers to one referent, which it does when $D = 1$.

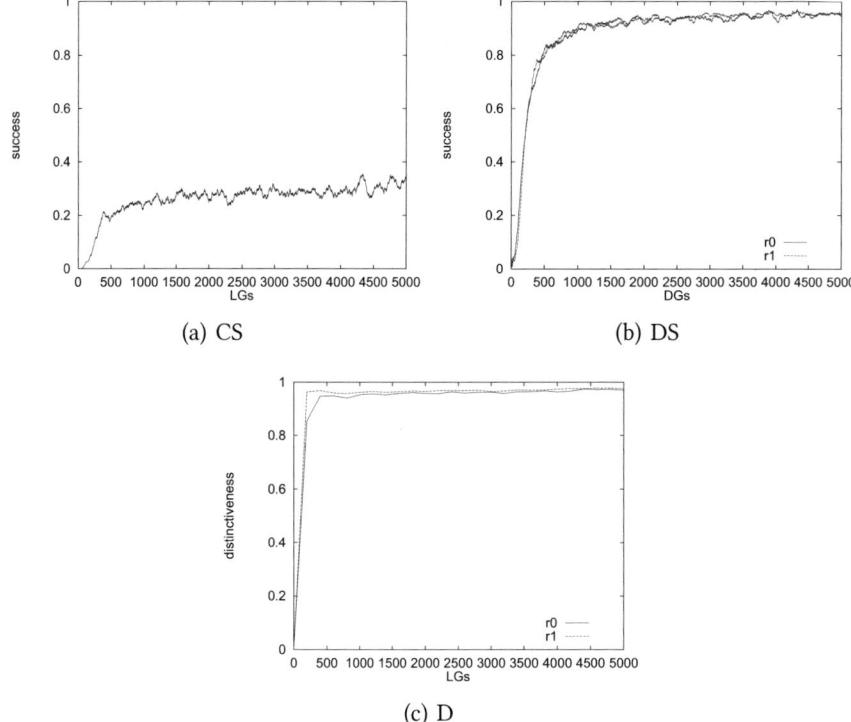

Figure 5.2: The evolution of the some measures for the binary subspace method.

5.1.3 Discussion

When the prototypes do not shift towards the central tendency as is the case in experiment NS, the communication system that is developed is qualitatively about the same. So, in the current set up, the dynamics of categories does not add any other functionality than possibly a more realistic model.

There is psychological and linguistic evidence that categories overlap making way for a fuzzy approach to categorisation. An experiment has been done where categories can overlap near their edges (or even near their centre when they are very close to each other). The discriminative success is significantly worse than in the basic experiment and the communicative success improves slightly but this is not very significant. It was predicted that parsimony and consistency would improve since the robots get a better chance to choose meanings or word-forms more consistently. This however has only been observed for the parsimony; the difference in consistency was insignificant.

The binary subspace method is performing worse than the basic set-up, which is a bit surprising. The communicative success is lower than chance and the discriminative success is lower than originally. The latter observation has much to do with a slow start. If an agent has constructed a category at a particular feature space in the prototype method, the agent can categorise every segment at this layer and sensory channel. This is because a feature is categorised with the category that is *closest* to the feature value. In the binary subspace method, this is not the case because each category has a fixed size and a feature space $\mathcal{F}_\lambda$ needs not to be covered completely with categories. Since a feature value must be *within* the sensitivity of an existing category, a segment may not always be categorised. At a later stage, the feature spaces are covered to a higher degree, so the discriminative success increases towards the end.

The system's distinctiveness is significantly different, but for the other measures parsimony, specificity and consistency the differences are much less significant or maybe not at all. So, in the binary subspace method more one-to-many relations between referent and meaning emerge than in the prototype method.

5.2 Impact from physical conditions and interactions

In the basic experiment, the robots decided to stop after two rotations based on finding a maximum intensity of infrared on the left back infrared sensor. Another method described is letting the robots align each other using infrared taxis (Section 2.3). Besides longer experimental time (due to more error-prone physical behaviour), the taxis has no influence on the grounding process, since the taxis is applied *after* the sensing. Two experiments are done where taxis is used to align the robots. In the first experiment it was observed that the gearing of the robots were worn off. In the second experiment the gearing were replaced

5 Varying methods and parameters

by new ones. These experiments show how co-ordination abilities and physical fitness may influence the quality of interactions.

In Steels & Vogt 1997 the robots did not rotate twice aligning back-to-back while doing the sensing, but only once aligning face-to-face. This experiment has been repeated to see what the differences are.

The adaptation of an agent to its environment and the agent's ability to detect the environment with enough precision is likely to be very important. In one experiment the environment and robots are changed such that the resolution of the robots' sensing decreases.

In all the experiments so far there were constantly 4 light sources present in the robots' environment. What happens when in each situation there are only 3 light sources present, while the robots' niche has 4 light sources? The last experiment of this section investigates this.

5.2.1 The experiments

The experiments of this section all investigate the impact from physical interactions and conditions on the robots' ability to ground a lexicon. Again all the experiments are variants of the basic experiment and hence implement the guessing game. The following experiments are defined:

Worn-off gearing (WOG) In this experiment the gearing of the robots were completely worn-off. As a result the robots had difficulties in rotating during the sensing task. Taxis is applied to re-align the robots after sensing.

New Gearing (NG) The robots in this experiment are equipped with brand new gearing. Like in WOG, taxis is applied to re-align the robots.

Acceleration (A) In the original implementation, the robots rotate only once starting face-to-face (Steels & Vogt 1997) rather than rotating twice and starting back-to-back. When the robots rotate once they immediately start the sensing and first have to accelerate, thus the spatial view initially is somewhat warped. When rotating twice they start sensing when the rotating robot faces its opponent. This way the robot is already moving at a constant speed, whereas in the original implementation the robots first have to accelerate.

Reducing distinctiveness (RD) In this experiment the difference in heights were reduced to 1.9 cm instead of 3.9 cm. This way the environment is reduced. Figure 5.3 shows the characteristics of the sensors as measured for different distances when facing a light source. It is obvious that the further a robot gets away from the light source, the closer the different sensor readings are. Furthermore, it should be clear that when the distance between robot and light source is larger, correspondence between sensor and light source is unreliable. Hence, the feedback mechanism is unreliable. Interesting to see is that when the robot is close to the light source the non-corresponding sensors hardly sense light, but the intensities increase up to 40 cm. This is because at close distance the light source is invisible for these sensors and at larger distance the divergent light emission falls on the sensors. Naturally it is expected that the robots have more difficulty in discriminating and identifying the light sources.

Dynamic environment (DE) In this experiment there were only three light sources present in every recorded situation. The height of the light sources were the same as in the basic experiment. After every few games, one of the light sources was removed and the one that was already out of the environment has been placed back. Whereas in the other experiments all light sources stayed roughly at the same place, the position of the light sources changed in this experiment as well. This way a dynamic environment was created.

5.2.2 The results

For all the experiments, different sensory data had to be recorded. Investigating the sensory data revealed the statistics given in Table 5.3.

Looking at Table 5.3, one can already see some interesting results. The WOG experiment reveals highest potential understandability. It also has a context size closer to 4 than in the other experiments. Apparently, the robots detect the four referents better when they rotate slower.

The NG experiment reveals data similar to the basic experiment. This is not surprising, since the only methodological difference with the basic experiment is taxis, which should not influence the grounding. Moreover, the basic experiment is recorded immediately after this experiment, so the physical condition of the gearing were similar. Experiment A has lower understandability. Apparently the warping during acceleration has some influence. RD has most influence on the data. Although the context size is similar (and thus the a priori success), the potential understandability is much lower. It seems there is more confusion. Making the environment dynamic (DE) has a logical consequence that the context size is almost 3, making the a priori success ±35%. The understandability is lower

5 Varying methods and parameters

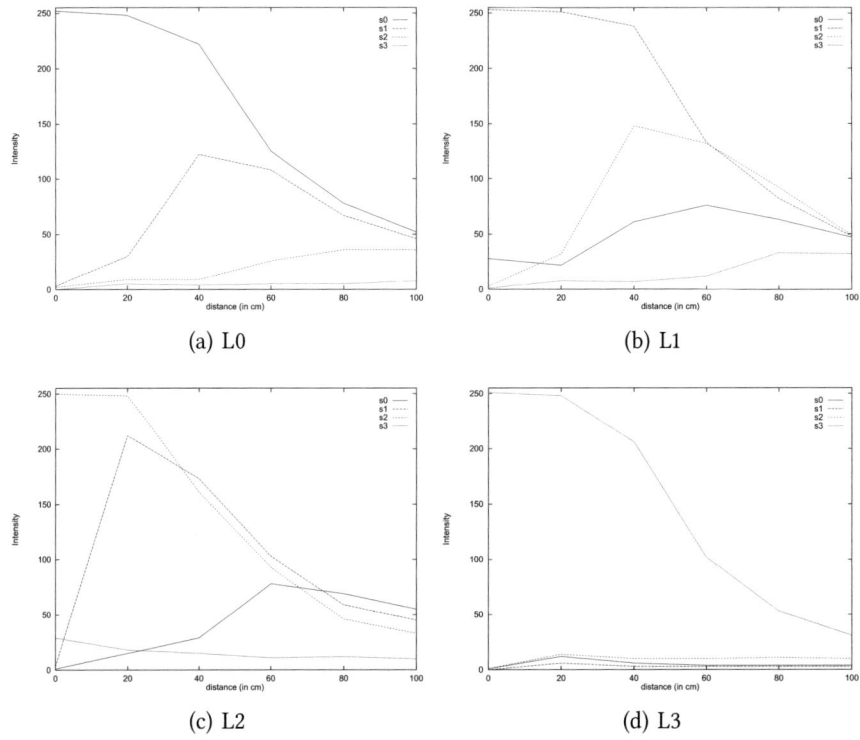

Figure 5.3: The characteristics of sensors $s0$, $s1$, $s2$ and $s3$ of robot $r0$ while looking at light sources (a) L0, (b) L1, (c) L2 and (d) L3. The light sources are placed at heights with a difference of 1.9 cm in between. Note that the characteristics of L3 may be inaccurate since the characteristics is quite different from all other characteristics.

than in the basic experiment. So, how does the ontology and lexicon evolve in these experiments? The results are shown in Figure 5.4 and Table 5.2.

5.2 Impact from physical conditions and interactions

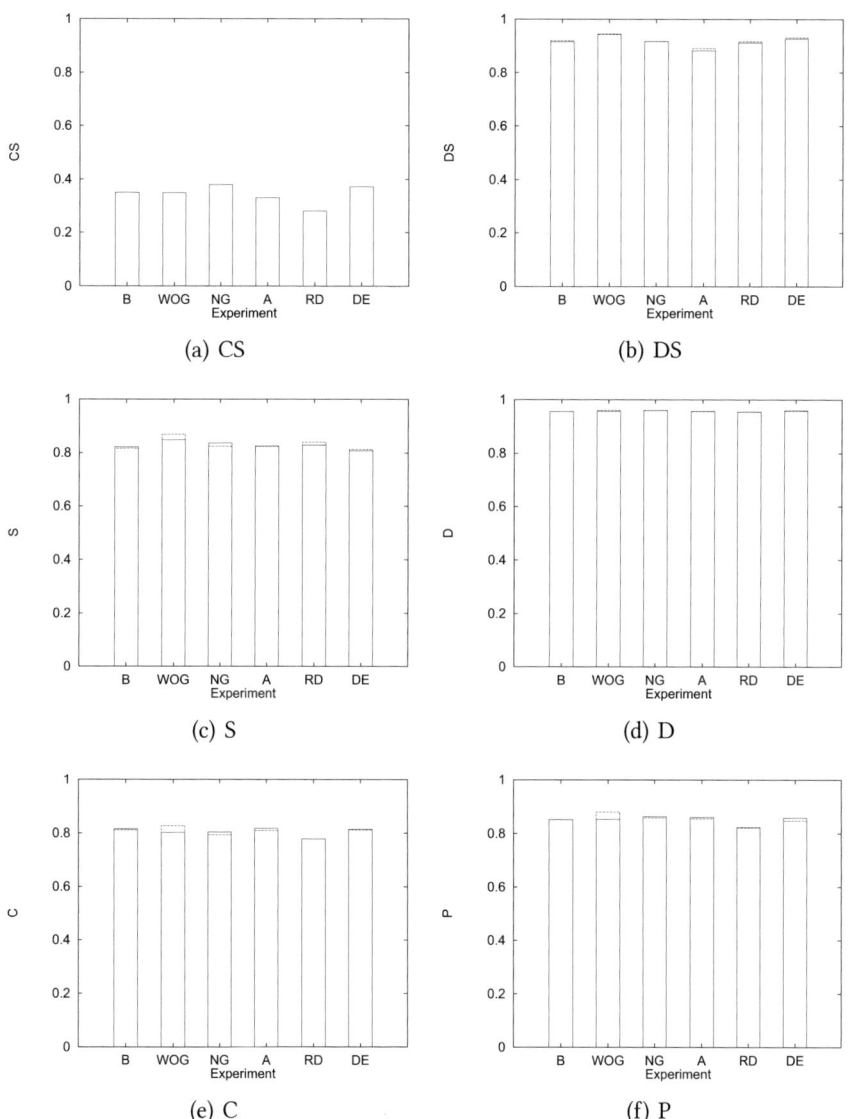

Figure 5.4: An overview of the results of the experiments presented in this section. Experiments WOG, NG, A, RD and DE are compared with the basic experiment (B).

5 Varying methods and parameters

Table 5.2: The global averaged results of the experiments concerning physical conditions and interactions.

	B	WOG	NG
CS	0.351 ± 0.01	0.350 ± 0.00	0.379 ± 0.013
DS0	0.916 ± 0.00	0.945 ± 0.00	0.918 ± 0.003
DS1	0.920 ± 0.00	0.944 ± 0.00	0.917 ± 0.003
D0	0.956 ± 0.00	0.956 ± 0.00	0.959 ± 0.000
D1	0.955 ± 0.00	0.960 ± 0.00	0.960 ± 0.001
P0	0.852 ± 0.00	0.852 ± 0.00	0.864 ± 0.001
P1	0.851 ± 0.00	0.880 ± 0.00	0.858 ± 0.002
S0	0.822 ± 0.01	0.849 ± 0.00	0.837 ± 0.014
S1	0.817 ± 0.01	0.869 ± 0.01	0.824 ± 0.018
C0	0.816 ± 0.00	0.802 ± 0.00	0.803 ± 0.006
C1	0.811 ± 0.00	0.828 ± 0.00	0.794 ± 0.004
	A	RD	DE
CS	0.331 ± 0.00	0.281 ± 0.00	0.372 ± 0.018
DS0	0.883 ± 0.00	0.913 ± 0.00	0.927 ± 0.005
DS1	0.891 ± 0.00	0.917 ± 0.00	0.932 ± 0.003
D0	0.957 ± 0.01	0.954 ± 0.00	0.959 ± 0.000
D1	0.956 ± 0.01	0.955 ± 0.00	0.958 ± 0.000
P0	0.861 ± 0.01	0.823 ± 0.00	0.858 ± 0.003
P1	0.855 ± 0.00	0.822 ± 0.00	0.847 ± 0.001
S0	0.826 ± 0.00	0.829 ± 0.01	0.807 ± 0.009
S1	0.823 ± 0.00	0.840 ± 0.01	0.812 ± 0.007
C0	0.818 ± 0.00	0.778 ± 0.00	0.814 ± 0.008
C1	0.809 ± 0.00	0.778 ± 0.00	0.812 ± 0.008

5.2 Impact from physical conditions and interactions

Table 5.3: The statistics of the sensory data of the experiments investigating the physical interactions and conditions. The columns display the experiments (Exp), the number of situations recorded (#Sit), the context size of robots r0 and r1 ($\langle |Cxt| \rangle_r$), the a priori success (APS) and the potential understandability of the two robots (U_r). The basic experiment (B) is added for comparison.

Exp	#Sit	$\langle \|Cxt\| \rangle_{r0}$	$\langle \|Cxt\| \rangle_{r1}$	APS (%)	U_{r0} (%)	U_{r1} (%)
B	1017	3.33	3.54	29.1	81.1	78.0
WOG	606	3.64	3.83	26.8	89.7	82.4
NG	934	3.28	3.49	29.6	80.9	77.9
A	1360	3.55	3.35	29.0	72.2	76.4
RD	953	3.53	3.48	28.5	63.9	67.9
DE	980	2.86	2.90	34.7	75.7	73.8

Table 5.4: The results of the basic experiments using only 606 situations from the basic data set.

Score	Avg
CS	0.354 ± 0.016
DS0	0.794 ± 0.009
DS1	0.816 ± 0.008
D0	0.959 ± 0.000
D1	0.960 ± 0.001
P0	0.869 ± 0.004
P1	0.877 ± 0.002
S0	0.849 ± 0.019
S1	0.853 ± 0.007
C0	0.820 ± 0.014
C1	0.831 ± 0.014

5 Varying methods and parameters

WOG The WOG experiment is in most ways similar to the basic experiment. Only the discrimination game is more successful (approximately 2 %, $p = 0.0004$). Specificity is higher and consistency is lower, but their significance is low ($p = 0.1704$ and $p = 0.2798$, respectively).

So, although the gearing of the robots were really at their ends, the communication system that emerges is not worse than the basic experiment. Question is if this result is biased by the fact that this data set only consists of 606 situations rather than 1,000. Table 5.4 presents the results of the basic experiment using 606 situations taken from the basic data set used. The table shows that using only 606 situations does not alter the results of the basic experiment very much, so the smaller data set does not really bias the experiment.

NG When the robots have new gearing, the communicative success is 2.8 % better than the basic experiment. However, its significance is low ($p = 0.1230$). It is also better than the taxis experiment with old gearing with a significance of $p = 0.0752$. The discriminative success is more or less equal compared with the basic experiment and is ±2.5 % lower for the old gearing ($p = 0.0008$). There are no significant differences when comparing the distinctiveness, parsimony, specificity and consistency with experiments B and WOG. So, using new gearing does not influence the ability for the robots to construct ground a language very much.

A The acceleration experiment seems to have little effect on the results. The discriminative success is about 3 % lower, which is significant ($p = 0.0000$). Also the communicative success is lower: 2 %, but with $p = 0.0770$. All other differences are insignificant. So, the onset of acceleration cannot be observed as an important difference.

RD Reducing the environmental distinctiveness has great impact on the lexicon grounding. The communicative success is around the a priori value; its significance in comparison to the basic experiment is $p = 0.0000$. The discriminative success is similar to the basic experiment.

The distinctiveness seems approximately the same as in the basic experiment, but its p-value is $p = 0.0114$, which is not very high. It seems likely that the two experiments yield different distinctiveness, but its difference is not large (≤ 0.002). Since the difference is so small, no further implications will be made.

Besides the specificity which does not show a significant difference, the parsimony and consistency ($p = 0.0068$ and $p = 0.0028$, respectively) are significantly different and lower than in the basic experiment. Obviously this has to with the large overlap in the sensory characteristics. Recall that these results are difficult to interpret, since the method for evaluating the feedback and thus the communicative success is unreliable due to the new characteristics of the sensors.

DE When changing the environment dynamically, the communicative success is about 2.5 % higher than the a priori value. It is about 2 % higher than in the basic experiment, but this is not very significant ($p = 0.0892$). Distinctiveness, specificity, parsimony and consistency show no significant difference with the basic experiment. Discriminative success looks higher than in the basic experiment, but its significance is low: $p = 0.0630$.

5.2.3 Discussion

Clearly, the quality of the physical behaviour influences the lexicon grounding. This is best illustrated by the fact that the potential understandability in most experiments is only around 80 %. However, it is difficult to investigate the impact structurally when the physical behaviour of the robots are difficult to control. This is because the robots physically behave reactively.

For example experiments WOG and NG are qualitatively more or less similar to the basic experiment. Differences in discrimination success in the taxis experiment with old gearing may lie in the fact that this was the first experiment after the sensors have been calibrated. It is not unlikely that the accuracy of the sensors becomes less reliable through time.

The experiment where the robots rotate only once (A) and where there are only three referents present (DE) are also qualitatively similar as the basic experiment. So, the slow onset of movement has little impact on the robots performance in these experiments. Furthermore, the robots seem to be well capable of dealing with a dynamic environment. Although the a priori success is higher, the robots appear to perform as if there are four referents. All these experiments show that the data recording can be repeated without influencing the experiments very much.

When the environment is changed such that it is less distinctive, the performance is significantly worse than the basic experiment. Surprisingly this does not hold for the discrimination success. It seems to have more impact on the ability to provide reliable feedback. However, the results might indicate the importance of agents' physical adaptation to their environment as a basis for language origins.

Physical interactions are also a part of how joint attention and feedback can be provided to the agents. However, these processes additionally require cognitive capabilities. Experiments investigating the influence of these interaction strategies are presented in the next section.

5.3 Different language games

This section investigates the impact from joint attention and feedback on the lexicon formation. The non-linguistic information used by human language learners is very much debated in the literature (see e.g. Bowerman 1988; Barrett 1995). The experiments presented here will show that the availability of joint attention and feedback has much influence on the grounding process. The games investigated are the guessing, ostensive, observational and xsl game.

5.3.1 The experiments

The four different language games have been introduced in Section 3.4.3. The properties of the four different language games are summarised in Table 5.5.

Table 5.5: A schematic overview of the experiments discussed in this section. The table gives the properties of the different language games.

Exp	Game	Joint attention	Feedback
ii	ostensive	Yes	Yes
xi	guessing	No	Yes
ix	observational	Yes	No
xx	XSL	No	No

Note that the guessing game (experiment xi) is the basic experiment. All experiments use the basic data set as sensory data, i.e., the same sensory data that has been used in the basic experiment and most other experiments.

5.3.2 The results

In the experiments where no feedback is used, the communicative success is different than the actual success. Therefore the results (Figure 5.5 and Table 5.6) employ the actual success for the first time. From the actual success, it becomes clear that the xsl game xx does not work. Although the other measures have similar values as the guessing, the actual success is 5 % lower than the a priori success and about 11 % lower than the basic experiment ($p = 0.0000$).

Table 5.6: The experimental results of the xsl game (xx), the guessing game (xi), the ostensive game (ii) and the observational game (ix).

	xx	xi	ii	ix
CS	0.818 ± 0.006	0.351 ± 0.010	0.671 ± 0.004	0.847 ± 0.003
AS	0.241 ± 0.008	0.351 ± 0.010	0.671 ± 0.004	0.667 ± 0.003
DS0	0.912 ± 0.004	0.916 ± 0.004	0.935 ± 0.002	0.937 ± 0.001
DS1	0.915 ± 0.005	0.920 ± 0.004	0.936 ± 0.002	0.941 ± 0.004
D0	0.959 ± 0.000	0.956 ± 0.002	0.959 ± 0.000	0.960 ± 0.000
D1	0.958 ± 0.000	0.955 ± 0.002	0.960 ± 0.000	0.960 ± 0.001
P0	0.866 ± 0.002	0.852 ± 0.004	0.856 ± 0.001	0.858 ± 0.002
P1	0.860 ± 0.003	0.851 ± 0.002	0.851 ± 0.002	0.851 ± 0.000
S0	0.808 ± 0.031	0.822 ± 0.017	0.647 ± 0.046	0.684 ± 0.144
S1	0.810 ± 0.031	0.817 ± 0.011	0.647 ± 0.045	0.688 ± 0.132
C0	0.814 ± 0.005	0.816 ± 0.008	0.823 ± 0.037	0.772 ± 0.117
C1	0.812 ± 0.005	0.811 ± 0.007	0.821 ± 0.026	0.787 ± 0.099

The ostensive game and the observational game appear to be much better than the guessing game. This increase in performance is measured by the actual success,[1] which is almost 30 % (!) better ($p = 0.0000$). However, the specificity is much lower: 0.18 for experiment ii and 0.14 in ix ($p = 0.0000$). This low specificity indicates that the lexicon is not stable and it must bear much polysemy.

The difference in consistency of the observational game is insignificant ($p > 1$). The consistency of ii is hardly different than the basic experiment. Note that the standard deviations of experiment ix is about 0.1 for both the specificity as the consistency. The results of the experiments vary a lot from run to run. The worst run has a consistency of 0.401, whereas the best one has 0.856. The basic experiment had all its values in between and a standard deviation of 0.007. Similar

---

[1] The communicative success of the observational game is much higher because this is measured when both robots 'think' they are successful. This happens when both robots identified a form-meaning association consistent with their categorisation. It is independent of whether both robots referred to the same referent.

5 Varying methods and parameters

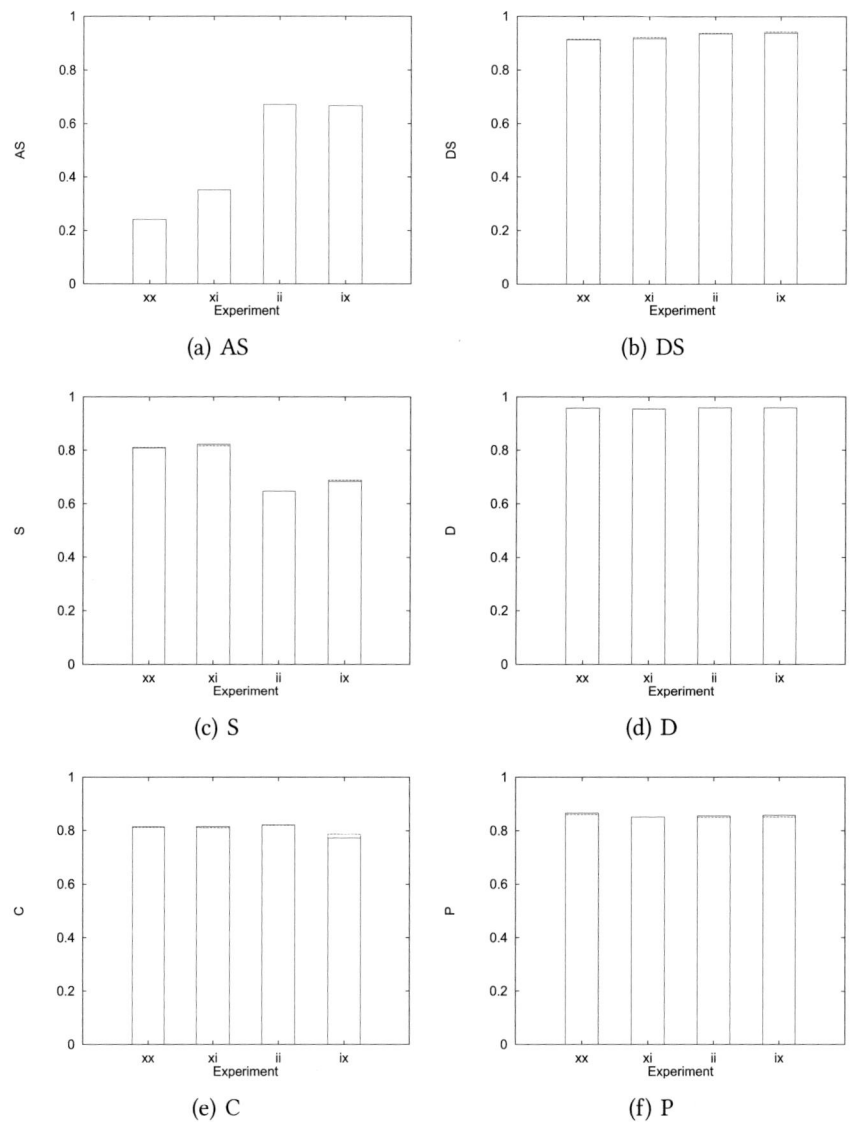

(a) AS

(b) DS

(c) S

(d) D

(e) C

(f) P

5.3 Different language games

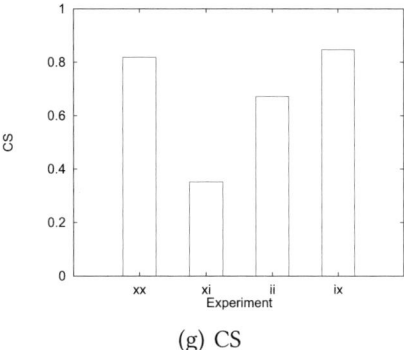

(g) CS

Figure 5.5: Results of experimenting with the different types of language games. Note that the first plot (a) shows the actual success, while the communicative success is plotted in the last Figure (f).

findings are also valid for ii that has standard deviation of about 0.05 for the specificity and 0.03 for consistency.

The discriminative success of ix and ii is slightly higher than the basic experiment ($p = 0.0000$), but this has to do with the higher communicative success, which influence the discriminative success. The differences of D and P are both small and insignificant.

5.3.3 Discussion

When looking at the results, some important observations can be made. A language game needs some extra-linguistic information. As expected, no effective lexicon gets off the ground in the XSL game.

It seems that a more informative lexicon emerges in the guessing game. It is more informative because the specificity and consistency are higher than in the ostensive and observational game. More information seems to have a cost in these experiments, namely a lower actual success. The actual success of the games that incorporate joint attention, on the other hand, is high. This also has a cost, namely a lower specificity.

To understand why the experiments that use joint attention have higher actual success and lower specificity (and to some extend consistency), it is instructive to look at an example: Suppose a robot has a (part of a) lexicon as in Figure 5.6. If the robot is a speaker and R1 is the topic, it would select F2 as the utterance inde-

143

5 Varying methods and parameters

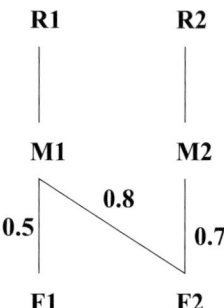

Figure 5.6: The semiotic landscape of one agent in the example that is described in the text.

pendent of the type of game.[2] If R2 is the topic, it would also select F2. Remember that the robots select the associations that have highest scores.

Suppose that this robot is a hearer, and it hears F2. If the robot plays a guessing game, it would select M1 and consequently R1 will be its topic. If however, the speaker intended to name R2, the game is a failure; there is a mismatch in referent. The score σ_{M1F2} between M1 and F2 is decreased.

But now suppose that the robot plays observational or ostensive games. If the speaker's topic is R2, the hearer will also have R2 as its topic, conform the joint attention principle. If the hearer now hears F2, it will select M2 as its meaning (since this categorises the only potential topic) and the language game is a success. Not only communicative, but also actual. Now the scores are adapted as follows: σ_{M2F2} is increased and σ_{M1F2} is decreased.

If such games will continue for a while, there will ideally emerge a preference where R2 is named with F2 and R1 with F1. But if, at some point before this happens, the robot is again the speaker and it chooses to name R1, it will still choose F2 to name M1. If a guessing game is played, there is a reasonable chance that the game ends in failure. The hearer (i.e. the other robot not shown in the figure) will have a similar but not equal competition of association scores and it might already be at the point where F2 will preferably be interpreted with meanings categorising R2. So, the speaker will decrease σ_{M1F2}. When, on the other hand, an observational game is played, and the robot names R1 with F2, it is very likely that the game will end in success. This is because the hearer knows what the topic is. So, if it as an association where F2 relates to some meaning M which categorises R1, the game is a success. As a consequence the association

---
[2] Remember that the guessing game is compared with both the ostensive and observational game, since what is important is the joint attention.

score σ_{M2F2} of the speaker increases again, whereas competing association scores decrease. The attempt to disambiguate F2 in favour of R2 has to start again.

This way the observational game allows more polysemy, yielding lower specificity. The same argument holds for the ostensive game. Since the robots easily establish actual success this way, the actual success is relatively high. So, it seems that establishing joint attention decreases the pressure to exploit the complete space of possibilities during selection. This is not surprising since joint attention makes linguistic communication redundant.

5.4 The observational game

In Section 5.3, an experiment with the observational game has been presented. It has been observed and explained that the specificity is low. So, the lexicon is unstable and allows much referential polysemy and some synonymy. But since the actual success is high, it is interesting to see whether it is possible to achieve good results for specificity and consistency as well.

While looking for working implementations it also has been found that lateral inhibition is a crucial source of lexicon development. This is conform with the findings of Oliphant (1997), Steels (1999), de Jong (2000) and Kaplan (2000). To investigate this a variant of the observational game of the previous section is presented in which lateral inhibition is absent.

5.4.1 The experiments

The experiments are compared with the observational game.

Creation probability ix_p In all experiments up to now, the word-form creation probability has been $P_s = 0.02$. In this experiment $P_s = 0.4$. This way the speaker is less modest in inventing new word-forms when it cannot produce an utterance.

Lateral inhibition ix_{li} In this experiment lateral inhibition of the association scores is not used. So, when an observational game is considered successful by the robots, only the "winning" association score is increased. All other scores are unaltered. For the rest this experiment is equal to experiment ix.

5 Varying methods and parameters

5.4.2 The results

The results are presented in Table 5.7 and Figure 5.7, where experiments ix_p and ix_{li} are compared with the observational game (ix) presented in Section 5.3.

Table 5.7: The results of the variants of the observational game.

	ix	ix_p	ix_{li}
CS	0.847 ± 0.003	0.827 ± 0.005	0.830 ± 0.001
AS	0.667 ± 0.003	0.657 ± 0.005	0.651 ± 0.002
DS0	0.937 ± 0.001	0.960 ± 0.001	0.937 ± 0.003
DS1	0.941 ± 0.004	0.963 ± 0.001	0.936 ± 0.003
D0	0.960 ± 0.000	0.960 ± 0.000	0.960 ± 0.001
D1	0.960 ± 0.001	0.961 ± 0.001	0.961 ± 0.000
P0	0.858 ± 0.002	0.853 ± 0.001	0.830 ± 0.001
P1	0.851 ± 0.000	0.848 ± 0.001	0.827 ± 0.000
S0	0.684 ± 0.144	0.927 ± 0.002	0.617 ± 0.094
S1	0.688 ± 0.132	0.927 ± 0.002	0.622 ± 0.095
C0	0.772 ± 0.117	0.838 ± 0.003	0.709 ± 0.114
C1	0.787 ± 0.099	0.839 ± 0.003	0.707 ± 0.112

For experiment ix_p the communicative success and actual success are more or less similar as in the experiment of the previous section, and so are the distinctiveness and parsimony. The difference in consistency is not very significant ($p = 0.1432$). The discriminative success is about 2.5 % higher when $P_s = 0.4$ ($p = 0.0000$). However, this is an artefact of the method for calculating the discriminative success. Because the speaker invents forms more often, the hearer plays discrimination games more often. Recall that the hearer only categorises when it receives an utterance. Since the discriminative success is a function of language games rather than of the discrimination games, the discriminative success is higher.

More important for experiment ix_p is the increase of specificity by 0.24 ($p = 0.0000$). Apparently the system reduces polysemy when P_s is higher. This is nicely shown by the form-referent competition diagrams of the two experiments (Figure 5.8). These diagrams show the competition for a word-form that is used very frequently in both experiments. The two diagrams clearly show the difference between experiment ix and ix_p. The word-form of experiment ix is used for all four referents almost equally often. The word-form displayed for ix_p clearly evolves to name LO pretty stable and specific.

5.4 The observational game

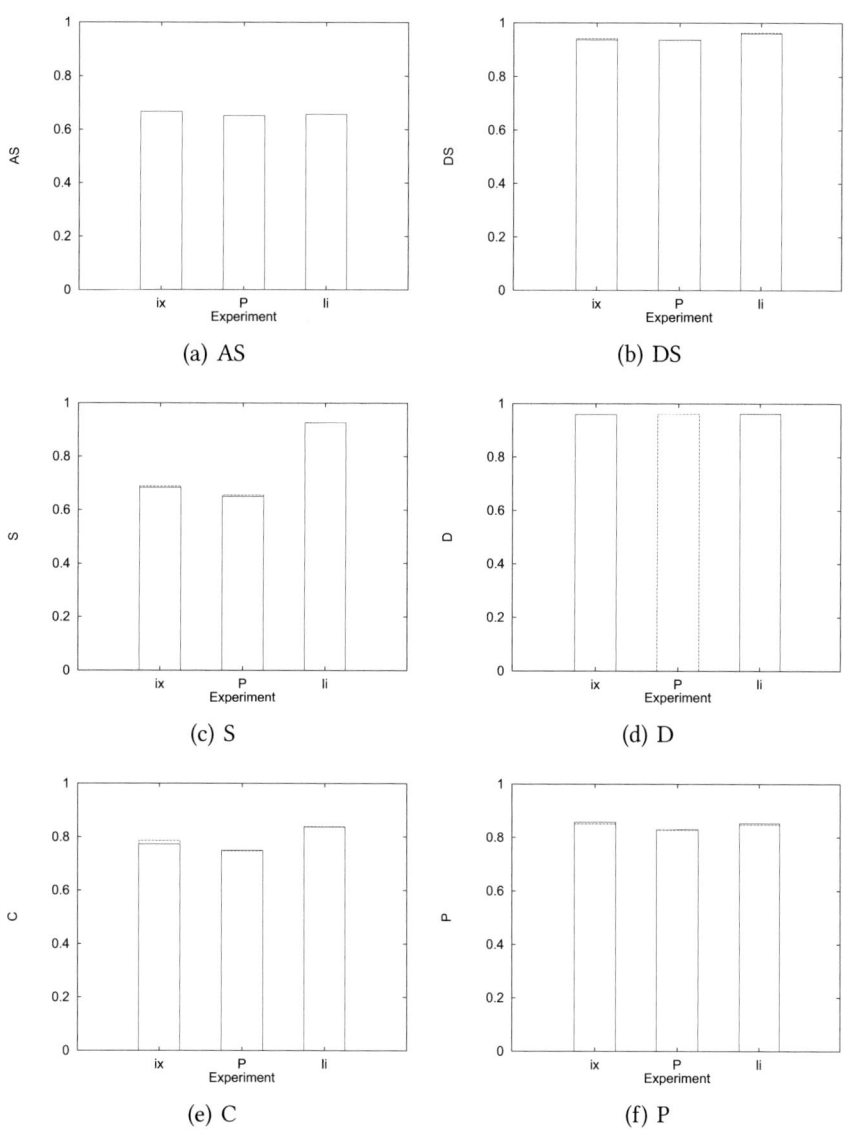

5 Varying methods and parameters

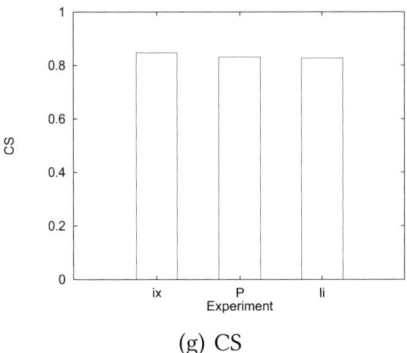

(g) CS

Figure 5.7: The results of experimenting with different observational games.

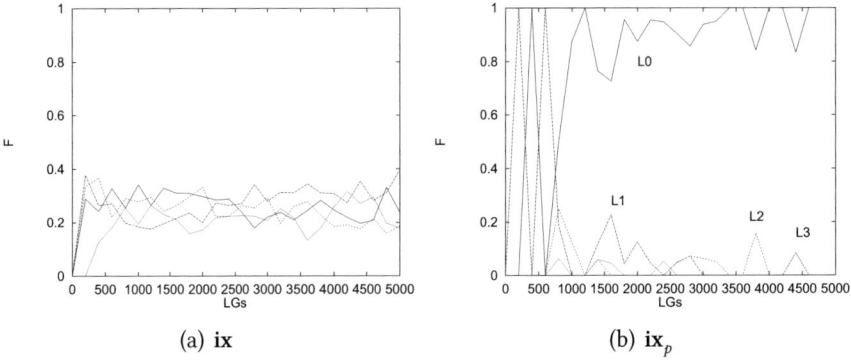

(a) ix (b) ix_p

Figure 5.8: The form-referent competitions of experiments **ix** (preceding section) and **ix**$_p$ for some form.

In the experiment where lateral inhibition is absent, most measures are also similar to *ix* from the previous section. However, both specificity and coherence is lower than in experiment *ix*. Hence when there is no lateral inhibition, more polysemy and synonymy emerges in the system.

5.4.3 Discussion

When the creation probability is higher, specificity is also higher. This can be explained as follows: When P_s is low, and the speaker cannot name some meaning, the probability is high that it will not invent a new word-form. This leaves the meaning unassociated, which increases the likelihood that the meaning will be associated with an already existing word-form. This may happen in a later game by means of word-form adoption when the robot is the hearer. This way the word-form increases its amount of one-to-many mappings and apparently its polysemy as well. When the P_s is higher, this effect is less, thus increasing the specificity.

It is interesting to note that the high average actual success is likely to be mainly caused by the joint attention mechanism and the easiness of establishing communicative success when joint attention is used. Note that, like in the ostensive game, joint attention makes the linguistic communication redundant. The ostensive game does not differ very much from the observational game. The feedback that it provides is more or less the same information that is provided by the joint attention mechanism.

Recall that the potential understandability is approximately 79 %. When multiplying this value with the average communicative success of approximately 83 %, this yields 66 %, which corresponds nicely to the average actual success. So, it appears that the difference between communicative success and actual success is caused by the inability of the robots to construct a coherent context as explained in Chapter 3. This indicates that there are still other mechanisms that are responsible for the imperfect communication.

The observational game is inspired by the experiments done by Mike Oliphant (1997; 1998; 1999), although they are not exactly the same. A big first difference is inherent on the use of robots.

Oliphant's agents have access to both the signal and the meaning of it during a language game, which he calls observation. The learning mechanism tries to converge an ideal communication system based on the word-meaning associations. This is also done in our experiments. However, the robots have, in principle, no access to the meaning of a signal other than to its referent. Another difference is in the learning algorithm (or the update of the scores). Where Oliphant uses Hebbian and Bayesian learning (among others), a different update rule is used here.

It is clear that the robots can ground a reasonable communication system with a reasonable success without the availability of feedback. However, this only works when joint attention is established and the word-form creation rate is sufficiently high. This confirms the work of Mike Oliphant (1997) and Edwin de Jong (2000). De Jong also showed in simulations that the naming game needs no feedback on the effect of a game. Like Oliphant (1997), Luc Steels (1999) and Frédéric Kaplan (2000), De Jong argues that lateral inhibition is an essential ingredient for success. The experiment without lateral inhibition again confirmed this finding. Without lateral inhibition all competing associations can be strengthened

5 Varying methods and parameters

in successful games. So, the competition between form-meaning associations is less effective. It is left as an exercise for the reader to invent an example.

5.5 Word-form creation

As has been observed in Section 5.4.1, the word-form creation probability P_s may have an enormous impact on the lexicon formation. In the basic experiment $P_s = 0.02$, which is a setting based upon earlier experiments (Vogt 1998b). In this section, the influence of the word-form creation probability is investigated more structurally.

5.5.1 The experiments

The creation probability is varied over 11 experiments. P_s is varied from 0.0 to 1.0 with intermediate steps of 0.1. The experiments further implement the guessing game and is therefore a variant of the basic experiment.

5.5.2 The results

The results are shown in Figure 5.9. It is trivial that communicative success, specificity, distinctiveness, consistency and parsimony are 0 when $P_s = 0$. When no word-forms are created, no communication can take place. All mentioned measures are only calculated when linguistic communication can take place. The discriminative success is approximately 50 % because only the speaker now performs a discrimination game and the discriminative success is calculated as an average discriminative success per language game. Since the robots can in principle discriminate almost perfectly (see Figure 4.3, page 112), the discriminative success is almost 50 %.

Figure 5.9 shows that there is hardly any difference in the experiments when P_s is varied between 0.1 and 1. The discriminative success and specificity are slightly increasing, as it appears monotonically. The communicative success also seems to be increasing, but it also shows some local minima and maxima. It seems that when $P_s = 0.9$, the communicative success is highest, but when $P_s = 0.4$, the communicative success is second best. There does not seem to be a relation: distinctiveness, consistency and parsimony seem to be indifferent for the variation of P_s.

When $0.1 \leq P_s \leq 1.0$, then the system outperforms the basic experiment. Although distinctiveness, parsimony and consistency are more or less the same as in the basic experiment; the communicative success is about 5–9 % higher,

5.5 Word-form creation

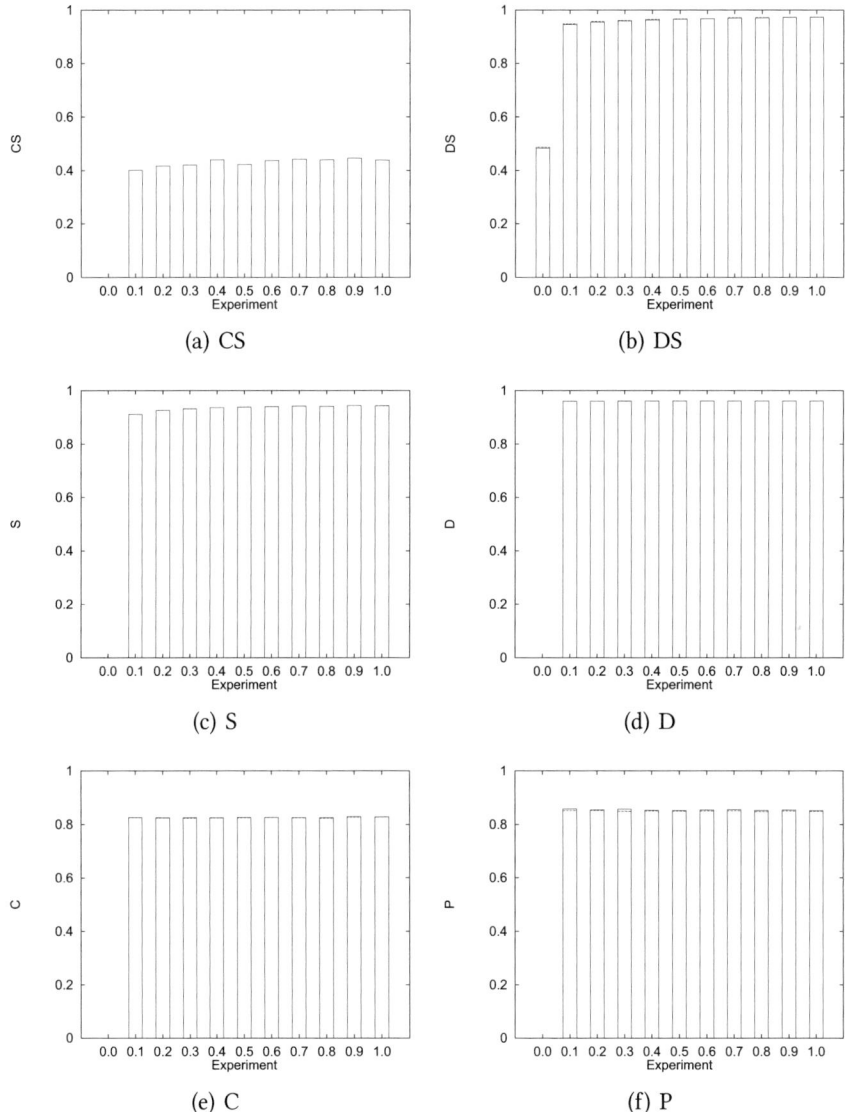

Figure 5.9: The results of a series experiments where creation probability P_s is varied from 0 to 1 with steps of 0.1.

5 Varying methods and parameters

discriminative success is 4 % higher and specificity is approximately 0.09 higher. All these differences are significant ($p = 0.0000$).

It is interesting now to see how the number of words grow in the communication system. Figure 5.10 shows the growth of the number of word-forms that are used successfully in the experiments. It is clear that the number of word-forms grows faster when the creation probability increases. Recall that the number of word-forms in the basic experiment grew to only 8 word-forms. When $P_s = 0.1$ this already increases to 25 word-forms, and when $P_s = 1.0$ there emerge more than 80 word-forms. As a comparison, the basic experiment finished with 12 word-forms. Remember that there are only 4 referents in the robots' environment!

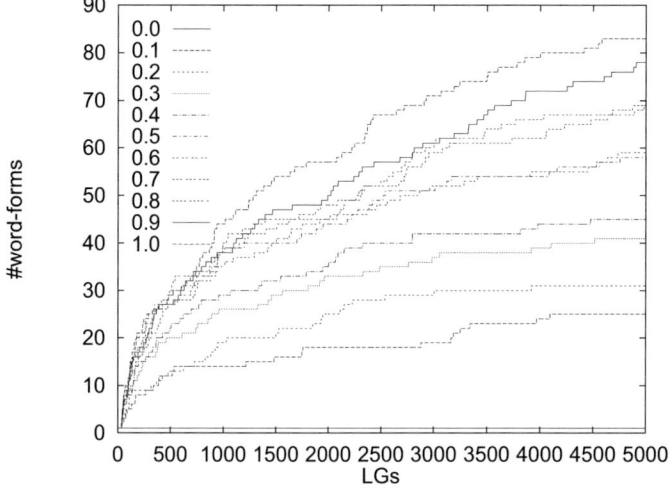

Figure 5.10: The lexicon growth for different values of the creation probability P_s, which is varied from 0 to 1 with steps of 0.1.

5.5.3 Discussion

The small differences between the results when $P_s = 00.1$ and $P_s = 1.0$ has also been observed in simulations on the naming game (Kaplan 2000).

From Figure 5.10 it can be inferred that the rate of synonymy thus increases very much, although this is not obvious from the consistency.[3] However, the robots do significantly better in learning to commentate than when $P_s = 0.02$

---

[3] Recall that consistency is weighted over the frequency of occurrences of referent-word-form pairs.

152

as in the basic experiment. This may be a side effect of the fact the agents optimise their lexicons for word-meaning associations rather than word-referent associations. When there are more word-forms, there is less need for many-to-many relations at the form-meaning level. But due to the fact that there is a high level of one-to-many relations between referent and meaning, synonymy is also relatively high.

As also observed in Section 5.4, the specificity is higher when P_s is higher. This is not surprising, since there are more word-forms to name the different meanings, thus decreasing the level of one-to-many relations between form and meaning. And since the different meanings are distinctive to a high degree, these word-forms refer to a unique referent more and more. A higher creation probability also yields a higher communicative success. The cost however of a higher creation probability is that there are more word-forms to name the same number of referents.

5.6 Varying the learning rate

The adaptation scores are adapted using a walking average. These scores are adapted for the category scores v, the effectiveness scores ρ and the association scores σ (Chapter 3). The formula by which the scores s are adapted is repeated here for clarity:

$$(5.1) \qquad s = \eta \cdot s' + (1 - \eta) \cdot X$$

where η is the learning rate and X is the success factor. The type of score is dependent on the game being played and so is X. This equation is used to update category, effectiveness and association scores.

In the basic experiment, the learning rate has been set to $\eta = 0.99$. This score has been chosen to be this value based upon early experiments, which was before the current implementation has been finished. What would happen if η is varied.

5.6.1 The experiments

The experiments implement the guessing game. The learning rate η is varied from 0.0 to 1.0 with steps of 0.1.

5.6.2 The results

Figure 5.13 shows the results of these experiments. The experiments where $\eta = 0$ and $\eta = 1$ perform very poor, poorer than in the basic experiment ($p = 0.0000$

5 Varying methods and parameters

in both cases). If $\eta = 0$, the scores are completely dependent from the previous language game where the element is used. When $\eta = 1$ the scores are not updated at all. Obviously, the robots cannot learn the communication system properly taking only the last game into account. Neither can it be learned when the scores are not updated. The communicative success when $\eta = 1$ is about 5 % lower than when $\eta = 0$ ($p = 0.0000$). So, taking only the last game into account is better than doing nothing. Figure 5.11 shows that these communication systems no longer learn after game 500. That some games are successful is caused by the fact that form-meaning associations do get formed as normal and the rest is more or less coincidence.

When $\eta = 0.1$, the communicative success is higher than in the basic experiment ($p = 0.0000$), but it is lower than when $0.2 \leq \eta \leq 0.9$ ($p = 0.0000$ when compared to $\eta = 0.2$). Furthermore, in this experiment the discriminative success and specificity are lower than when $0.2 \leq \eta \leq 0.9$ (again $p = 0.0000$ when compared to $\eta = 0.2$). However, Figure 5.12 shows that the communication is learned when $\eta = 0.1$ as well as when $\eta = 0.2$. It only takes longer, so the global averages are lower. Strangely enough the discriminative success and specificity are also lower when $\eta = 0.1$ than when $\eta = 0.0$. It is not understood why this is the case.

Figure 5.13 (a) shows that when $0.2 \leq \eta \leq 0.9$ the communicative success seems to be increasing slightly. Differences, however are hardly significant. When comparing the case where $\eta = 0.2$ with $\eta = 0.9$, the difference has a significance of $p = 0.0892$. Nevertheless, the increase really appears to be there.

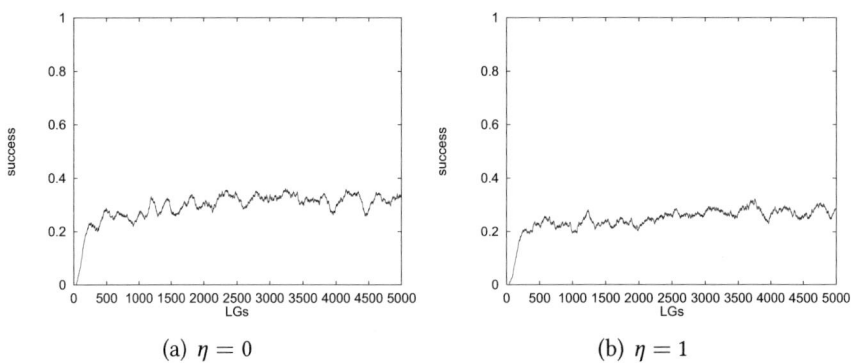

(a) $\eta = 0$ (b) $\eta = 1$

Figure 5.11: The evolution of the communicative success when (a) $\eta = 0$ and (b) $\eta = 1$. It is clear that the communication system is not learned.

5.6 *Varying the learning rate*

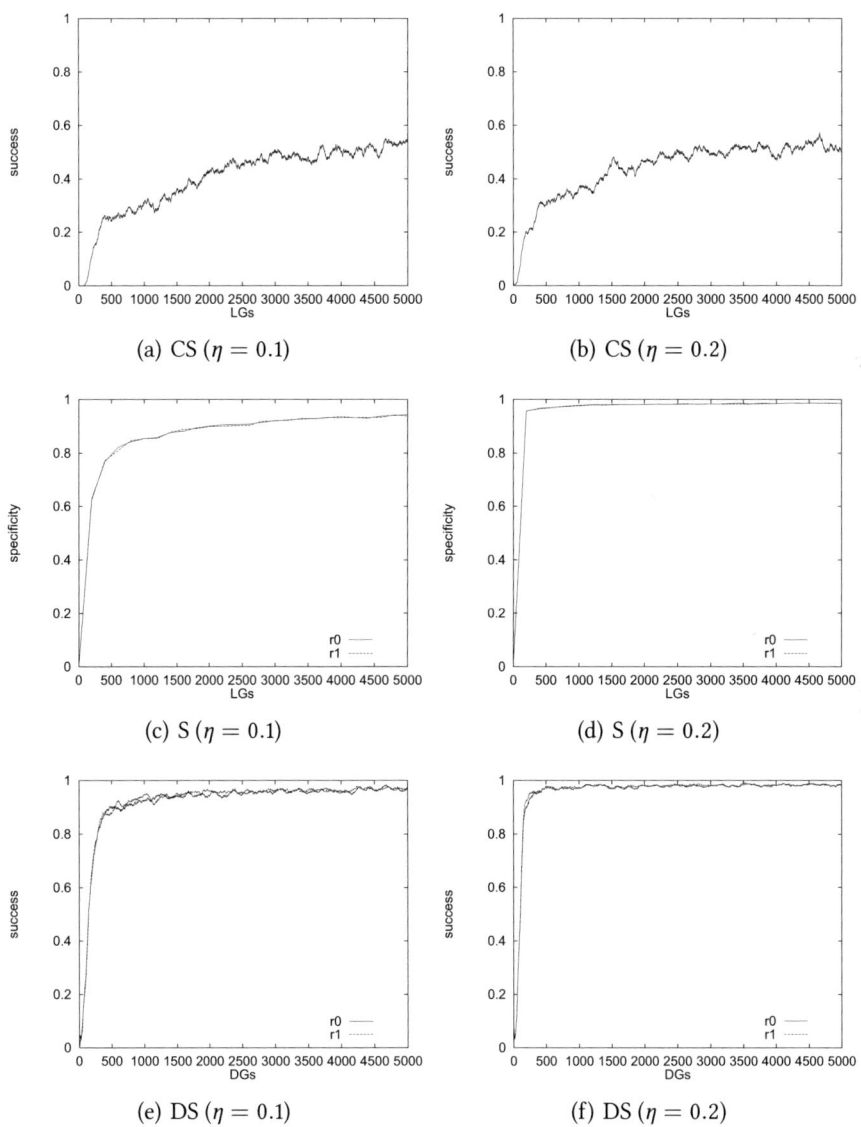

Figure 5.12: Comparing the communicative success, specificity and discriminative success in the cases where $\eta = 0.1$ and $\eta = 0.2$.

5 Varying methods and parameters

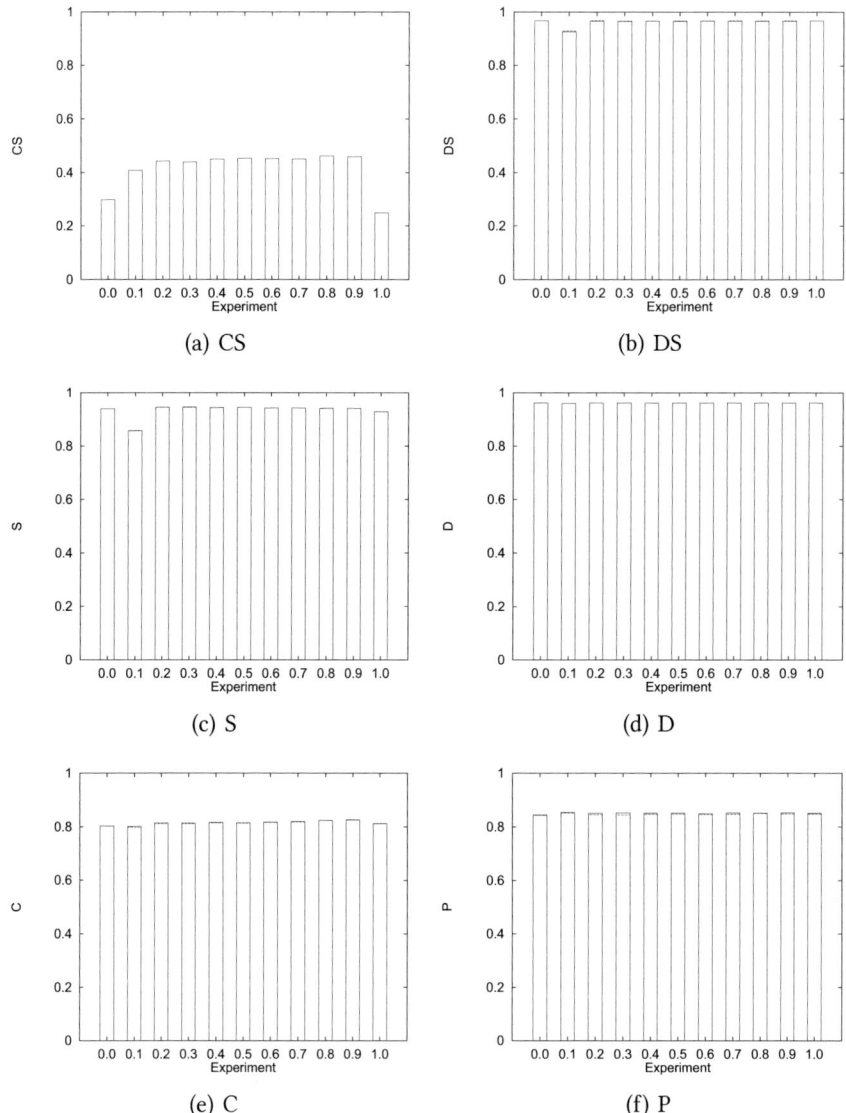

Figure 5.13: The results of a series of experiments where the learning rate η has been varied from 0 to 1 with intervals of 0.1.

5.6.3 Discussion

The results showed that a successful lexicon cannot be learned when the scores are not adapted. Neither can it be learned when the memory of a past interaction lasts only one re-occurrence of the association.

It is surprising that the system develops more or less equally well when $\eta = 0.2$ than when $\eta = 0.9$. In the first case the last few interactions have much more influence on the selection than the complete history of interactions. When $\eta = 0.9$ the vice versa is true. It is not clear why this is the case.

The results of this section show that the difference between the weight with which past success influences the experiment is high. When the learning rate η varies between 0.1 and 0.9, the success of the language games is higher than when $\eta = 0.99$. In that case the system is too much based on the past and as a result the system learns too slowly.

5.7 Word-form adoption

In the basic experiment the hearer only has to adopt a new word-form when it cannot find a matching form-meaning association. This happens when either the form is unknown to the hearer or when its meaning(s) do not match a distinctive category of a possible topic. In the Talking Heads, a word-form may also be adopted when there is a mismatch in referent (Steels 1999), i.e., when the hearer did find a matching form-meaning, but the thus identified topic does not cohere with the speaker's topic. Intuitively, this strategy seems to be beneficial. If the hearer misinterprets the speaker, it should learn what the speaker meant.

5.7.1 The experiments

Three experiments are done that investigate the impact from the extra word-form adoption. All experiments implement the guessing game. It differs from the basic experiment in that the uttered word-form is adopted by the hearer when the language game ends in a mismatch in referent. In that case the hearer identifies a topic. How this topic is selected is subject to variation. If this topic is not the same as the hearer identified before, the word-form is adopted according to the rules explained in Section 3.4.3.

The three experiments vary in the way the topic is selected:

Random (R) The topic is selected at random, like is the case when the hearer adopts a word-form in the basic experiment.

5 Varying methods and parameters

Correspondence (T) The topic is identified via the correspondence criterion, like is done when joint attention is established. This is only done when there is a mismatch in referent.

Double correspondence (TT) Like in experiment T, but now the hearer uses the correspondence criterion *every time* it adopts a word-form. This is conform with the Talking Heads (Steels 1999).

5.7.2 The results

The results in Table 5.8 and Figure 5.14 show that the communicative success is 5 to 6 % higher than in the basic experiment. These differences are significant with p-values of $p = 0.0040$, $p = 0.0188$ and $p = 0.0400$ for R, T and TT, respectively.[4] In all cases the discriminative success is about 3 % higher with a significance of $p = 0.0000$ for all experiments.

Table 5.8: The results of the experiment where the robots also adopt word-forms in case of a mismatch in the language game. In experiment R the hearer's new topic is selected at random. Topic information is used in experiments T (only in case of mismatch) and TT (any time).

	R	T	TT
CS	0.416 ± 0.051	0.415 ± 0.014	0.398 ± 0.004
DS0	0.958 ± 0.001	0.953 ± 0.002	0.957 ± 0.001
DS1	0.958 ± 0.002	0.953 ± 0.002	0.959 ± 0.002
D0	0.960 ± 0.000	0.956 ± 0.001	0.959 ± 0.000
D1	0.960 ± 0.000	0.956 ± 0.002	0.960 ± 0.000
P0	0.837 ± 0.001	0.826 ± 0.003	0.831 ± 0.001
P1	0.836 ± 0.002	0.825 ± 0.004	0.828 ± 0.001
S0	0.705 ± 0.075	0.660 ± 0.062	0.669 ± 0.023
S1	0.711 ± 0.071	0.659 ± 0.063	0.683 ± 0.016
C0	0.825 ± 0.025	0.833 ± 0.007	0.825 ± 0.013
C1	0.825 ± 0.023	0.834 ± 0.010	0.838 ± 0.016

Consistency is about 0.01 higher, but these results are insignificant. Distinctiveness is nearly the same as in the basic experiment. The parsimony is approximately 0.02 lower; differences with significance of $p = 0.0000$, $p = 0.0504$ and

---

[4] Note that only 9 runs of 5,000 language games have been run in experiment TT.

$p = 0.0400$ for R, T and TT, respectively. The specificity is 0.10 to 0.17 points lower ($p = 0.0004$, $p = 0.0078$ and $p = 0.0000$, respectively). Although the communicative success increases in comparison to the basic experiment, the cost appears to be a higher level of referential polysemy. This is not really a surprise, since the robots now construct more form-meaning associations with already existing word-forms. Thus representational polysemy increases, and apparently also the referential polysemy.

The above comparisons are made in contrast to the basic experiment. When comparing the results with each other, the differences have a significance with p-values that are higher than $p = 0.4894$. Hence no significant differences are observed.

5.7.3 Discussion

According the communicative success, the results improve when the hearer uses more opportunities to adopt existing word-forms. However, this strategy has a negative side effect. As word-forms are adopted when there is a mismatch in referent, this means that the hearer already had a lexical entry with this form. Hence the level of representational polysemy increases. In turn this increases the chance for referential polysemy when the different meanings categorise different referents.

Remains the question which experiment has performed best. Intuitively, one would say TT, then T and finally R. However, the results indicate otherwise. But since the observed differences are insignificant, no such conclusions can and shall be made. In more complex environments it is not unlikely that the (halfway) random strategies (R and T) will fail.

5.8 Summary

Starting from the basic experiment introduced in Chapter 4, this chapter has been used to investigate different interaction and learning strategies as variations on the basic experiment. Some variations have not shown much difference in performance whereas others have.

In Section 5.1 the influence of different categorisation schemes have been introduced and it appeared that the scheme applied in the basic experiment worked more or less the best. This categorisation scheme will be used in this chapter.

Varying physical interaction schemes on the robots contributed mainly in strategies that had negative influence on the performance (Section 5.2). Although the

5 Varying methods and parameters

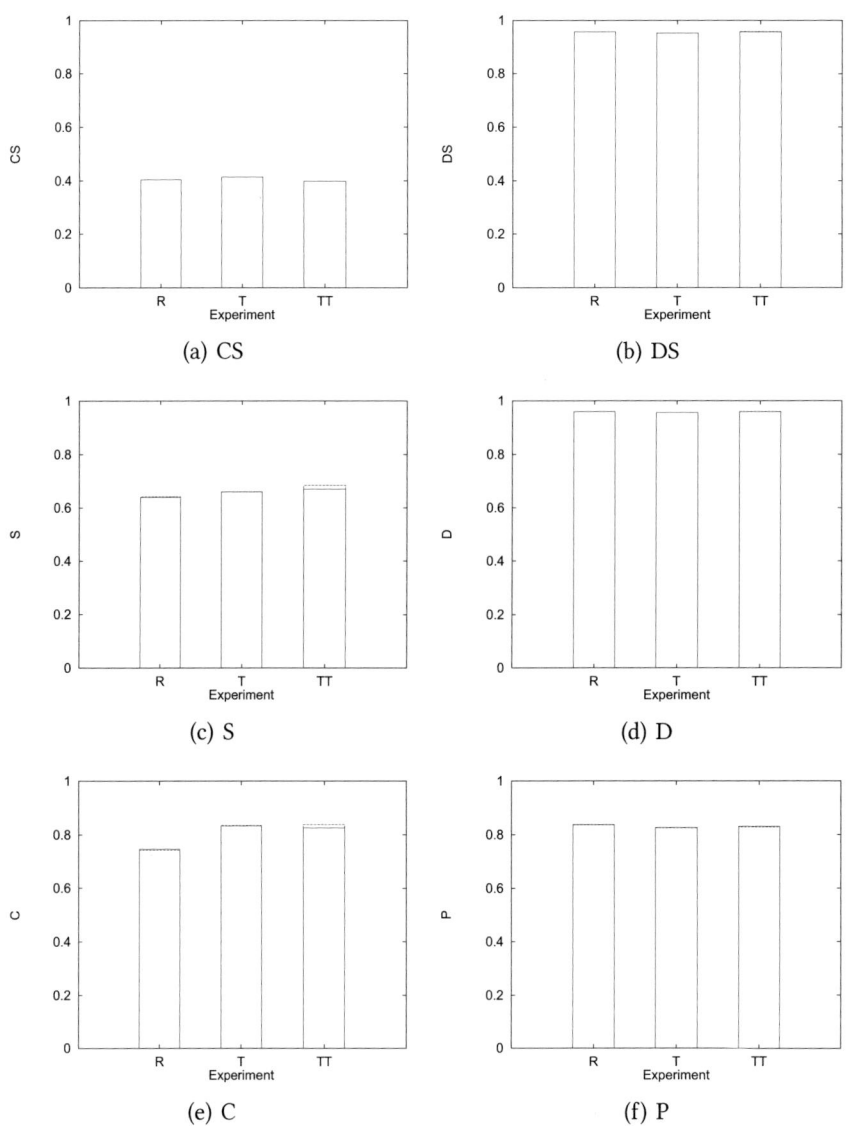

Figure 5.14: The results of the experiments varying the word-form adoption strategy.

significance was small, the case where taxis has been applied when the robots had new gearing appeared to be best.

In Section 5.3 the influence of joint attention and feedback has been explored. It appeared that when joint attention was applied the success rate increased enormously. However, the cost was a lower specificity.

When investigating the observational game in more detail, the specificity could improve under a higher word-form creation probability P_s. This latter finding has also been observed when the creation probability has been varied in the guessing game (Section 5.5). It appeared that the previously used probability of $P_s = 0.02$ was much too low. When this parameter varied between 0.1 and 1.0, not many differences are found in the success, but the lexicon grows drastically when P_s is high.

Like the creation probability, the learning rate η has been investigated on its impact. The experiments revealed that the adaptation of scores is crucial. Furthermore, the scores should be adapted fast enough (the initial value of $\eta = 0.99$ was much too slow), but not too fast.

Besides varying the mentioned parameters, three different word-form adoption schemes have been investigated. When the hearer is allowed to adopt the speaker's utterance when the hearer misinterpreted the utterance (i.e. when the hearer's topic referred to a different light source than the speaker's topic), the results were observed to work best. The topic with which the utterance may be adopted can be selected at random or by the criterion of correspondence.

Naturally, more parameters and methods could be investigated. Some of these variations have been investigated, but did not reveal interesting results and have been left out this book for clarity. For additional analyses of parameters and methods that are involved in the language games, see de Jong (2000) and Kaplan (2000).

6 The optimal games

In the previous chapters various aspects of the different language games have been investigated. Chapter 4 introduced the basic experiment. Variations that have been investigated in Chapter 5 indicated some possible improvements on the basic model. This chapter combines some proposed improvements in the most interesting language games: the guessing game and the observational game.

The first set of experiments that will be investigated involves the guessing game. Although not most successful at first sight, the guessing game scenario is an important scenario that is also applied in the Talking Heads experiment. To enable a fruitful discussion with the Talking Heads experiments, this scenario is investigated first and in most detail. This experiment is investigated in Section 6.1.

The observational language game is explored as a second experiment in Section 6.2. The results of this experiment in Chapter 5 were very promising, and it is possibly a very common strategy in language development.

Instead of doing 10 runs of 5,000 language games, each experiment is done with 10 runs of 10,000 language games. This will make it harder to compare these experiments with previous experiments. On the other hand the resulting systems can be investigated more reliably, because many systems were still learning after 5,000 games.

6.1 The guessing game

6.1.1 The experiments

The two experiments presented in this section implement the guessing game. The basic experiment has been optimised by changing the following strategies and parameters:

- The categorisation is unaltered, i.e., the prototype method is used, because no drastic improvements have been observed in the other methods and the implemented method is relatively fast.

6 The optimal games

- The physical interaction is improved by applying new gearing on the robots. Although the differences were not very significant, the results were better than the basic data set.

- The creation probability is set to $P_s = 0.4$ in one experiment (P.4) and $P_s = 0.1$ in another (P.1), because these values revealed most promising results in Section 5.5.

- Learning rate η is set to $\eta - 0.9$, a value that holds a relatively long history of interactions and allows sufficiently fast learning.

- Word-forms are adopted under all proposed circumstances, i.e., when novel word-forms are encountered, or the matching meaning does not match the relevant topic. The topic with which the form is adopted is selected at random, since no overt differences have been observed in the experiments of Section 5.7.

The differences are summarised in Table 6.1. Instead of 10 runs of 5,000 games, 10 runs of 10,000 games are played. The two experiments of this section are now defined as above with the two variants:

P.1 Word-form creation probability $P_s = 0.1$.

P.4 Word-form creation probability $P_s = 0.4$.

Table 6.1: The set-up of the optimal guessing game.

Type of change	Value
Data-set	new gearing
P_s	0.1 and 0.4
η	0.9
Adoption strategy	random

6.1.2 The results

The experiments are done with 10 runs of 10,000 guessing games. Figures 6.1 and 6.2 show the evolution of the qualitative measures and the averaged results of both experiments are shown in Table 6.2. The two experiments are qualitatively

6.1 The guessing game

very much the same. Only the specificity differs from each other significantly $p = 0.0000$. The specificity in experiment P.1 is 0.075 higher as in the basic experiment ($p = 0.0000$). In P.4 the specificity is even 0.12 higher. As discussed in the previous chapter, the higher specificity has to do with the higher P_s. When comparing the evolutions of the specificity in Figures 6.1 (c) and 6.2 (c), it is clear that the specificity in experiment P.1 is still increasing towards the end. So the difference becomes less near the end.

Clearly, the communicative success approaches the potential understandability of 80 % in both experiments. After 10,000 games, the csis approximately 75 % on the average. The discriminative success is on the average about 97 %, thus approaching 100 % at the end of the experiment. On the average the distinctiveness is about 0.02 higher than in the basic experiment. Parsimony is only a little higher than in the basic experiment (0.861 vs. 0.851). Consistency is about 0.045 higher than in the basic experiment. All these differences have a significance of $p = 0.0000$.

Table 6.2: The averaged results of the optimal guessing game experiment.

Score	P.1	P.4
CS	0.624 ± 0.008	0.628 ± 0.001
DS0	0.972 ± 0.001	0.976 ± 0.001
DS1	0.972 ± 0.001	0.977 ± 0.001
D0	0.979 ± 0.000	0.979 ± 0.000
D1	0.979 ± 0.000	0.979 ± 0.000
P0	0.864 ± 0.001	0.864 ± 0.001
P1	0.859 ± 0.000	0.859 ± 0.000
S0	0.898 ± 0.005	0.941 ± 0.002
S1	0.894 ± 0.005	0.940 ± 0.003
C0	0.860 ± 0.001	0.860 ± 0.002
C1	0.857 ± 0.002	0.860 ± 0.001

So, the system finally becomes very good in constructing a lexicon by which the robots can communicate about the things they detect in their environment.

The run that will be discussed in more detail below resulted in the lexicon that is displayed in the semiotic landscape shown in Figure 6.3 and is taken from experiment P.1. This figure shows the connections with a strength that represents the frequency of connections that are successfully used. Ideally, the connections

6 The optimal games

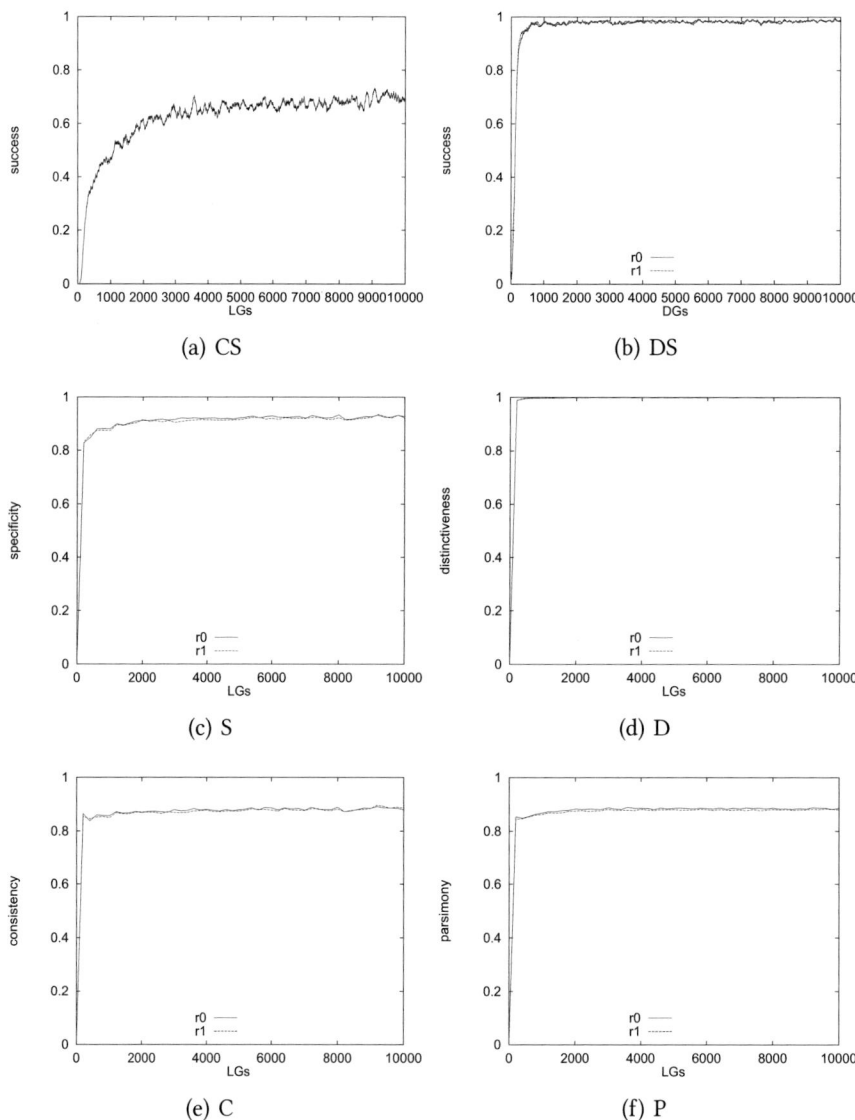

Figure 6.1: The evolution of the optimal guessing game experiment P.1.

6.1 The guessing game

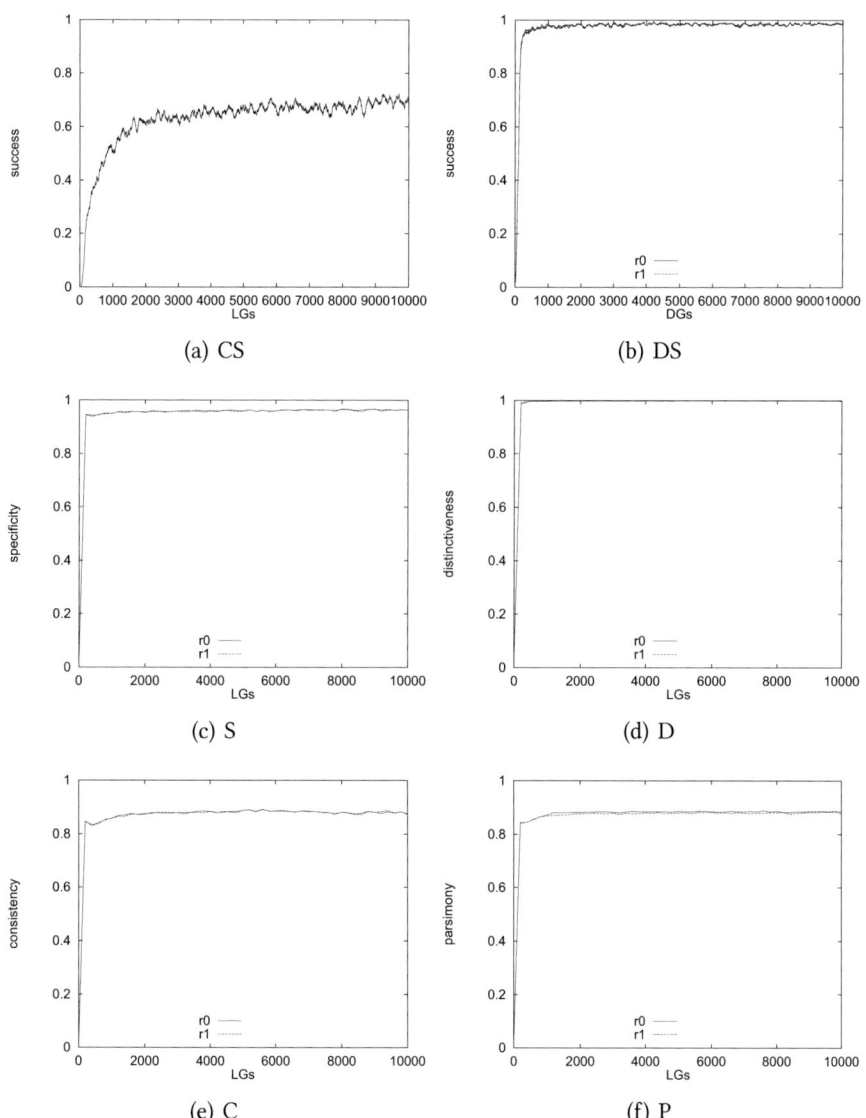

Figure 6.2: The evolution of the optimal guessing game experiment P.4.

6 The optimal games

between referent-form-referent would be orthogonal, i.e., the couplings of a referent and its form should not cross-connect with other referents.

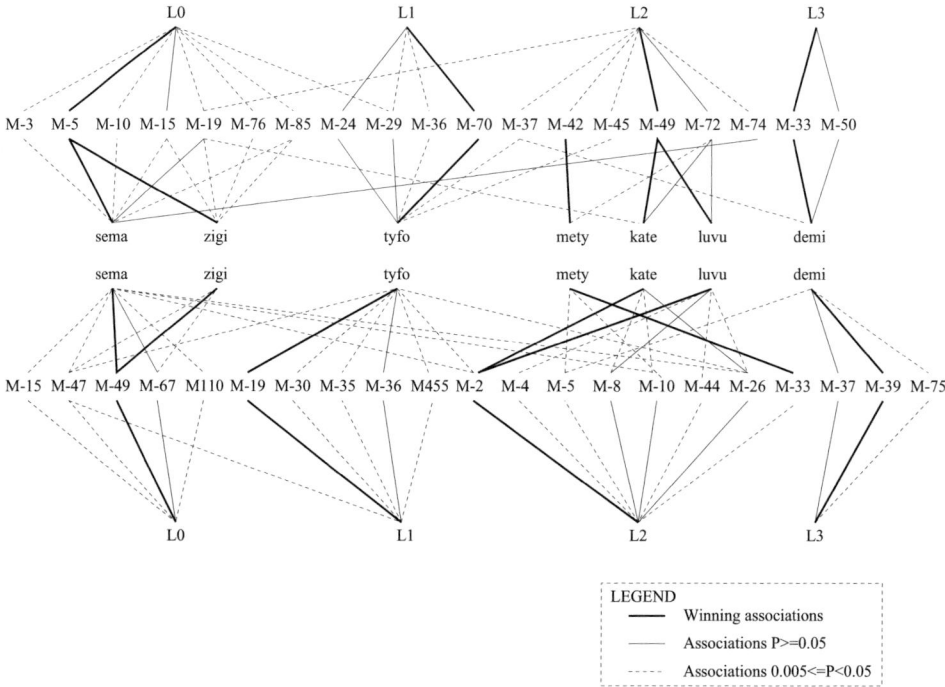

Figure 6.3: The semiotic landscape of the optimal experiment with $P_s = 0.1$.

This orthogonality criterion is achieved for *mety*, *luvu* and possibly *zigi*. The word-forms *kate* and *demi* have cross-connections, but these are relatively unimportant because they have low frequencies. More referential polysemy is found for *sema* and *tyfo*. As will be shown in the discussion, *tyfo* gets well established to name L1 almost unambiguously. *sema* however, provides some instability in the system.

Comparing this landscape with that of the basic experiment (Figure 4.8 at page 121), the system shows more orthogonality and there are less word-forms. L0 and L2 have synonymous connections, but these are not a big problem, since the different forms are most frequently used to name one referent, i.e., they show low polysemy.

One important result of experiment P.1 is that the number of word-forms the agents use *successfully* in the language is much lower than in P.4. The robots used 16 word-forms successfully at the end vs. 34 in P.4 (Figure 6.4 (a), solid lower line). Furthermore, the number of word-forms does not grow after approximately 3,500 games, whereas the vocabulary size increases until the end when $P_s = 0.4$.

6.1 The guessing game

The number of word-forms that have been created by the robots is only slightly above the number of word-forms that have been successfully used. Apparently the robots tend to have more time to adopt word-forms correctly when $P_s = 0.1$.

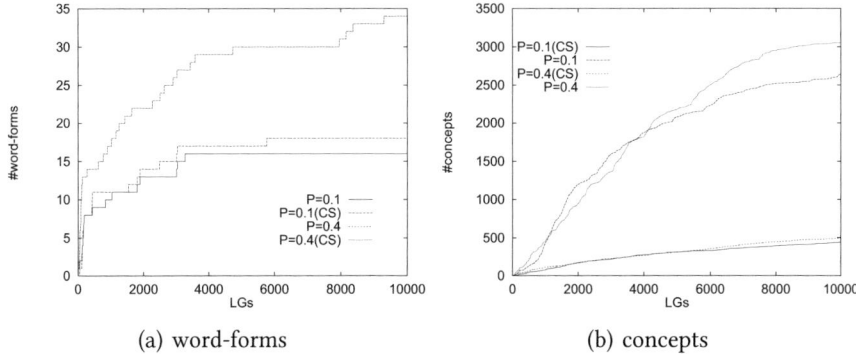

(a) word-forms   (b) concepts

Figure 6.4: The vocabulary and ontological growth of experiments with P.1 and P.4. The growth is shown for successful usage (indicated with cs) and just those elements that are used. The concepts that are just used are those that have found to be distinctive.

The one-to-many relations between form and meaning of both systems is high as can be derived from Figure 6.4. Figure 6.4 (b) shows the ontological growth of categories that are distinctive and of those that are successfully used in the communication (as indicated by "(cs)") for creation probabilities $P_s = 0.1$ and $P_s = 0.4$. The total numbers of distinctive categories that the agents categorised are ranging from 2,600 for P.1 and 3,100 for P.4. The number of meanings (categories that are used in communication) they successfully use is around 500, which is substantially lower than the number of concepts that could be used. So, the number of successfully employed concepts is roughly 15 times higher than the word-forms that are used when $P_s = 0.4$ and it is 31 times higher when $P_s = 0.1$. It appears that in case when the creation probability is lower, the robots have more time to associate existing word-forms with meanings rather than to create new ones. This way the amount one-to-many relations between form and meaning increases as a possibly beneficial side effect. The cost of this is that there appears to be a higher level of polysemy. To see whether this is problematic, it is instructive to look at the various competition diagrams of experiment P.1. This is done in the discussion that follows.

6 The optimal games

6.1.3 Discussion

The results make clear that with the current settings and strategies, the robots construct a communication system that meets its limits. The communicative success is in the end nearly as high as the potential understandability.

Both the discriminative success and distinctiveness are very close to 1, and the specificity is also close to 1. When a robot uses a symbol successfully, it almost always refers to the same referent. The polysemy is very low. The parsimony and consistency are somewhat lower. Hence, there are some one-to-many relations between referent and meaning and between referent and form in the system. The semiotic landscape already showed that most of the synonymy does not necessarily mean that the communication is difficult. Usually, the hearer can rather easily interpret any speaker's utterance. The landscape also shows that a one-to-many relationship between form and meaning does ot necessarily mean polysemy. It is also beneficial, since it antagonises the one-to-many mapping of referent to meaning for a great deal. This is nicely illustrated by the following discussion of some competition diagrams that are taken from the same run as the semiotic landscape. The discussion also explains some of the dynamics of the language games.

6.1.3.1 One-to-many relations between form and meaning

Figure 6.5 shows various competition diagrams of robot r0, relating to referent L1 in one of the runs of experiment P.1. Figures (a) and (b) show the referent-form competition. In Figure (a) the co-occurrence frequencies of referent and form independent of their success are displayed. Figure (b) shows the successful co-occurrence of referent and form. Very infrequent occurrences are left out for clarity. Where Figure (a) shows that form *tyfo* clearly wins the competition, Figure (b) shows that in successful games, this form is nearly used uniquely[1]. Hence light source L1 has very little synonymy.

Although there is hardly any synonymy, there is substantial conceptual synonymy. This is nicely shown in the referent-meaning diagram for L1 (Figure 6.5 (c)). Two meanings are used rather frequently, M24 and M70. When looking at the form-meaning diagram for word-form *tyfo* (Figure (d)), a similar competition is observed. The frequent meanings that co-occur with *tyfo* are M24 and M70. So, the lexical one-to-many relations between form and meaning antagonises out the negative side effect of the one-to-many relations between referent and meaning,

---

[1] Note that this diagram is the same for robot r1, since it shows successful co-occurrences only. By definition of the success, they must be the same for both robots.

6.1 The guessing game

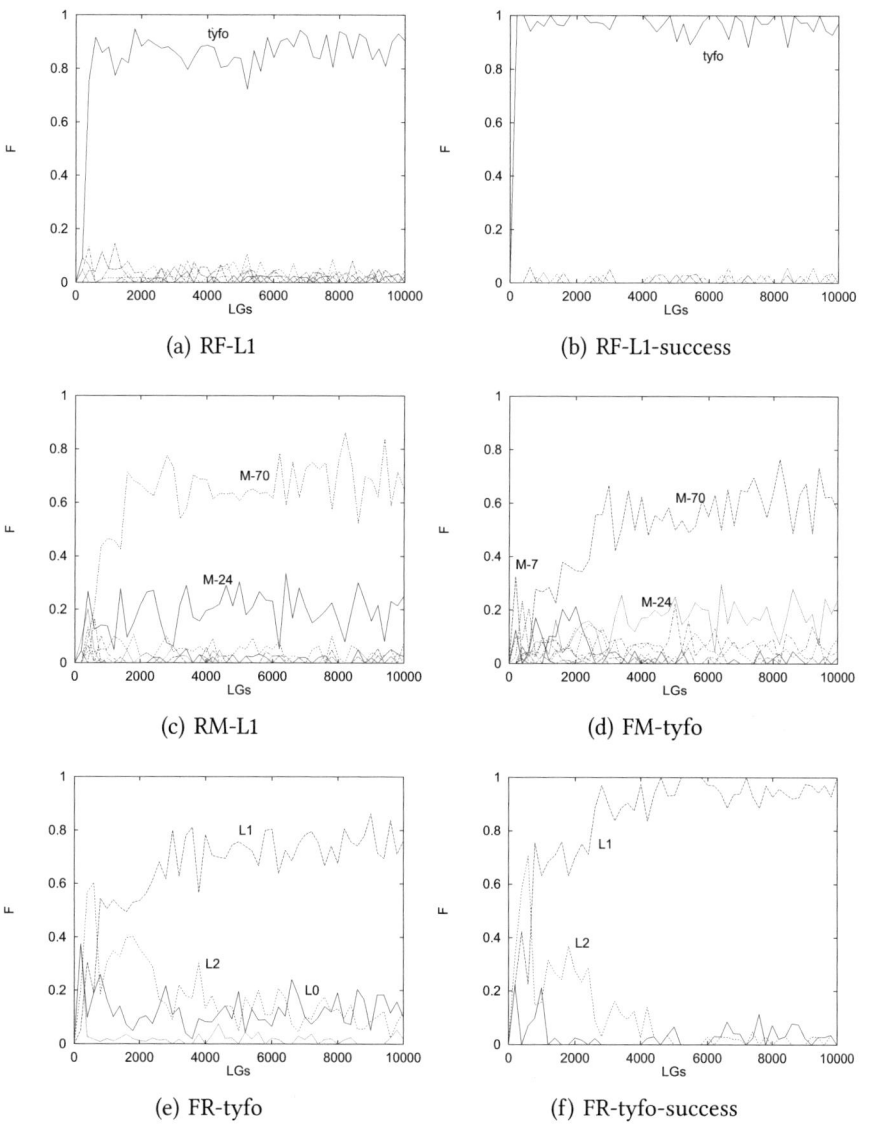

Figure 6.5: Some competition diagrams of robot $r0$ in one run of experiment P.1. Figures (a) and (b) show referent-form competitions for L1, (a) show its use and (b) shows the successful use. Figure (c) shows the referent-meaning competition for L1 and (d) shows the form-meaning competition for *tyfo*. Both Figure (c) and (d) show the use. Figures (e) and (f) show the form-referent diagrams for *tyfo*, where (e) shows its use, and (f) its effective use.

6 The optimal games

yielding almost one-to-one relations between form and referent. So, there is little synonymy and polysemy.

That there is hardly any polysemy can be seen in Figures 6.5 (e) and (f). These figures plot the form-referent diagrams for used (e) and successfully used (f) co-occurrence frequencies. Although some polysemy can be observed, it is hardly present in successful games after, say, 4,000 language games. Table 6.3 shows the legend of some of the meanings that are discussed. Note that most meanings are uniquely used to stand for a particular referent. So, there are mostly one-to-one relations between meaning and referent, which drives the distinctiveness near 1, cf. Figure 6.6.

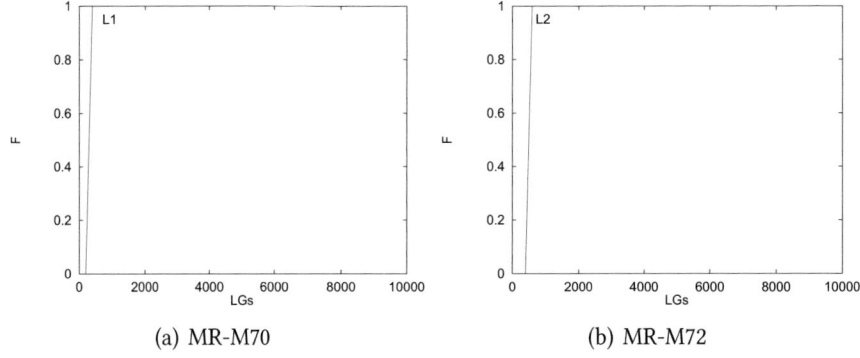

(a) MR-M70 (b) MR-M72

Figure 6.6: Meaning-referent competition of r0 for meanings M70 and M72.

6.1 The guessing game

Table 6.3: The legend of some meanings of robot r0 in the optimal guessing game as represented by their prototypes. It should be clear that the meanings mostly bare the invariant property that the sensory channels have values (near) 1 corresponding to the referents they are used for which has values in the middle. This meaning acts at feature space $\mathcal{F}_0$, which can only be distinctive if there is only 1 referent in the context of a language game. This meaning is mainly used to categorise L0, although not very frequently. The semiotic landscape (Figure 6.3 shows that M19 (in the upper half) is also used to categorise L2. Another interesting meaning is M37, which has high values in dimensions WL2 and WL3. It has been used most frequently to categorise L2 in the beginning of the experiments. Later it has been used less frequently. M49 shows that the sensory channel WL3 adjacent to the corresponding sensory channel WL2 reads relatively high values when the robot detects L2. This can be inferred from the fact that both dimensions WL1 and WL3 have high values. That this does not happen all the time is shown with M72, which has low values in each dimension that does not correspond with L2.

M-5	$(0.96, 0.01, 0.03, 0.05)_1$
M-15	$(0.96, 0.60, 0.03, 0.05)_1$
M-19	$(0.53, 0.19, 0.71, 0.20)_0$
M-24	$(0.38, 0.99, 0.03, 0.05)_1$
M-33	$(0.03, 0.01, 0.03, 0.96)_1$
M-37	$(0.03, 0.01, 1.00, 0.96)_1$
M-49	$(0.03, 0.01, 1.00, 0.46)_1$
M-50	$(0.03, 0.01, 0.28, 0.96)_1$
M-70	$(0.03, 0.99, 0.03, 0.05)_1$
M-72	$(0.03, 0.01, 1.00, 0.05)_1$

6 The optimal games

6.1.3.2 Polysemy and lexical dynamics

That relations and competition between referent, meaning and form are not always as nice as in the case above is shown in Figure 6.7. The competition is taken from the same run as the semiotic landscape and the previous example, so $P_s = 0.1$.

Figure 6.7 (a) shows the referent-form diagram of successful co-occurrences of referent L2 with some forms. After an initial period in which *tyfo* is used, the diagram is dominated by a competition between *luvu* and *kate*. It appears as if *luvu* is the most dominant of the two. To investigate this competition in more detail, one should look at the referent-meaning diagram (Figure 6.7 (b)).

The referent-meaning diagram shows that there appear to be two meanings which are used more or less equally frequent: M49 and M72. There are more meanings that compete at the bottom of the graph. Apparently there is a strong one-to-many relation between referent and meaning.

Figures (c) and (d) show the MF diagrams of the two dominant meanings. It should be clear that a weighted superposition of the two diagrams resemble the referent-form diagram very much. Hence these diagrams also show the dynamic competition between *luvu* and *kate*. So, the synonymous referent-form competition cannot directly be explained by the fact that L2 is categorised by two meanings. These meanings themselves show similar mappings between referent and meaning. This is not so odd, since light source L1 (Figure 6.5) was not named with two forms, whereas it is related with two meanings.

The apparently unstable competition returns in the form-meaning diagrams of the two relevant forms (Figures 6.7 (e) and (f)). *luvu*, which appears to be the most dominant form for L2, evolves in a competition between M49 and M72. The competition for *kate* appears to be more chaotic. This is probably due to the fact that *kate* is used infrequent in the period where it shows most chaos (between game 6,000 and 7,000).

It is difficult to tell exactly what factors cause the dynamic competition. There are many factors that can influence the dynamics of language games that it seems impossible to explain what happened. The most important factors are the adaptation of association scores, its lateral inhibition, the one-to-many relation between referent and meaning, the different ontologies and lexicons of the robots, the different contexts and situations, language game failures and possibly many more. The observed dynamics are probably caused by an interaction between these factors.

Although it is not completely understood, here follows a possible explanation. In the periods where *kate* is more (or even most) dominant in the competition,

6.1 The guessing game

M49 appears to be the most dominant meaning in the form-meaning competition for *kate* and least dominant for *luvu*. Check the periods around games 4,000 and 8,000. This is also observable in the MF competition for M49.

If one looks at the meaning-form competition for M72, *kate* is the dominant form in the period between 3,000 and 4,000, just before it becomes dominant for M49. In this period, the other robot (r1) must have acquired *kate* and uses it also to name L2. Through the linguistic interactions it is not unlikely that our robot (r0) starts to use *kate* also successfully for M49. The association scores are laterally inhibited, so when *kate* is successfully used to name M49, this association is strengthened, but the associations between *kate* and M72, and *luvu* and M49 are inhibited.

If such dynamics continues, there will be a break point where there is a trade off between the dominant associations. At that point, *kate* may become dominant M49, and *luvu* becomes dominant for M72. This dominance is very stable until the end of the run where *kate* starts to win again. A short while after *luvu* became dominant for M72, it also started to win the competition for M49.

It seems as the dominance for one meaning is taken over by the dominance for the other meaning. This take over is antagonised with the take over of another form for the first meaning. This in turn can feed the competition similarly; thus a vicious circle emerges.

To finish the discussion, look at figures (g) and (h). These figures show the form-referent diagrams of successfully used occurrences of *luvu* (g) and *kate* (h). Clearly these forms are specifically used to name L2. So, there is huge competition showing one-to-many relations between referent and meaning, meaning and form, and form and meaning. However, there is little polysemy. Note by the way that *kate* is not used successfully at all around game 7,000.

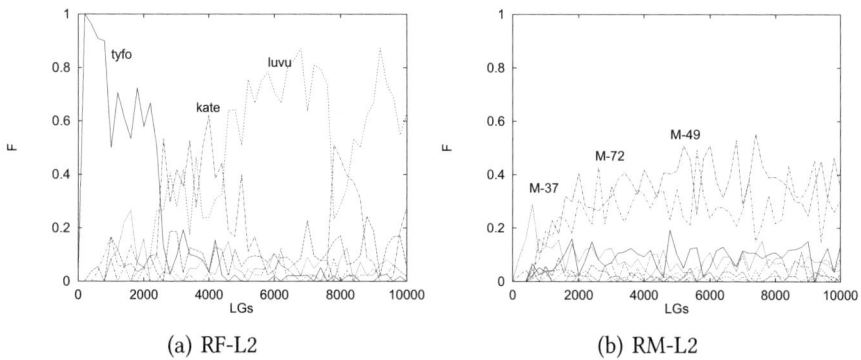

(a) RF-L2   (b) RM-L2

175

6 The optimal games

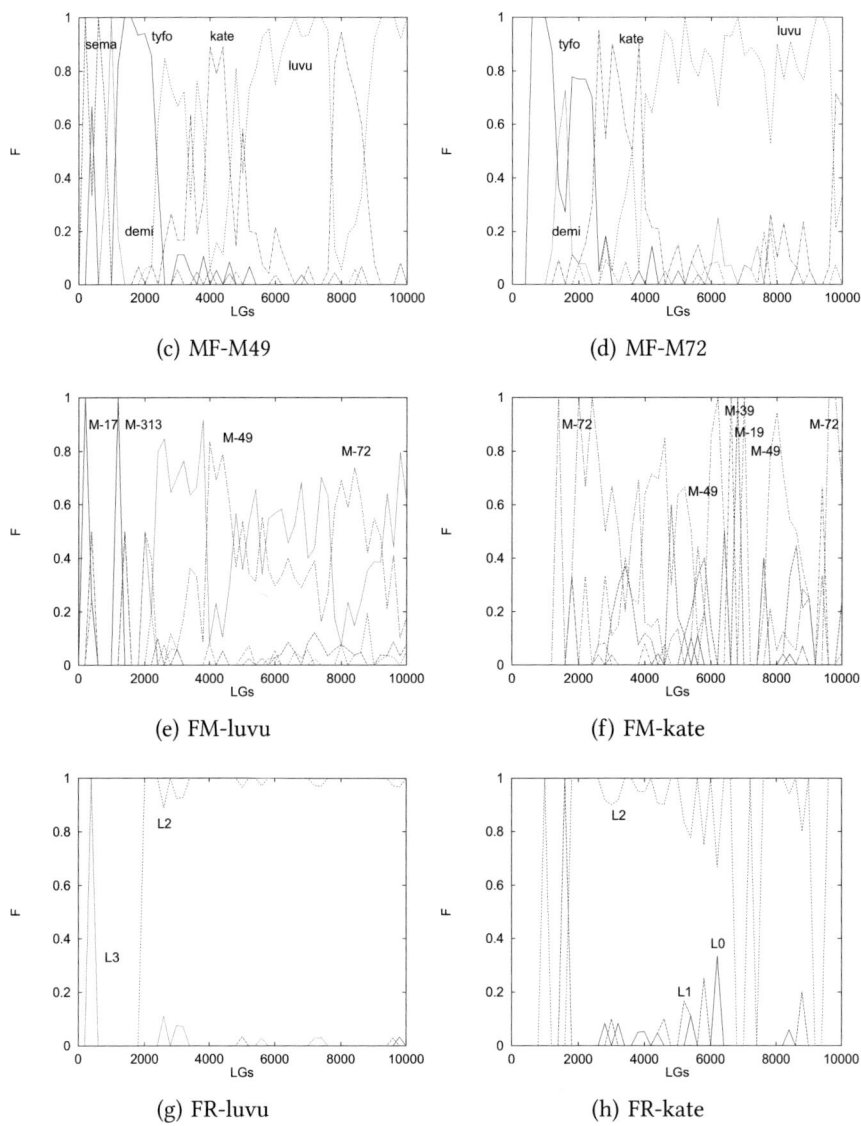

Figure 6.7: Various competition diagrams of r0 concerning light source L2. The referent-form (a) and form-referent diagrams (g) and (h) display competitions of successful occurrences. All other diagrams show competitions of used occurrences.

6.2 The observational game

6.2.1 The experiment

The final experiment that will be reported is the experiment in which there is joint attention, but no feedback available to the agents. Hence the robots play observational games. The experiment takes the same improved parameters as the guessing game (see Table 6.4). However, it only investigates form creation probability $P_s = 0.4$. Note that the robots have no extra word-form adoption, since for this mechanism the robots have to know whether they mismatched in referent. For this they would need feedback, which the observational game lacks. Besides the robots already know what the topic is, so they will not be able to find a mismatch in referent.

Table 6.4: The set-up of the optimal observational game.

Type of change	Value
data-set	new gearing
P_s	0.4
η	0.9
Adoption scheme	n.a.

6.2.2 The results

The results of this experiment are shown in Figure 6.8 and Table 6.5. As the figure and table make clear, the global measures have similar results as the guessing game. Except the actual success is about 6 % higher than the communicative success of this experiment ($p = 0.0000$). Note that the actual success of the guessing game is the same as its communicative success, because the feedback of the guessing game is provided by the correspondence criterion.

6.2.3 Discussion

Apparently the observation game yield better results than the guessing game. It seems that the robots are better at developing a lexicon when they know what the topic in advance rather than when they need feedback to guide their success. If the guessing game would not be able to construct a similar system is not proven. However, it would certainly take longer (compare Figure 6.2 with Figure 6.8).

6 The optimal games

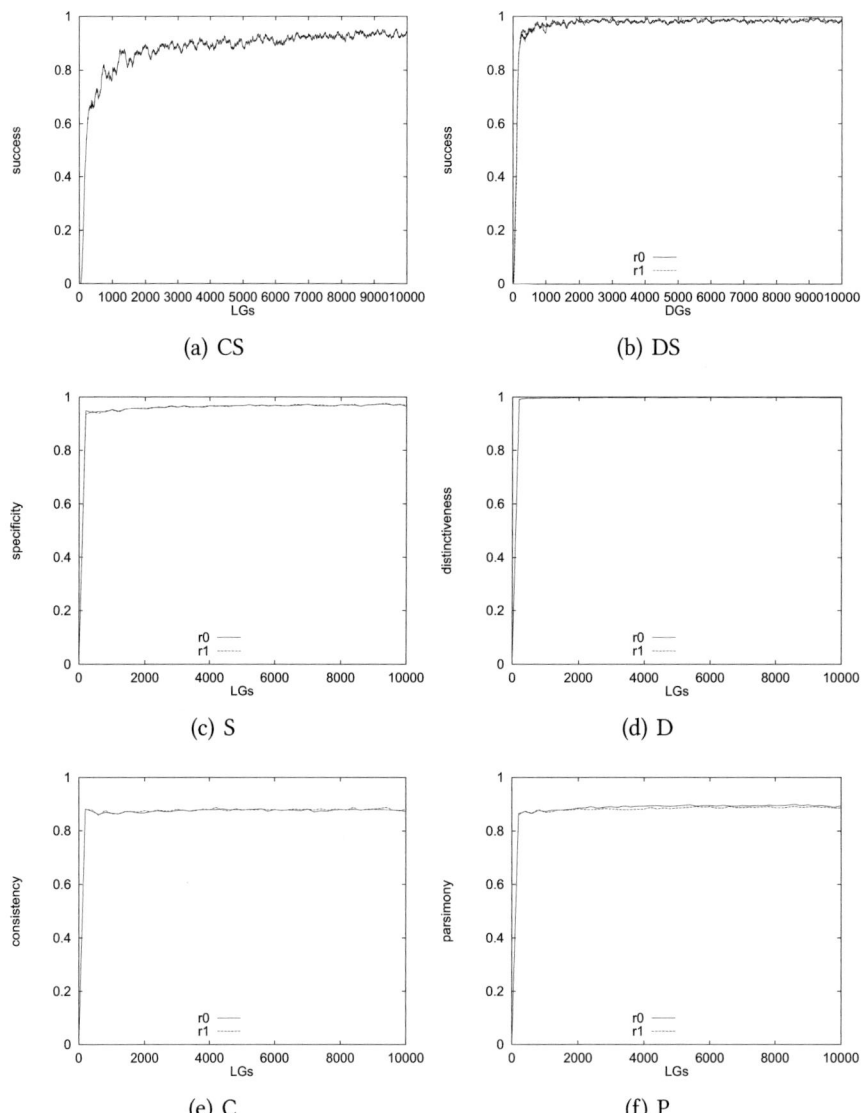

6.2 The observational game

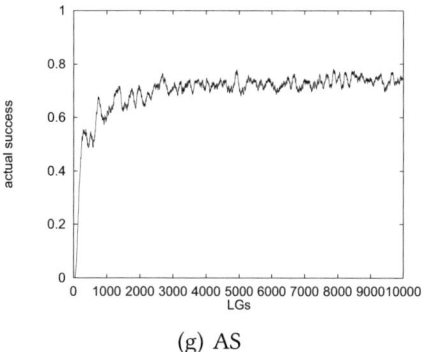

(g) AS

Figure 6.8: The results of the optimal observational game.

Table 6.5: The averaged results of the optimal observational game experiment.

Score	Avg
CS	0.879 ± 0.005
AS	0.698 ± 0.003
DS0	0.973 ± 0.000
DS1	0.974 ± 0.000
D0	0.979 ± 0.000
D1	0.979 ± 0.000
P0	0.873 ± 0.001
P1	0.867 ± 0.001
S0	0.946 ± 0.004
S1	0.946 ± 0.005
C0	0.860 ± 0.006
C1	0.862 ± 0.006

6 The optimal games

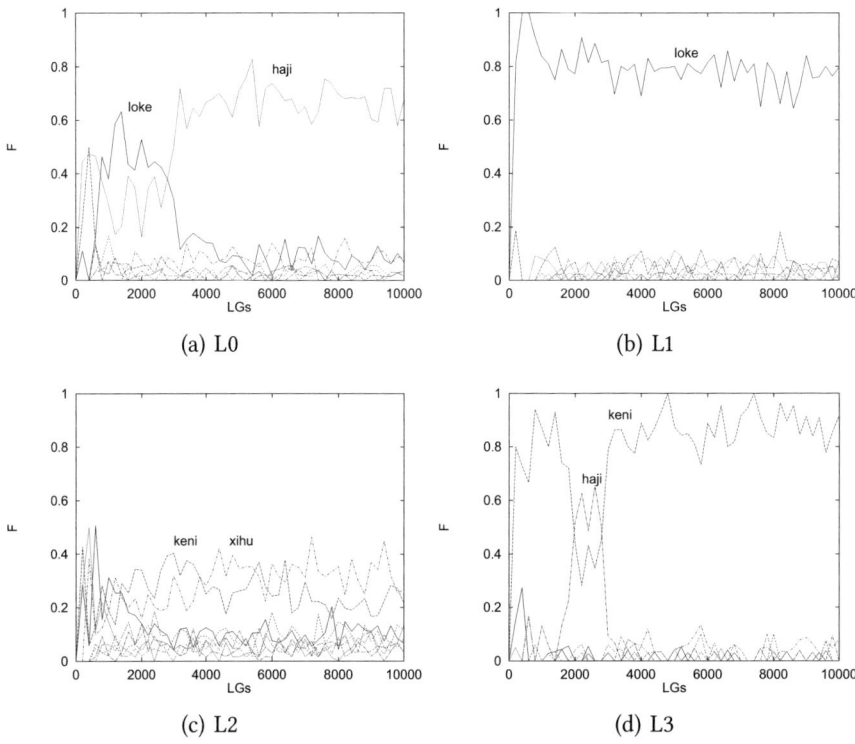

Figure 6.9: Referent-form diagrams of the observational language game.

Do the observational games yield a similar evolution of word-form and meaning? To see this, one can investigate the various competition diagrams. The referent-form competition diagrams (Figure 6.9) shows the successful co-occurrences of one of the runs of this experiment.

For three out of four referents there are clear winning word-forms, although light sources L0 and L3 both show a short period where another word-form takes over. L2 does not show a clear winning word-form. Two word-forms are used with almost the same frequency. One of these word-forms *keni* is used to name both L2 and L3. Hence there is apparently some polysemy, see also Figure 6.10. This has not been observed at this level in the guessing game.

Figure 6.10 shows that there is some polysemy, especially for *keni*. So, it would be interesting how the competition around *keni* evolves. It is good to begin with some referent-meaning diagrams of both robots for light sources L2 and L3 (Figure 6.11). From these figures it is clear that for L2 there is a high level of one-to-many mappings between referent and meaning, whereas L3 does not show this

180

6.2 The observational game

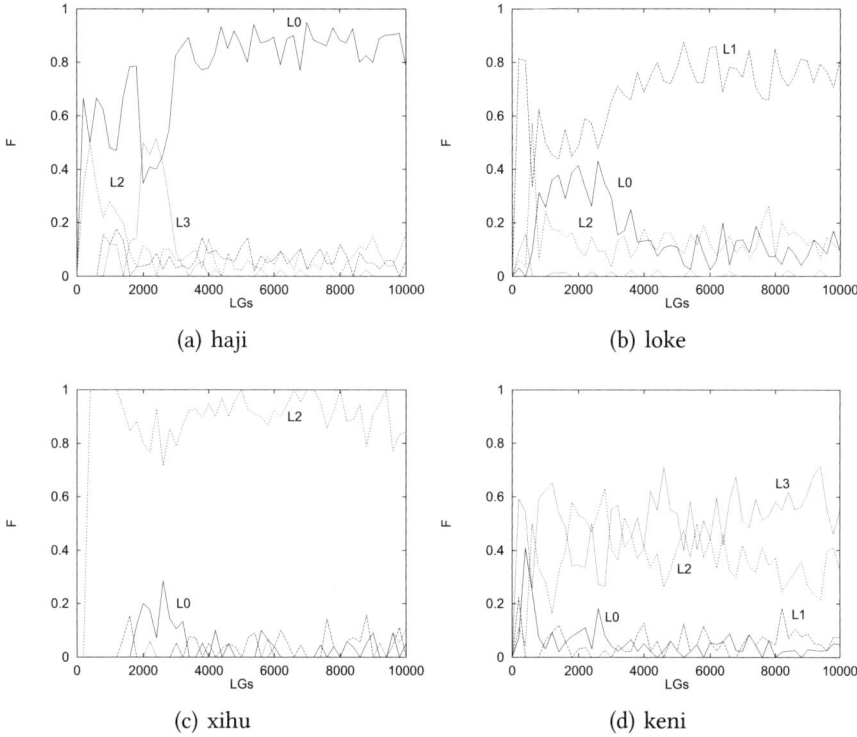

Figure 6.10: Form-referent diagrams of the observational games.

very much. Striking is that it is almost equally strong for both robots. Apparently, the synonymy in the lexicon reflects itself on these one-to-many relations between referent and meaning for both robots. It is not unlikely that one of the robots took over these one-to-many relations in its effort to disambiguate the synonymy initiated by the other.

For robot *r0* there are basically three meanings that compete for light sources L2 and L3. The meaning-form competitions of these meanings are shown in Figures 6.12 (a) to (c). Meaning M12, which is used to categorise L3 almost unambiguously, has very little synonymy and *keni* clearly wins the competition. This is not very surprising, since L3 is both categorised parsimonious and named consistent. The two meanings of L2 (M28 and M36) reveal more one-to-many relations between meaning and form. For M12, *keni* is most frequently used and for M36 this is *xihu*. In both cases the other name is also competing for these meanings, i.e. *xihu* is also competing for M12 and *keni* for M36. This competition, however is at a low level. The polysemy of *keni* is also found back at the lexical level (i.e. in the

6 The optimal games

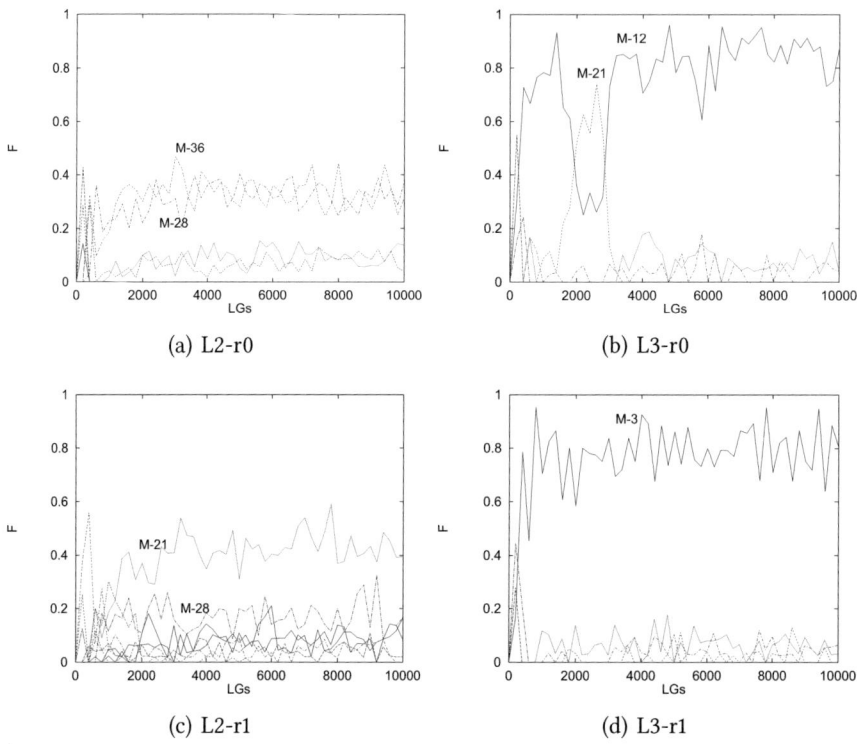

Figure 6.11: Referent-meaning competition for L2 and L3 of robots r0 and r1.

one-to-many relations between form and meaning), cf. Figure 6.12 (d).

Another striking observation when comparing the competition of this experiment with the competition in the guessing games is that at the bottom there is more and stronger competition here, compare e.g. Figure 6.7 (a) and Figure 6.9. Apparently, the observational game strategy is pretty well at developing a coherent lexicon, however the lack of directive feedback allows quite some synonymy.

So, although the update principle of the scores works relatively good (conform the naming of referents L0 and L1), the system still allows both many-to-many relations at each level of comparison, except between meaning and referent, which is almost one-to-one. Recall that the association scores are updated according to an association's use, since the robots consider themselves to be successful whenever they communicated an association. Apparently the use alone cannot disambiguate very strong competitions that are structurally present in the communication.

6.3 Summary

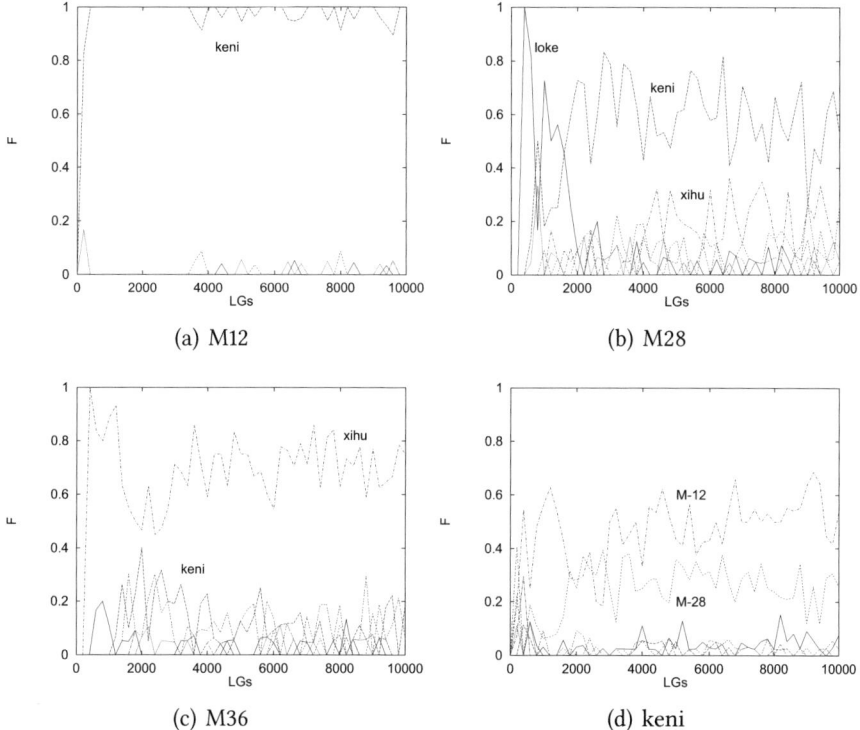

Figure 6.12: Meaning-form competition of robot r0 for (a) M12, (b) M28 and (c) M36. Figure (d) shows the form-meaning competition of *keni*.

6.3 Summary

In this chapter the experiment has optimised two games: the guessing game and the observational game. Several parameters and methods that were found to improve the system in Chapter 5 were combined in these experiments.

The optimised experiments revealed that the robots are well capable of developing an ontology and lexicon by which they can communicate pretty well. The important features of the optimised experiment are: (1) using new gearing, (2) adopting word-forms additionally when the robots misidentified the topic, (3) a different learning rate and (4) a higher creation probability.

Furthermore it has been shown that the robots learn the communication system almost up to its potential when they play an observational language game, a result that is not yet reached in the guessing game.

6 The optimal games

Establishing joint attention prior to the linguistic communication, however, has a cost. The lexicons that emerge under this condition show a higher level of synonymy. It seems that the pressure to disambiguate is too small because the joint attention makes communication more or less redundant.

The results of the experiments reported here shall be discussed more thoroughly in Chapter 7.

7 Discussion

Up to now this research is presented first by describing the model, followed by the presentation of a series of experiments. The model is built such that the robots can engage in language games, for which the physical interactions have been pre-programmed. The language games consists roughly of four parts: (1) the robots detect their surroundings, (2) the sensing is categorised, (3) the speaker names one topic and the hearer tries to understand the speaker's utterance, and (4) the robots adapt their ontologies and lexicon.

An important feature of the experiment is that the robots do not have any prior knowledge about the ontology or lexicon. They only have knowledge how they can communicate and how they can invent, adopt and select ontological and lexical items that enables them to develop a coherent communication system.

The main questions raised in the introduction of this book were:

1. Can the symbol grounding problem be solved with these robots by constructing a lexicon through individual adaptation, (cultural) interaction and self-organisation? And if so, how is this accomplished?

2. What are the important types of extra-linguistic information that agents should share when developing a coherent communication system?

3. What is the influence of the physical conditions and interaction on developing a grounded lexicon?

Question (1) can reasonably be answered with *yes*, at least within the current application and experimental set-up. There are some drawbacks on this answer, because some important assumptions have been made and the physical capabilities of the robots prevent to enable perfect sensing and communication. The two assumptions were that the robots could establish joint attention and provide feedback on the outcome of a language game. Previous experiments on physical pointing revealed that this method does not work with the currently used robots (Vogt 1998b), and hence the robots still need to have a way in doing so. In the experiments the robots were able to inspect each other's internal feature vectors. This way the robots were able to construct a shared and grounded lexicon. The

7 Discussion

symbol grounding problem has been solved in the experiments reported by a number of subtasks as will be discussed in the next section.

The answer to question (2) is not complete, because not all possible forms of information have been investigated. Nevertheless, some important forms have been found. It appeared that establishing joint attention is very important in the development of a coherent lexicon. When joint attention is not established, feedback plays a crucial role.

The last question is harder to answer, because not all experiments yielded astonishing results. However, there are some important conclusions that can be drawn. The sensing and segmentation resulted in set of situations in which approximately 20 % did not have a coherent context. So only in 80 % of the language games the robots could establish communicative success, because in the other cases the hearer did not detect the topic that the speaker was communicating. The impact from varying physical conditions has not been shown convincingly in all proposed directions, although they indicated some influences.

This chapter will discuss the results in more detail, and will compare the findings with other literature on the topic. Section 7.1 will discuss how the grounding problem is solved. The effect of joint attention and feedback will be the topic of Section 7.2. The experimental results will be discussed around psychological issues about joint attention and feedback in language learning. The influence of the physical interactions will be discussed in Section 7.3. Especially the robots' adaptation to the environment (or vice versa) is the key issue. In Section 7.5 the results will be compared with other experiments on grounding language, especially the Talking Heads (Belpaeme, Steels & van Looveren 1998) and the work of Billard & Hayes (1997).

7.1 The symbol grounding problem solved?

The key problem that had to be solved for physical robots to develop a shared lexicon about the things they detect is the symbol grounding problem (Harnad 1990). The problem is how seemingly meaningless symbols can become meaningful in the real world. In Chapter 1 three sub-problems of the grounding problem have been identified from (Harnad 1990). These sub-problems are:

1. Iconisation

2. Discrimination

3. Identification

7.1 The symbol grounding problem solved?

The three sub-problems will be discussed in more detail below. Solving the symbol grounding problem is known to the roboticists as a fundamentally hard problem (see, e.g., Pfeifer & Scheier 1999). It is especially hard, because the robots have different sensings of some real world object when detected under different circumstances. It appears to be very hard to acquire invariant categorisations of these different sensings.

The symbol grounding problem has been attacked with a semiotic view towards symbols (or signs). In this Peircean view a symbol is a semiotic sign where its form is either arbitrary or conventionalised. The sign is a triangle of which the edges resemble a referent, a meaning and a form. It has been argued that a robot can ground a symbol when a semiotic triangle can be constructed successfully. Its success is measured with the success of a language game, but it can also be measured otherwise. When the symbol is used successfully in a language game, the form is said to be conventionalised.

In the experiments the real world consists of light sources about which the robots try to *construct* a lexicon. The word-forms and referents are the overt part of the symbols that the robots ground. The covert part is a hybrid chain of internal and possibly external structures from which the meaning is constructed. Part of these structures are activated by the robot's sensing. The sensing is segmented and feature vectors are extracted. These feature vectors are then categorised. The robots were able to successfully incorporate the distinctive categories that constitute the meaning in language use (i.e. in naming the referents). It should be clear that when the robots communicate successfully, the utterance refer to one of the light sources their environment. Whether or not this justifies to conclude that the robots have meaning in the philosophical sense (where meaning is often ascribed in terms of intentionality and consciousness) remains a philosophical question. Technically, the robots closed the semiotic triangle (or square) and conventionalised the form. Hence the physical symbol grounding problem is solved by these robots.

7.1.1 Iconisation

Iconisation is the first step in solving the symbol grounding problem. It is related to the following question: How does the analogue sensation of a referent project on an internal representation of the robot? This representation is still sub-symbolic. Iconisation is solved in the presented application through sensing, segmentation and feature extraction. Segmentation of the raw sensory stimuli results in a set of segments that are supposed to relate to sensed real world objects. The segments consist of for noise filtered raw sensory data. Feature extraction result in a vector of features that describes each segment with invariant properties of the sensing of a real world object. This latter process is very crucial for the result of the grounding problem. Although this issue has not been a key issue in this book, the problems became clear during the development of the system.

First of all, the segmentation process has to identify those regions that are interesting and should relate to the sensing of a referent. Ideally, segmentation should identify each referent that could be detected. The robots move around in their environment and the lighting conditions may change or something can obscure (a part of) the environment. Therefore, the sensing of the different robots are not likely to be identical and neither are the different sensings in different situations. A rather simplistic segmentation scheme has been used, which is prone to errors.

Segments are identified when the sensor value of a certain sensor exceeds a pre-determined noise value. But when, for instance, two light sources are detected shortly after each other with the consequence that one or more sensors did not get back to drop below the noise value, the two light sources will be taken as one segment. This is one of the reasons why the robots do not establish a coherent context. "Why not identify only the top of the peaks? This way you solve this problem." is an often heard remark. However, the sensors are not extremely reliable and show fluctuations during the sensing of a region of interest, resulting in local maxima when looking for real maxima. Thus yielding the same problem of context incoherence. One region of interest may be segmented in several regions, making it hard to solve discrimination and identification. Increasing the noise level would cause the robots to miss light sources that are further away.

When a segment is found, the sensory data of such a segment is transformed into a multidimensional feature vector, where each dimension corresponds to one sensory channel. This is done by means of feature extraction. The feature extraction is done by a real valued function from the sensory channel space to the feature space. The feature space is typically taken as a real valued domain between 0 and 1 in all dimensions. The goal of this feature extraction is (1) to reduce the amount of sensory data and (2) to extract information that is ideally invariant in the different situations. In the current implementation, all maxima that are found for the different sensory channels inside a segment are normalised to the maximum intensity of the sensory channel that has the highest maximum intensity in this segment. The absolute maximum of a sensory channel in a segment tells the observer to which light source the segment corresponds. Applying the feature extraction to this sensory channel results in a feature with a value of 1. Application to the other sensory channels yield values lower than 1. After feature extraction, the segment can be described with a low dimensional vector with a value of 1 where the sensory channel has the highest intensity. The other features have, depending on the distance of the robot to the corresponding light source, a value between 0 and 1. This is most often close to 0.

So, the segmentation and feature extraction is an important pre-process in the process of solving the grounding problem. This is a widely accepted phenomenon that is applied both in (computer) vision (Cotter 1990) and speech perception (Damper 2000). Cotter notices the fact that in a survey amongst different animal species, the optic pathways where the initial filtering takes place differ in details, although there are fundamental similarities:

> Such differences – differences in size of the pathways and development in nuclei in visual centres – represent variations on a theme that are due to the evolution of the visual system, the accentuation of specific sensory systems and ultimately the attainment of a specific ecological niche by individual species. (Cotter 1990: 11)

This makes it plausible that pre-processing of visual stimuli is very important for categorisation. Furthermore, it sheds light on the nature of embodiment. Different ways of sensing yield different categorisations. Obviously, the feature extraction functions could be evolved genetically as is shown in Belpaeme 1999, and once primitive functions are present, the feature extraction functions could also be developed onto-genetically into more complex ones as shown by de Jong & Steels (1999).

In spite of its importance, the segmentation and feature extraction is not a key issue of this book. The segmentation and sensory channels are relatively simple and not very well developed.

7.1.2 Discrimination

The second part of the solution of the grounding problem is discrimination. Harnad (1990) applies the notion of discrimination to the level of sensing. According to Harnad, discrimination should find out how the perception of something differs from the perception of something else. This can already be done at the perceptual level. This perceptual level can be compared to the sensing, segmentation and feature extraction in the current application. Although some of the discrimination is already done with segmentation and feature extraction, it is mainly pursued at the categorisation level. Segmentation yields the different sensings of the different referents. The feature extraction describes what properties the

7 Discussion

different segments have. However, it is only at the categorisation level that the model proposed tells the robots how the different segments differ.

In the current book, discrimination is solved by modelling discrimination games (Steels 1996d). In a discrimination game, an individual robot categorises the feature vectors that relate to the segments. Then the agents select categories that can distinguish a segment from the other segments in the context. So, the resulting distinctive categories only are distinctive in contrast to the context. This is conform with a pragmatic approach. As a consequence, part of the meaning is in the robot's environment, making it a situated approach (Clancey 1997). Since the meaning is constructed based on the robot's experience, it is embodied (Lakoff 1987). This dialectic approach favours what Jordan Zlatev (1997) called situated embodiment. It is also an argument for talking about the *physical symbol* grounding problem rather than the physical grounding problem (Brooks 1990) or the symbol grounding problem (Harnad 1990).

So, discrimination already starts at the segmentation level. At this level, the different interesting regions are identified, thus distinguishing one region from another. However, this does not answer the question how one segment is different from another. This can be answered more constructively at the categorisation level.

The first step of the discrimination game is categorising the feature vectors of the segments. The main method that has been used was the prototype method. Here the categories are represented by prototypes, and the feature vectors are categorised with those prototypes that are nearest to the feature vectors in the different feature spaces. The categories are organised in different feature spaces to allow categories that resemble more generalised and specialised samples of a feature vector.

The second step in the discrimination game is to extract the categories that distinguish one segment from the other segments in the context that a robot has constructed in a language game. This phase is the actual discrimination.

Initially, there are no categories at all. When the discrimination fails, new categories are created for which the features of a feature vector acts as exemplars. These prototypical categories are organised hierarchically in the different versions of the feature space. Each version of the feature space has a different resolution, thus allowing generality and specificity of the categories. In de Jong & Vogt 1998 no such hierarchical layering was imposed and the robots had great difficulty in developing a coherent communication system.

The categories have been made dynamic in the sense that the prototypes move in the feature space and thus their sensitivity range changes in time. It is thought

7.1 The symbol grounding problem solved?

that this would let the prototypical categories evolve towards a more representative sample of the feature vectors that have been extracted. In turn, this is supposed to increase the quality of the categorisation and discrimination. The experiment where this dynamical mechanism has been left out showed that this does not necessarily contributes to a higher performance. This, however, may be due to the simplicity of the robots' visual environment. Perhaps in a more complex environment it may well be very beneficial to have dynamically changing categories.

The feature vectors that the robots extract from the segments are categorised in each feature space with that category that is nearest to the feature vector. The prototypes of a feature space cover the entire space. This has the advantage that whenever there is a category in some feature space the feature vector will be categorised. When the categories are constructed with the binary subspace method, or in the binary tree method (Steels 1996d) as is the case in the Talking Heads, a category is only activated when the feature vector to be categorised falls inside the sensitive region of a category. This is because these categories do not necessarily cover the entire feature space. Furthermore, the binary category, once established, is not dynamic, i.e. its sensitivity does not move. Whether these are problems is not really shown. The fact that in the prototype method explored here, the robots can exploit more categories in the discrimination games increases the chance of success. This is probably the main reason why this system outperforms the experiment incorporating the binary subspace method.

Although it might be beneficial allowing fuzzy boundaries on the categories' sensitivity, this has not been observed in the experiment which investigated this. No big and significant differences have been observed, except in the discrimination success, which was slightly lower. The reason for this can be found in the fact that in the fuzzy approach a feature vector can be categorised in more ways than in the non-fuzzy prototype method. This increases the probability that more feature vectors share the same categories. Hence discrimination would be more difficult. Applying the fuzzy boundaries in more complex environments, might still be beneficial, but the problem in applicability lies in the increase of computational power.

The discrimination works well. In the basic experiment the discrimination success was already approximately 92 %. It has been argued in Chapter 4 that the discrimination success did not go to a 100 % because: (1) A success-rate of 100 % simply cannot be reached. (2) The discrimination success is partly a function of the number of language games and the hearer does not play a discrimination game every language game. When the speaker did not utter a word-form or

7 Discussion

when the hearer does not know the word-form no discrimination game is played. These reasons are confirmed with the results of letting the agents only playing discrimination games. It appeared now that the average discrimination success rose to 98.7 %.

The meanings that emerge are used very distinctive. In all experiments the distinctiveness is higher than 0.95 and usually ends up with a value of 1. So, when a distinctive category is used in the communication it refers to the same referent with a high certainty. It is well shown in the meaning-referent competition diagrams that after a very short period, the meanings that are used in the language refer to the same referents about 100 % of the time. The parsimony however is lower. The probability that when trying to categorise a referent with a previously used category is around 0.85. It can be explained by the fact that in different situations the segments differ and hence are categorised differently, thus yielding a strong one-to-many relationship between a referent and the distinctive categories.

In these experiments, the categories all bear the invariant property that the dimension of the feature vector with value of 1 corresponds to a unique referent. In the Talking Heads invariance is filtered out using the notion of saliency. However, as the statistics of the sensory data revealed (Appendix C), saliency does not guarantee to find the invariance. This is because another dimension of the feature vector might have a value very close to 1, which may not be most salient. However, there may be selection criteria in the discrimination or naming game that allows a more controlled categorisation of invariant properties of the different feature vectors. A possible mechanism preference could be the selection of categories that have maximum values at their sensory channels. However, this would require to implement more knowledge on the categorisation, which is against the non-nativist approach that is pursued. On the other hand, selection for maximum intensity is so simple and uniform that such a selection principle could have evolved genetically. Still another selection criterion may be how well a feature vector correlates with a prototype. I.e. an agent may prefer those categories of which the extracted feature values best resemble the categories. This way a prototype effect (Rosch et al. 1976) could be modelled. Naturally, these different criteria could be combined yielding a hybrid mechanism.

According to Harnad (1990), one of the aims of discrimination is to reduce the amount of symbolic structures that relates to a certain referent. As Figure 6.4 showed, the number of distinctive categories that have been proposed can increase up to more than 2,500 for categorising 4 referents! Although it has not been shown in this book, it has been observed that when counting all different (non distinctive) categories that has been proposed before discrimination was applied, more than 5,000 (sometimes even 10,000) categories were constructed. So, the discrimination already yields a substantial reduction in the amount of categories that relate to the different segments. The naming phase further reduces the number of categories to, say 500 meanings that are used successfully in the communication. Of these 500 meanings, most are rarely used, while a few are used most frequently as observed in the various competition diagrams. It should be clear that discrimination games alone cannot solve the grounding problem sufficiently. Still too many distinctive categories are categories for the four referents.

7.1.3 Identification

A final process in symbol grounding is identification. Identification is reducing the symbolic structures relating to a segment even more than is the case in discrimination yielding invariant symbols. As argued before, the identification process of symbol grounding takes place at the language level. In other applications or types of problem solving, identification may take place at a different level depending on the type of problem to be solved. For planning a path, for instance, a robot also has to identify symbols with which it can reason. Then identification succeeds when the robot successfully incorporates the symbols to plan a path. In language this is at the communication level. When a language game is unsuccessful, at least one of the robots failed to identify the referent and it is not sure which robot failed to do so. Therefore, identification is successful when the language game is a success.

It is at the identification level that a distinctive category becomes a meaning. As argued, a meaning is some categorisation that is used in language. It is a part of the symbol that has been defined in semiotics. There the meaning is the *sense* that is made of the symbol. According to Wittgenstein (1958) the meaning can only be interpreted by its use in language. Therefore, it should be related with a form that can be used in a language game. This trinity (referent, meaning and form) is what Peirce called a symbol.

The basic experiment already showed that the robots solved the grounding problem in successful language games. They successfully identified symbols that stand for a referent. However, there was still quite some polysemy. Although higher than the a priori success, the communicative success-rate was relative low. In Chapters 5 and 6 it has been shown that the success could increase and thus identification improved. The main factors that improved the success were: assuming joint attention, increasing the form creation rate and learning rate, and assuming a different form-adoption scheme.

7 Discussion

The influence of the form creation probability (P_s) has been shown in Section 5.5. It appeared that increasing the creation probability increased the success in communication. It also increased the specificity, i.e. the likelihood that when a word-form is used it would refer to the same referent it previously referred to increased. Increasing the creation probability, however revealed a major drawback: the number of word-forms used increased proportionally up to 83 when $P_s = 1.0$. This sums up to more than 20 word-forms per referent, which is not very efficient. The point is that a high creation probability decreases the amount of many-to-many relations between meaning and form, which in turn increases the specificity because the meanings uniquely refer to a particular referent. This is nice, but it increases synonymy. The number of word-forms used are much lower when $P_s = 0.1$ and the communicative success is not much lower than when $P_s = 1.0$ (only a few percent, but significantly). Now only 25 word-forms are used, yielding slightly more than 6 word-forms per referent.

When, in addition, the hearer is allowed to adopt the speaker's word-form when it misinterpreted the speaker's utterance, the success grows even more and the number of word-forms used decrease even more. In the optimal guessing game experiment ($P_s = 0.1$), where also the learning rate is different from the basic experiment, the number of word-forms used are 16, most of them used rarely. Inspecting the experiment more closely, there are only 6 word-forms that are used frequently. The communicative success grows up to approximately 75 % after 10,000 language games. So, it seems that adopting the word-forms after misinterpretation is one of the necessary factors of the model. Furthermore, in less reliable robots, a modest creation probability is very useful: It allows the word-forms to be associated with more meanings, thus increasing the amount of one-to-many relations between form and meaning. The adaptation of the association scores and lateral inhibition causes improved selection and through self-organisation a more coherent and invariant lexicon emerges. This way referential polysemy and synonymy remain low.

A high learning rate, controlling the adaptation of the association scores, increases the influence of past success and has low influence on failures. When the learning rate is too high ($\eta = 0.99$), the system does not find a suitable equilibrium in the scores. Failures are not punished and will be made again, thus the success does not increase. Lateral inhibition is small and the lexicon does not converge well enough to an attractor. A suitable lexicon also does not emerge when the learning rate is too low, i.e. when $\eta \leq 0.1$. If there is no word-form adoption when the hearer misinterpreted the speaker, the self-organising effect that the score adaptation should control does not reveal itself.

So, identification in the language games takes place at the language level. The invariance of the symbols are therefore to be found in the consistent use of these symbols in the language. This way the ambiguous categorisation of the various sensings of some referent is disambiguated in the successful use of the symbols in the language games.

7.1.4 Conclusions

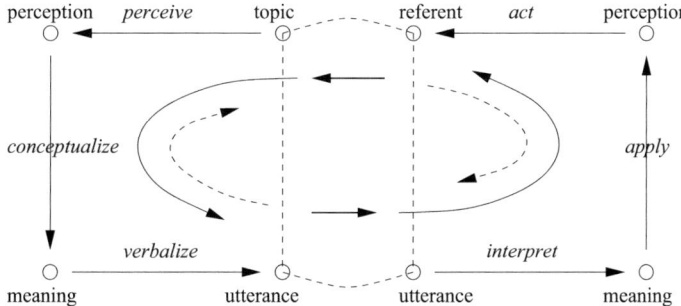

Figure 7.1: The semiotic square of the language games.

The hybrid processes of sensing, segmentation, feature extraction, categorisation, discrimination, naming and feedback transforms the symbol grounding in the formation of a semiotic coupling (or structural coupling) between the robots' environment, their internal states and their mutual interaction. Some of the lexicons that result from the experiments have been plotted in semiotic landscapes showing the structural couplings that emerged. These landscapes showed that the many-to-many relations between form and meaning can serve cognitive agents to decrease the amount of polysemy and synonymy that is necessary to ground their sensing of the environment invariantly.

The meaning of the utterances are always in contrast to the rest of the context as a result of the discrimination game. However, the experiment with only three of the four light sources present in every situation showed that the robots acquired a lexicon similarly to the basic experiment. Hence the system learns to communicate about the four referents in their world, while only sensing three in their environment. Nevertheless, the use of the language depends on the situation that the agents are in.

So, the symbol grounding problem is solved by a hybrid of relative simple mechanisms: sensing, segmentation, feature extraction, categorisation, discrimination, naming and feedback. The principles are based on interactions of the

7 Discussion

agents with their environment and each other, individual adaptation and self-organisation. A complex structure of couplings emerges from the co-evolution of language and meaning, and can well be used to communicate about the agents' environment. Summarising, the three phases of the symbol grounding problem are modelled by the following:

1. Iconisation: Sensing, segmentation and feature extraction
2. Discrimination: Discrimination game
3. Identification: Naming and adaptation

One of the main findings was that the robots tend to categorise the various sensings of a particular referent differently. Thus yielding one-to-many relations between referent and meaning. This is not problematic as long as this is cancelled out by one-to-many relations between form and meaning. This results in low, or ideally no polysemy and synonymy as illustrated in Figure 7.2 (a). The proposed model is pretty well capable of doing just this. Figure 7.2 shows how a symbol thus can be visualised by a set of semiotic triangles. These types of symbolic structures may well explain the notions of family resemblance (Figure 7.2 (b)) and object constancy (Figure 7.2 (c)).

Family resemblance (Wittgenstein 1958) is the observation that seemingly different things are called the same without being ambiguous, like the meaning of *games*. Where soccer and chess are typical games, a game like swinging is not typical. Swinging lies near the border of the "conceptual space" of games. It has no direct resemblance with games like soccer and chess (referents R1 and R2 Figure 7.2 (b)), but it has some resemblance with other games that in turn do have resemblance with soccer and chess. Such categorisation process can be explained with the one-to-many relations between form and meaning. The word "games" is associated with different meanings of soccer, chess and swinging. The successful use of these meanings in different situated language games allows the system to emerge a family of resemblance.

One of the reasons that makes the symbol grounding problem hard is the notion of object constancy. How can an object be recognised as being the same when different sensings of such an object results in different sensory stimuli, for instance because it is partly obscured? In the experiments, the robots detect the light sources from different positions, resulting in different sensings as the continuum of sensings P in Figure 7.2 (c) shows. This may also yield different meanings. Nevertheless, the system identifies the objects pretty consistently, because the one-to-many relations between form and meaning is damped at the level of form and referent. That the robots actually learn to identify the referents has been shown in an experiment where there were only three of the four referents available in each situation. The robots could learn to name all referents equally well as in the basic experiment whereas they only could detect three of them in a situation.

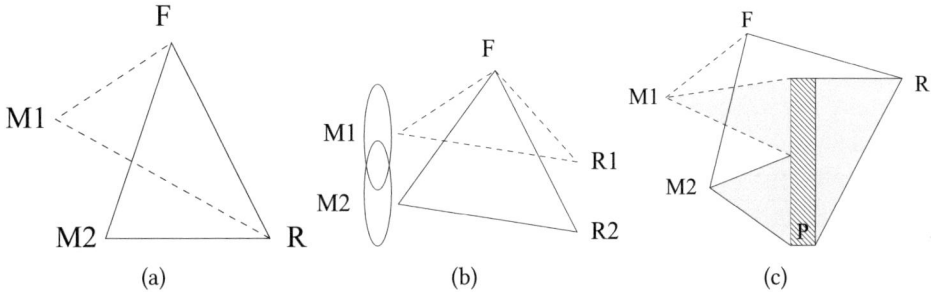

Figure 7.2: Illustration of three semiotic relations between referent R, meaning M and form F. Figure (a) shows how one-to-many relations between referent and meaning cancels out synonymy and polysemy by one-to-many relations between form and meaning. Figure (b) shows how the model may explain family resemblance. The ovals should be interpreted as Venn–diagrams of the meanings R1 and R2. In Figure (c), the continuum of possible sensings P of referent R are displayed as a rectangle. Some part of the rectangle may be interpreted by M1 and another by M2. When both meanings relate to the same form, this mechanism may solve the problem of object constancy.

7.2 No negative feedback evidence?

The experiments in Chapter 5 showed the importance of either joint attention or feedback in the language formation. One experiment has been done in which neither are present: the XSL game. In this experiment the robots used association scores based on the co-occurrences of word-meaning associations to select them. A XSL game was considered to be successful when the hearer "thought" it understood the speaker. The communicative success from the robots' viewpoint was around 82 %, but the actual success was in fact less than 25 %, which is lower than the a priori success.

7 Discussion

Many psycholinguists hold that children learning language hardly get any feedback on their language use. This is the so-called "no negative feedback evidence" (see e.g. Braine 1971 or Bowerman 1988).[1] Other psycholinguists claim that, when children make (structurally the same) mistakes, they do get feedback from their language teachers like their parents (Demetras, Nolan Post & Snow 1986). Furthermore, the influence of feedback on language acquisition is thought to be crucial by some scientists (Clancey 1997; Demetras, Nolan Post & Snow 1986; Clark & Clark 1977; Tomasello & Barton 1994). The results of the guessing game and the XSL game make clear that this model seems to be unable to work without feedback. The fact that the robots' mismatch in referent word-form adoption benefits the communicative success provides a strong reason why feedback is needed in the guessing game.

Although less successful in communication than the observational game, or perhaps only slower, the guessing game appears to converge best on the lexicon. Mostly, a clear winning name is used by the robots and the competition at the bottom is not successful. Since the hearer has no knowledge about the topic prior to linguistic communication, it has to trust completely on the linguistic information. The robots have to disambiguate the lexicon for which feedback is required. When the feedback only depends on the co-occurrence of word and meaning as is the case in the XSL game, the robots cannot disambiguate the system well. The feedback must be on the success of the language game. Since communication in the guessing game is not redundant as in the ostensive and observational games, there is more pressure to disambiguate. Hence the robots are better at it.

When joint attention is established prior to the communication, directive feedback appears to be less important. Experiments revealed that when the robots established prior topic knowledge (or joint attention prior to the communication) the lexicon formation improved, whether or not feedback was used.

The observational language game has been inspired by the work of Mike Oliphant (1997) and appears to work best. In this game no directive feedback is required. The agents use feedback based on the use of word-meaning pairs, not on their success in the game. This strategy works provided the agents have prior topic knowledge, established through some joint attention mechanism, and provided that scores are updated with lateral inhibition. This is conform with the findings of Oliphant (1997; 1998) and confirmed by Edwin de Jong (2000). Oliphant found that lateral inhibition is important in a comparison experiment where the associations were updated following (1) Willshaw learning and (2) Heb-

---

[1] Recall that feedback in this book is about the effect of a language game; not to correct one another.

bian learning. Hebbian learning uses lateral inhibition, which allowed Oliphant's agents to establish a coherent lexicon, whereas the Willshaw method that does not use lateral inhibition did not.

When investigating a lexicon developed by the observational language game more closely, it appeared that the system still allows quite some polysemy and synonymy, especially at the bottom of the competition. If the no negative feedback evidence argument is correct, this might explain why children tend to use overgeneralisations during their lexicon development. Having more examples and directive feedback (possibly evaluated from the environment by the language learners themselves) could disambiguate such overgeneralisations. It is interesting to note that each type of language game revealed some level of overgeneralisation at the beginning of the experiments. Usually there was quite some referential polysemy in the beginning of the experiments, which died out after approximately 1,000 language games.

So, in what way does this reflect on our knowledge of child language acquisition, it has been found in several observations of mother-child interactions that joint attention is established prior to the linguistic act (Schaffer, Hepburn & Collis 1983; Harris, Jones & Grant 1983; 1984; Tomasello & Todd 1983; Tomasello, Mannle & Kruger 1986 as cited in Barrett 1995). In particular Tomasello & Todd (1983) and Tomasello, Mannle & Kruger (1986) found that there was a positive relation between the period of joint attention and the child's later vocabulary size.

Although children seem to be able to select the right referent, there is no complete consensus how. It is likely that there is some trade-off between using ostensive and non-ostensive contexts in the lexical acquisition phase. The guessing game on the one hand and the ostensive and observational on the other hand showed that robots can learn a lexicon in both the ostensive and the non-ostensive case. This is conform with Tomasello and Barton's (1994) results. Tomasello and Barton investigated children's language acquisition under conditions that are similar to those in the guessing game and observational game. In addition, Barrett's (1995) conclusions that the lexicon is learned better under joint attention prior or simultaneously to the linguistic act hold as well. This is also conform the discussion placed at the 2000 *Evolution of Language* conference by Jean-Louis Dessalles (2000).

To put the conclusion in light of the empirical data available in the psycholinguistic literature as from Braine (1971), Demetras, Nolan Post & Snow (1986) and Tomasello & Barton (1994), it is likely that infants (and probably humans in general) use a combination of strategies to learn and develop a language. For instance

7 Discussion

when the context is clear and the child has a high likelihood of identifying the topic (possibly prior to the communication), feedback on the outcome of a game is not necessary. When such a precondition is not satisfied and a child makes structural mistakes, feedback on the success becomes more important, and may be provided by adult speakers. Other strategies for associating words with meanings are likely to exist, like the filling up of knowledge gaps by language learners when the context is clear (Clark 1993).

Joint attention and feedback were simulated in the current experiments. Therefore, the question how joint attention and feedback are established is left as an open question. Probably there are several strategies. For instance, pointing can be used to draw attention or to provide feedback. But also gaze following, attention monitoring, novelty and evaluative rewards on a language game may be sources of establishing joint attention or feedback.

The feedback provided on the outcome of language game is the same for both robots. Naturally, this is not very plausible. It is interesting to investigate how robots can establish joint attention and evaluate feedback autonomously. For this it would be good to have a more task oriented approach, where joint attention and feedback are implicit in the accomplishment and success of the task.

7.3 Situated embodiment

As obvious the influence of the physical interactions and the body of the robots is very important. Especially the results of Chapters 4 and 5 must have made this clear. First, the physical condition and the bodily adjustment of the robots relevant to the task appear to have some influence. And second, the most important influence seems to be in *how* the robots interact with their environment, including each other.

Due to the fact that the robots have unreliable control, they have difficulties in co-ordinating their interaction physically. This is one of the reasons for the robots' poor ability to construct a coherent context. In turn, this has set a limit to the potential understandability around 80 %. Using more reliable robots could solve this problem to some extent. However, the physical unreliability is not the only reason for context incoherence. More fundamental is the problem, that the robots are at different locations from which they cannot sense the same. Since the robots only communicate the "here and now", this problem cannot be solved in principle.

The idea that the robots physical condition and bodily adaptation to the robots' environment appears to be trivial to some people, but this is not so. Why is it that humans are the only creatures on earth that use language? Answering that they have a different body, which enables them to learn language is simply not enough. It presumably has a lot to do with it, but to what extend and in what ways? When the robot's visual apparatus could not neatly detect the world with enough resolution, the robots performed much worse at grounding the language. The communicative success was around the a priori value. And when the robots had new gearing, the performance increased a little bit. Although these results were not significant, the robots can rotate more smoothly, giving noise in the sensing less chance. It is likely that physical fitness and co-ordination abilities are important ingredients in language learning. Humans are organisms that have great co-ordination abilities, which especially become handy in setting up coherent contexts and joint attention.

The most important influences observed came more from the experiments where different strategies of joint attention and feedback were investigated. Many of the results have already been discussed in the previous section, so they will not be discussed again.

To obtain reasonable results in the experiments the methods for obtaining joint attention and feedback have been simulated. The result of the simulations were that the robots could inspect the internal states of each other. Obviously this is not very plausible. These mechanisms did not change the principle of language acquisition, but it required the assumption that the robots had a mechanism by which they could establish joint attention extra-linguistically. This requires that the problems of establishing joint attention and evaluation of feedback on the robots still needs to be developed. It should be clear that establishing joint attention requires good physical co-ordination of the agents' bodies.

The different results showed the importance of a good co-ordination of the robots in their environment. Hence the importance of the robot's *interaction* with the world is made clear. Language is not only linguistic communication, but also heavily depends on co-ordinated interaction of agents with their environment as has been made clear in the situated cognition paradigms (Clancey 1997).

7.4 A behaviour-based cognitive architecture

For the development of a robotic system that is able to fulfil a relatively complex task that the language game is, an architecture is constructed that is based on a behaviour-based architecture. Examples of behaviour-based architectures are the subsumption architecture (Brooks 1990) and PDL (Steels 1994c). These architectures mostly control reactive behaviour as "direct" couplings between sensors and actuators. It is most prominently based on the "vehicles" proposed by Valentino Braitenberg (1984). Behaviour-based architectures have become very popular in robotics in the past ten years. However, these architectures could not show much more complex behaviour than e.g. wall following, phototaxis and obstacle avoidance. Although these behaviours have interesting emergent functionalities, they cannot be used for accomplishing more complex tasks that involve planning. The dual dynamics architecture (Jaeger & Christaller 1998) could, but there the planning is implemented implicitly in the reactive processes. It is therefore less controllable and thus prone to errors.

To deal with explicitly planned behaviour, a behaviour-based cognitive architecture has been developed. The cognitive architecture is an extension of PDL. The planning is coded in finite state automata. Each state activates or inhibits separate behaviours using "motivations" that can be set "on", "off" or the "inverse".[2] The behaviours that are "on" control in parallel the emergent behaviour an agent shows. This approach is very similar to the architecture proposed by Barnes et al. (1997). The transition from one state to another happens when the final condition of the state is satisfied. When another robot has to transfer to the next state simultaneously, the first robot can send a radio signal to do so. Each state has a timer and when a robot tries to achieve a goal for too long, the state is left and the default state is entered, thus the task fails.

The architecture has basically three parallel operating layers between the sensors and actuators of the agents. The first layer bears the finite state automata that control planning. The second layer consists of behaviours that control the reactive behaviour of a robot, like phototaxis. And thirdly, there are cognitive processes that for instance control categorisation and naming. The processes in the two final layers are controlled by the motivations set in the first layer. A distinction is made between the reactive and cognitive processes. This is done, because calculating reactive processes are faster than calculating cognitive processes. The reactive processes demand a fast response, because a moving agent cannot wait to respond when, e.g. it is close to a wall it has to avoid. In the control architecture that is used in this application, the sensor readings and actuators are updated and processed 40 times per second. The cognitive processes can take in principle as long as they need, because they can be processed (physically) in parallel. In the current implementation this has been accomplished by doing off-board processing later on. When all processes are run in real time, this should

---

[2] In principle motivations can have any value between -1 and 1 controlling the strength of a certain behaviour. These motivations have been incorporated before in PDL, see e.g. Steels 1994a; 1996b.

either ask for a physically parallel process or incorporate a good timing protocol that works on the clock process. When this is not done, unwanted side-effects will occur as has been observed while implementing a real time language game where robots tried to develop a lexicon about their actions (Vogt 1999; 2000b). In these experiments it has been observed that robots collided with a wall and did not avoid it because they were busy processing the categorisation or naming.

The cognitive behaviour-based architecture that has been developed for these experiments is a general-purpose architecture for doing cognitive robotics. It has been used to implement various language games on the mobile robots that incorporate fundamentally different behaviours. In the current implementations, the behaviours have been pre-programmed, including the planning. It might well be possible that the planners are learned or created dynamically, see e.g. Barnes et al. (1997). Furthermore, new layers may be introduced when necessary.

7.5 The Talking Heads

Before discussing the results obtained in the previous chapters in relation to the Talking Heads and other related experiments, it is good to summarise the differences between the different experiments. The main sources from which the discussions are based are the book *The Talking Heads experiment: Volume 1. Words and meanings* by Luc Steels (1999) and the PhD thesis *L'émergence d'un lexique dans une population d'agents autonomes* of Frédéric Kaplan (2000).

7.5.1 The differences

In the Talking Heads several agents can *materialise* their cognitive structures into a set of cameras, each representing the physical body of a robot. Different sites are placed around the world and are connected via the internet. Agents can travel from one site to another and engage in guessing games with each agent that is present at a certain site. Furthermore, human users can launch new or existing agents to travel the net. In a guessing game the robots look with their cameras at a white board at which various geometrical figures are pasted. The cameras cannot move around freely, they can only move there cameras in a pan-tilt manner. In addition, the cameras are calibrated such that they can identify co-ordinates at the white board reliably. This information is used to implement pointing. So, although not completely perfect, the robots can reliably point to a referent on the white board thus providing feedback. In addition, the calibration is also used to focus the robots' attention, which is used to detect a context. This

7 Discussion

way the Talking Heads can detect (again more or less) reliably a coherent context. Since the Talking Heads cannot move from their place, the cameras observe a referent more or less similarly at different times. The differences they detect are mainly due to changing lighting conditions and possibly changes made on the white board by human intervention introducing new referents. Another source of difference lies in the fact that the robots can change bodies, and thus observe a particular area of the white board from different positions. However, these positions are limited to two at each site. The mobile robots can move freely in their environment.

Besides the different sensory apparatus (a camera instead of light sensors) and different referents (geometrical figures), there are already several important differences found:

1. The first fundamental difference is the number of agents that are in the language community. In the Talking Heads there is a dynamic flow of agents that learn the language at different sites, whereas in the experiments presented here, there are only two agents.

2. Another fundamental difference is that the agents cannot move freely in their environment, but they can only pan-tilt their movements and they can travel from site to site and from camera to camera. The mobile robots can move freely in their environment which is only at one site. The robots cannot change from body.

3. The third difference is that the Talking Heads have a calibrated world in which they can establish joint attention by means of pointing reliably. The calibration is also incorporated to detect a more or less coherent context, which is a flaw in the mobile robots implementation.

Another source of differences can be found in the segmentation, feature extraction and categorisation processes of the two applications. Besides the fact that the Talking Heads have cameras and a different environment of objects, the way information is extracted from the image differs in fundamental ways. In the mobile robots experiments the feature extraction is developed to identify classes of light sources that are placed at different heights. The Talking Heads have feature extractors that are more abstract and can be used for instance to name very different objects similarly by using information about their relative positions in a context. The feature extraction of the Talking Heads extracts features about colour, horizontal position, vertical position, relative object size and a filling ratio of the segmented area inside a rectangular bounding box. This way

7.5 The Talking Heads

the Talking Heads develop a language not to *recognise* objects directly on their shape, texture etc., but also on their relative position in a particular context. Such abstractions are not made on the mobile robots.

Categories in the Talking Heads are constructed using a binary tree, which splits subparts of the sensory channel space in equal halves of increasing granularity. Besides one experiment, the mobile robots' categories are represented as prototypical categories. In addition, the Talking Heads construct categories that start searching lexical elements with one dimensional categories. When it fails finding a good match, the Talking Heads look for all possible categories of dimension 2 etc. This continuous until a good match is found or until the naming game fails. In the binary tree method, the categories need not to be composed of elements from one hierarchical layer. They can also be composed with a combination of elements stored at different hierarchical layers. Remember that the binary tree method does not work with different versions of the feature space, but the different versions can be compared with different hierarchical layers. Thus the Talking Heads potentially looks for all possible configurations of categories. This process is guided by the naming game; when a suitable category is found in the lexicon either for production of utterances or understanding, the search for more complex categories stops.

Another feature of the category selection is guided by the notion of SALIENCY. After the discrimination game, a category that is most salient will be used in the naming game. This way, the Talking Heads have a more invariant and coherent way of categorising a certain scene. In the mobile robots it is opted to consider only categories that span all the dimensions of the feature space. This way the mobile robots are guaranteed to find a category that has the invariant property of the segment in it. As argued, exploiting saliency does not guarantee to find that information, whereas exploiting all dimensions of the feature space does.

Summarising, the differences found at the feature extraction and categorisation level between the Talking Heads and the mobile robots are:

4. The feature extraction of the Talking Heads extract more abstract information of the sensed image. Most notably are those of colour and spatial information.

5. The discrimination games in the Talking Heads explores categories that are composed of one or more dimensions of the feature space at possibly different hierarchical layers. It stops when a suitable match is found.

6. Saliency is incorporated in the Talking Heads to guide invariant and coherent categorisations. This is necessary because, among others, the Talking

7 Discussion

Heads have more abstract feature extractors (4) and categories may not span all the dimensions of the feature space (5).

In the naming part of the guessing game there are no large differences apparent. The only main differences are in the word-form adoption strategies, some parameter settings and the adaptation mechanisms of scores.

In the Talking Heads word-forms are adopted when there is a mismatch in the referents the two robots identified as the topic. In the mobile robots this only done in certain experiments. In both experiments word-forms are adopted when the hearer could not find a matching word-meaning pair that matches the categorisation. When word-forms are adopted in the Talking Heads, the speaker points to the topic and the hearer adopts the uttered word-form with the identified topic from pointing.

The word-form creation probability in the Talking Heads are always set to 1, whereas this was set initially in the basic experiment presented here this was set to 0.02. Kaplan (2000) investigated the different parameter settings of P_s. The experiments reported in Chapter 5 revealed that when $0.1 \leq P_s \leq 0.9$ the mobile robots system worked best.

The scores are adapted in the Talking Heads by a different scheme than incorporated in the mobile robots. The scores s are adapted according to the following equation:

$$\sigma = \sigma' + \delta \cdot X \qquad (7.1)$$

where σ' is the previous value, δ is a constant (usually set to 0.1) and

$$X = \begin{cases} 1 & \text{if association is used successful} \\ -1 & \begin{cases} \text{if association is lateral} \\ \text{if association yields mismatch} \end{cases} \end{cases} \qquad (7.2)$$

This equation allows the scores to vary rapidly in through time, thus allowing instability in some way. In addition, the method lets the scores to hold only a little information on past effectiveness of an association. The walking average method used on the mobile robots do not alternate heavily in time and it holds information about a longer period of use. In fact it holds all past experiences, although recent past experiences influence the scores more than experiences from long ago.

So, the naming game of the Talking Heads differs from the mobile robots mainly in the following features:

7. Word-forms are always adopted when there is a mismatch or misunderstanding in any way. In such cases, the speaker always provides the hearer with topic information by means of pointing. In the mobile robots word-form adoption is done always only in a few experiments. In the case of word-form adoption, the hearer randomly selects a segment to be the topic.

8. The word-form creation probability P_s is always set to 1 in the Talking Heads experiment. A lower value is used in the mobile robots.

9. The scores adapted in the Talking Heads are adapted differently than in the mobile robots. The method used in the Talking Heads allows more fluctuations and does not keep track of effectiveness in a longer history than in the mobile robots.

The differences between the mobile robots experiment and the Talking Heads are summarised in Table 7.1.

Table 7.1: The summarised differences between the mobile robots experiments and the Talking Heads experiments.

	MOBILE ROBOTS	TALKING HEADS
Referents	Light sources	Geometrical figures
Sensors	Light sensors without spatial information	Camera
Nr. of agents	2	Variable ≥ 2
Mobility	Mobile	Immobile
Calibration of world	Yes	No
Feature extraction	Not complex	Complex
Category span in n dimensional feature space	n dimensions	$\leq n$ dimensions
Saliency	No	Yes
Joint attention before form-adoption	No	Yes
Form creation rate	$P_s < 1$	$P_s = 1$
Score adaptation	$\sigma = \eta \cdot \sigma + (1 - \eta) \cdot X$	$\sigma = \sigma + \delta \cdot X$

7 Discussion

7.5.2 The discussion

When comparing the results of the Talking Heads (Steels 1999; Kaplan 2000) with the results obtained in this book (mainly reported in the guessing game in Chapter 6), a first observation is that the results quantitatively are similar. Discriminative success is also very high (Steels 1999) and the communicative success varies between 50 % and 80 % (Kaplan 2000). The main reason why the communicative success is low in the Talking Heads has been ascribed to the fact that there is a continuous flow of agents in the environment.

In more controlled experiments where there are two agents developing a lexicon, the success increases, although it still does not converge to 100 % as the system does in simulations (Steels 1999). The time of convergence, as far as there is convergence, is much faster than in the mobile robots experiment. The time of convergence is already achieved after 25 language games. In cases where there are more than two agents the speed of convergence is longer and complete success has not been obtained after 35,000 games (Steels 1999). An important source of failure is ascribed to the uncertainties that is part of the physical interactions. As in the mobile robots, experiment failures occur mainly when the robots do not detect a coherent context or when pointing used for feedback fails.

In the mobile robots experiment convergence is never achieved before 1,000 language games; it usually takes about 2,000 games in the optimal models. This is a rather long period, also when comparing the results with the experiments of Billard & Hayes (1999). Billard's robots learned a grounded lexicon in less than 30 language games. The difference with Billard's experiment is that one of her robots had its lexicon pre-programmed and the other robot learned this lexicon. In the current experiment the lexicon has to be developed completely from scratch; a task that is naturally much harder. The reason why convergence takes long in the mobile robots experiment has probably to do with the mobility of the robots. Due to this mobility the differences in sensing in different language games is larger than in the Talking Heads. Furthermore, the two robots participating a language game have larger differences in sensing as is the case in the Talking Heads.

Although there are main differences in the experimental set-ups between the Talking Heads and the mobile robots, the results are similar. The success of the mobile robots experiments is consistently lower than in the Talking Heads experiment with two agents. As argued, the communicative success of the mobile robots experiment cannot exceed 80 % because there is a large fraction of situations in which the robots do not share a coherent context. Due to more reliable context setting in the Talking Heads as a result of the calibration of the cameras orientation in relation to their environment, this fraction is much less in the Talking Heads. The communicative success of the mobile robots when subtracting the 20 % of failures due to context incoherence is very much similar to the success obtained in the Talking Heads.

The categorisation in the Talking Heads use different representations for the categories: a binary tree is used rather than a prototype representation. Assuming that the binary tree method is very similar the binary subspace method, the results presented in Section 5.1 showed that the binary tree method does not work just as well as the prototype method.

When a binary tree is being developed, the categories of the tree do not cover the complete feature spaces, whereas the prototypes do once they are formed at a certain space. Hence the binary tree method cannot always categorise a segment a every layer. When one of the segments cannot be categorised at a certain layer, this layer is discarded in the discrimination game. The latter is due to implementation limitations, which had been introduced for consistency reasons (investigating a conjunction of four categories at the same hierarchical layer). When looking at the success evolution of the discrimination games in the Talking Heads (e.g. Steels 1999) it is clear that the success evolves similar to the success of the prototype method presented in this book. In addition, de Jong (de Jong & Vogt 1998; de Jong 2000) showed that applying the ADAPTIVE SUBSPACE METHOD, also yield similar results.[3] This indicates that the power of categorisation lies not in the representation of categories, but rather in the methodology of the discrimination games. This methodology is strongly based on generation and selection of categories.

In the Talking Heads saliency is thought to be crucial in the establishment of a coherent lexicon (Steels 1999). The results of the mobile robots experiments showed that this can also be accomplished by preferring categories that span all the dimensions of the feature space. Depending on the type of information that needs to be categorised, one might prefer one method above another. When one wants to categorise a variety of abstract notions like spatial information of left/right, up/down or colour, one is interested in only one or more dimensions of the feature space. In such cases the method of saliency may be preferred. When the most information of an observation lies in the entire feature space, one might prefer categories that span all dimensions in this feature space. In this case saliency appears to be redundant. Furthermore, the sensory data revealed that saliency does not guarantee invariance filtering. In more complex systems

---

[3] Note that de Jong does not apply its experiments on the Talking Heads. de Jong's experiments are a simulation on the emergence of communication about SITUATION CONCEPTS.

7 Discussion

where there are many more different sensory channels, a combination of both might be useful.

In the mobile robots experiments it appeared that one-to-many relations between form and meaning can benefit the communication system as long as polysemy and synonymy is minimised. In his PhD. thesis Kaplan (2000) presented an experiment in which groups of categories are classified in a variant of the naming game. In this variant clusters of categories tend to be named with the same word-form. The categories are distributed as points in the CONCEPTUAL SPACE, cf. Gärdenfors (1996). When an agent cannot name a particular category, the agent can recruit the name of a category (or meaning) that is mathematically in the same cluster of the conceptual space. This way a classification of meanings emerge that are lexicalized with the same word-form. Although in the mobile robots experiment, such classifications emerge from the existing model, it may be beneficial for the agents to *explicitly* recruit neighbouring categories. This is because such classifications in the mobile robots experiment are in continuous competition with each other. They are thus exposed to antagonising forces. Hence a deliberate recruitment may overcome this effect.

When looking at competition diagrams, the diagrams in the Talking Heads look very similar to the ones presented in this book. This is not very surprising, since the competition between the different elements are very similar. Self-organisation at the word-meaning level is established mainly by the update of association scores. As reported in Steels (1999), de Jong (2000) and Kaplan (2000), the main source of self-organisation appears to be lateral inhibition. When a form-meaning association is used successfully, the score of the winning association is increased and the scores of other associations with either the word-form or meaning are inhibited. In the language experiments the lateral inhibition sharpens the difference between associations that are proven to be successful and connections that are less successful. This way punishment of possible failures of previously successful associations has little influence and the associations are still likely to be used again. If lateral inhibition is not used, less successful associations can easily take over effective ones, causing instability. Hence a more stable communication system is present.

According to de Jong (2000), lateral inhibition is more powerful than the rewards taken from the evaluated success. In an experiment where success was not evaluated, but where there was lateral inhibition, guided only by the *use* of associations, agents were well capable of learning a communication system. The observational games confirm the findings of de Jong. Lateral inhibition disambiguates the level of synonymy and polysemy to a large extend, as observed in Section 5.4.

7.5 The Talking Heads

That lateral inhibition is such a powerful mechanism in self-organising systems should not be a surprise. It has already proved to be a powerful mechanism of self-organisation in cognitive sciences. The Kohonen networks (or Self-Organising Maps) showed how topological maps emerge in connectionist models that are fundamentally based on lateral inhibition. When activation of certain neurons results in a desired response of the network, neighbouring neurons are excited and neurons that lie further away are laterally inhibited. Similar mechanisms are also used in Hebbian learning.

Kaplan (2000) reported an experiment in which the creation probability P_s has been varied between 0.1 and 1.0 in a series of simulations of the guessing game. The results showed a similar result as obtained in Chapter 5. There are hardly differences in the evolution of the communicative success. Nevertheless, the number of word-forms that enter the language does increase. Kaplan does not investigate what the influences are for the quality of the communication system that emerged other than reporting on the time of convergence of the system.[4]

In the Talking Heads P_s is usually set to 1. No negative side-effects have been reported on this. But recall that the meanings of the Talking Heads are more abstract (using e.g. spatial relations) and the aim of the experiment is to name these meanings. In the mobile robots experiment the aim of the robots is to name the referents with meanings that more directly correspond to the sensing, rather than naming the referents by using abstract and relative meanings. In the Talking Heads word-forms emerge that mean e.g. 'left', 'far left' or 'close left' and distinctions that have even more granularity. These word-forms can be used to name different referents depending on the context of the language game. In the mobile robots experiments the aim was that the robots learn to name the referents that are in their context (and categorisation is context-dependent), but *independent* of the orientation at which these are observed. To achieve this, a lower setting P_s is more effective, since it allows more one-to-many relations between form and meaning to cancel out the one-to-many relations between referent and meaning. This way a word-form better relates to one referent. Thus solving the symbol grounding problem more invariantly.

7.5.3 Summary

So, although there are many differences in the details between the Talking Heads experiment and the mobile robots experiment, the principles of the models used

---

[4] Convergence is established when the communicative success becomes 1. Kaplan measures the success of his experiments by the average time a system needs to converge.

7 Discussion

are the same. The results are therefore also very similar. Due to the fact that the Talking Heads are better controllable, the heads are better capable of constructing a coherent context. In addition the differences in sensing between two Talking Heads is smaller than in the mobile robots experiments. As a result of this, the maximum communicative success is much lower. Furthermore, arriving at a stabilised success takes longer in the mobile robots experiments.

Lateral inhibition is found to be crucial for the development of a coherent lexicon in the Talking Heads (Steels 1999; Kaplan 2000) and in simulation done by de Jong (2000). Experiments in the observational language game confirm this finding.

Although the details of the categorisation differs a lot in the different models used here, by Steels (1999) and de Jong (2000), the discrimination games explored in all these models reveal similar results. Hence the power lies in the model of the discrimination games rather than somewhere else.

A similar conclusion can be drawn from the naming game. Although different interaction schemes may be used, as well as alternative adaptation schemes, the results of the two experimental set-ups are rather similar.

Hence, most important observation is that the principle of generation, selection and (cultural) interaction is a strong tool in explaining grounded lexicon emergence.

7.6 Future directions

This book showed how the symbol grounding problem can be solved in a real-world multi agent system in which robots interact with their environment (including each other), adapt their ontology and lexicon individually and the resulting ontology and lexicon are formed through self-organisation. In the experiments, the symbols have been grounded in a lexicon, however the method of discrimination games can also be applied to other task oriented applications, like navigation. In such an application, the naming game can be replaced by another type of game, for instance a SELF LOCALISATION GAME.

Since the set-up of this experiment has many elements of a toy problem, it is necessary to scale up the models and test them in a more realistic real world environment. The Talking Heads experiment as it is does not suffice this requirement because the Heads' world consists only of geometrical figures. The experiments currently being investigated by Frédéric Kaplan (2000) are a better example. In his new experiment he uses a dog-like robot, the AIBO developed by Sony CSL in Tokyo, that learns a language from human-robot interaction in a world with real toys (furry animals and balls). More interesting would be an experiment with a mobile robot navigating in an office environment. In such an experiment the robot can ground "natural" landmarks like doors, paintings or whatever exists in an office environment. This way the robots can communicate about their whereabouts.

Another interesting direction that can also be applied in a navigation task is grounding a lexicon about actions, like going left and going right. A preliminary study on this has been published in Vogt (1999) and Vogt (2000b). In this study two robots engage in a FOLLOW ME GAME. The robots take turns in being the speaker and hearer. The speaker drives in front doing obstacle avoidance. The hearer follows the speaker by doing phototaxis on the light that the speaker carries. When the speaker changes its direction, it categorises the action and tries to produce a single word utterance. When the hearer receives the utterance, it also categorises its actions and tries to interpret the utterance. When the hearer understands the speaker and it is still following it, the game is successful. Later in the games, the hearer can try to follow the speaker only by using the speaker's utterances.

In this game, categorisation is done by what has been called the IDENTIFICATION GAME. By using reconstruction vectors of a time series (first proposed for categorisation by Rosenstein & Cohen 1998a) a segment of the time series is compared to the prototypes that it constructed. If there is a prototype close enough to the segment that corresponds to the robot's action, the identification game is successful. When the robot fails to identify such a prototype, it creates a new one, taking the segment as an example.

Integrating the "perceptual" language game, the follow me game and, for instance, the self-localisation game can result in an interesting experiment where robots learn to communicate about navigation. The result may be a PATH PLANNING GAME, where the robots learn a language during a navigation task in such a way that a path can be planned based on the grounded interactions. In addition, it should be possible that one robot can give route descriptions to another robot for going somewhere. Not by saying "go forward for 5 meter, then turn 90° left, go forward 3 meters ...", but by saying "go forward until you see a yellow painting, go left, at the red door ...". This idea has been proposed for a post-doctoral research at the University of Amsterdam in co-operation with the VUB AI Lab.

An interesting side effect of such an experiment is that it can be integrated with newly investigated models in which grammatical structures are developed (Steels 2000). In these new ideas, a procedural cognitive semantics is constructed, from which a grammar might emerge when applying new types of language games to the system.

7 Discussion

For all future experiments on (mobile) robots in this direction, it is advisable to use off-the-shelf robots when possible. It turned out that developing the current system was immensely difficult, and for a great deal the problems had to do with the unreliability of the sensorimotor board of the robots and the unreliable sensory equipment. Off-the-shelf robots are tested on their robustness and their sensorimotor equipment has been calibrated. Hence, modelling a cognitive system on such a robot is more easy. A disadvantage is that one has to cope with the physical limitations of the robots that are used.

Additional interesting future research areas are involved with categorisation, attention and feedback. For instance, is there a way to make a fuzzy categorisation system that benefits the grounding process? In this book the fuzzy system did not provide much improvement over the normal categorisation, but it has been mentioned that this might happen in more complex environment. Recruiting similar categories or meanings in the naming game (Kaplan 2000) might also be an interesting and beneficial strategy for selecting form-meaning associations and classification.

Can the categorisation improve when the phase space of the sensorimotor space is exploited using techniques from non-linear dynamics? In Rosenstein & Cohen (1998a) and Vogt (1999), such methods have proved to be successful in the categorisation of time series. Perhaps this could also be applied to the sensing of real world objects.

Besides the discrimination game, other strategies of categorisation could be investigated. Distinctions are not the only source of meaning. Identification is another. An identification game has already been explored in Vogt (1999; 2000b). When a segment is close enough to a prototypical category, the identification is completed. If it fails, new categories may be introduced in the ontology. Possibly similar strategies can be invented.

In the current implementations attention has been pre-programmed by means of internal inspection. It would be interesting to implement other more realistic strategies modelling attention. Saliency could be one source of attention selector, novelty could be another one. Several studies argue that humans tend to focus their attention at salient events in their surroundings and use these events as the topic of their conversation, see e.g. Dessalles 2000. Robotic studies could be made where such mechanisms are investigated. In addition, it is interesting to investigate ways how such mechanisms could be learned or perhaps acquired by genetic selection.

A similar argument can be given about the feedback. This has now also been implemented by means of internal inspection. Other more plausible methods should be developed. This is best done when having the agents operate and communicate in a task-oriented application. Then agents can evaluate the success of a language game based on the outcome of the task, which indicates the success of the language game.

To make the model physiological more plausible, a more biologically inspired structure of representation and processing should be investigated. A potential architecture would be the selectionist architecture proposed by Gerald Edelman and colleagues (1987). One language game model has already been implemented in the Neural Darwinism approach (Popescu-Belis 1997). Another more simple neuronal implementation of the language game is done by Dircks & Stoness (1999).

7.7 Conclusions

This book showed how the symbol grounding problem is solved in a particular experiment. In this experiment, two robots developed a shared and grounded lexicon about the light sources that they could detect in their environment. In the experiments the robots construct relations between the referents, meanings and forms so that they can communicate the referents by using forms efficiently. Conform with the theories on semiotics, the relation between a referent, meaning and form is called a symbol.

The model that has been developed lets the robots do a hybrid set of tasks: sensing, segmentation, feature extraction, categorisation, discrimination, naming, evaluating feedback and adaptation. This way the robots develop a shared lexicon based on three principles as hypothesised by Luc Steels (1996c): individual adaptation, cultural evolution and self-organisation.

Because the robots detect their environment differently under different circumstances, the categorisations of the light sources they try to name differ as well. However, the mechanisms that guide the lexicon formation (i.e. the naming game model) allow many-to-many relations between category (meaning) and form. Feedback or joint attention cause the robots to select relations in such a way that there emerges more or less one-to-many relations between form and meaning. This way the robots construct a lexicon that enables them to communicate the referents rather consistently. It appeared that the physical conditions of the robots influence their ability to co-ordinate their interactions, which in turn influenced their capability to ground a shared lexicon.

So, the symbol grounding problem has been solved for this particular experimental set-up, but there is still a long way to go for robotic agents to develop a grounded language within its full scope. Nevertheless, this book provides a good step forward on the road to understanding and modelling cognition.

Appendix A: Glossary

Actual success The actual success is a measure that calculates the average success of the past 100 language games. A language game is successful when both robots of a language successfully identified a symbol that has the same form and stands for the same referent. Often this is the same as the communicative success. In these cases, the latter measure will be used.

Binary subspace A binary subspace is a region in the feature space. Binary subspaces are constructed by splitting another subspace in two equal halves in one dimension of the feature space. A binary subspace is a possible definition of a category.

Categorisation Categorisation is the process in which a feature vector is related to one or more categories. In the experiments a category is defined by either a prototypical category or a binary subspace.

Category A category is defined by a region in the feature space.

Communicative success The communicative success is a measure that calculates the average success of the past 100 language games as evaluated by the robots themselves. This need not be the same as the actual success.

Context A context is the set of segments identified from a single sensing event.

Consistency Consistency is a measure that indicates how consistent the referents are named by some word-forms.

Discrimination Discrimination is a process where the robot identifies categories that relate to one feature vector, but not to another feature vector from the same view. This discrimination takes place at the category level. Harnad (1990) defines discrimination directly at the level of perception. Unless mentioned otherwise, the term *discrimination* is used at the category level.

Discriminative success The discriminative success is a measure that calculates the average success of the discrimination games of a robot in the past 100

A Glossary

language games. If a robot does not play a discrimination game in a language game, the discrimination game is considered to be a failure.

Distinctive category A distinctive category is a category that relates to some segment in a context, but not to any other segment in the same context.

Distinctiveness Distinctiveness is a measure that indicates to what degree the meanings used by a robot relates to the same referent as before.

Feature A feature is a value between $[0, 1]$ that designates a property of the sensed segment.

Feature extraction Feature extraction calculates some property of the sensed segment from the sensor data. It reduces the complexity of the segment and returns a set of values that designate features.

Feature space The feature space is an n-dimensional space where each dimension is related to some property that can be calculated from the sensory data that a robot can sense. In the experiments described here there are 4 dimensions, each relating to a property of a sensory channel. The domain of each dimension are real values between $[0, 1]$.

Feature vector A feature vector is an n-dimensional vector in the feature space that has as its elements the different features that are extracted from a segment. This way a feature vector is related to a segment.

Feedback Feedback is the process where the robots evaluate the effectiveness of a language game, i.e. whether both robots communicated the same referent. The feedback evaluated can be both positive as negative.

Form A form is an arbitrary string of characters from an alphabet.

Iconisation Iconisation is the forming iconic representations. It is a term that Harnad (1990) identifies as a subpart of solving the symbol grounding problem.

Identification Harnad (1990) defines identification as the invariant categorisation of sensing a real world phenomenon. In this book this means that both robots successfully related the referent to a meaning and a form. Although the meaning can be different, the referent and form must be the same for both robots.

Joint attention With joint attention is meant the state where both participants of a language game know the topic prior to the verbal communication.

Lexicon A lexicon is the set of form-meaning pairs that a robot has stored in its memory.

Meaning In the theory of semiotics meaning is the sense that is made of the symbol. The meaning arises in the interpretation of the symbol. In the experiments this is the category that a robot used in a language game to name a referent.

Parsimony Parsimony is a measure that indicates to what degree a referent gives rise to the use of a unique meaning.

Polysemy Polysemy is the notion that a form is used to name more than one referent.

Prototype A prototype is defined as a point in the n-dimensional feature space and it is used for defining a category.

Prototypical category A prototypical category is a category that is represented in the feature space by a prototype. It is defined by the region of which the points in the feature space are nearest to the prototype.

Referent A referent is that what the symbol "stands for". In the experiments, the referents in the robots' environment are light sources.

Segment A segment is a set of data from the sensory channels that is obtained by segmentation.

Segmentation Segmentation is the process in which the aim is, given a sensed data set, to construct regions that corresponds directly to a real world object. It is implemented by a process that identifies from a sensed data set connected areas that are uniform in some way.

Sensing Sensing is the process in which a robot records a view of its surroundings. In the experiments described here, the robots make a full 360° turn while recording. Sensing results in a set of data points given on the sensory channels.

Sensory channel A sensory channel is the channel in which the numeric output of a particular sensor flows.

Specificity Specificity is a measure that indicates to what degree forms are used to name a unique referent.

A Glossary

Symbol The definition of a symbol is adopted from C.S. Peirce's theory on semiotics. A symbol is defined as the relation between a referent, a meaning and a form. This relation is often illustrated with the semiotic triangle.

Synonymy Synonymy is the notion that one referent is named by more than one form.

Topic The segment that is the subject of a discrimination game and/or language game is called the topic.

Word-form See *form*.

Appendix B: PDL code

In this appendix the PDFL program that runs on the physical part of the robots is presented. Its purpose is to sketch how the behaviour-based cognitive architecture presented in Chapter 3 can be implemented in PDL.

The language game scenario that the program implements has partly been introduced in Chapter 3. The scenario is extended with the part in which the robots can find each other autonomously, as discussed in more detail in Steels & Vogt (1997) and Vogt (1997).

The program is adapted such that there is more readability than the original program. This means that some debug facilities are left out, as well as some by-passes, which have been made to solve some not yet understood peculiarities of the robots' behaviours. In addition, although no actual implementation has been made in PDL, it is sketched how the cognitive part of the language game may be implemented in PDL. This sketch, however, leaves away the critical parts of the segmentation, discrimination and naming processes.

PDL has been introduced in Chapter 2. PDL is implemented in ANSI C. Part of the code is in C, but it should be readable also for non-C programmers. Remarks are given between /* and */ or behind a double slash: //. PDL processes are defined as functions, which are usually preceded by a void.

```
/* Here are some include files with libraries for PDL, SMBII and C.
   Also some definitions and declarations are present.
   These are all left out for clarity.
*/


#define NoPulse 25
#define Relax 15

const float ON=200.0f,
   OFF=1.0f;

/*PDL declarations of quantities.
  The network is constructed at the end of the program.
*/
```

B PDL code

```
quantity Identity;
quantity LFBumper, RFBumper, LBBumper, RBBumper;
        //Left- and Right- Front and Back Bumpers
quantity L0,L1,L2,L3; //The white light sensors.
quantity LeftIR, FrontIR, RightIR;
quantity LM, RM;//Left- and Right Motors
quantity IREm0,IREm1,IREm2,IREm3;//IR emitters

/*Basic behavior processes

  Touch Based Obsacle Avoidance (TBOA) */

void touch_based_obstacle_avoidance(){
  int T,DL=1,DR=1;

/*If both front bumpers are active one of the directions to turn
  is randomly chosen. The appropriate direction DL(eft) or DR(ight)
  is set to 0. */

  if ((value(LFBumper))&&(value(RFBumper))){
    T=random(2);
    if (T)
      DL=0;
    else
      DR=0;
  }

/*If LFBumper and MotTBOA (motivation for obstacle avoidance
  are active, then LM:=-Retract and RM:=-LargeRetract
  For the RFBumper it is the other way around*/

  add_value(LM,
    -DL*value(LFBumper)*MotTBOA*(Retract+value(LM)));
  add_value(RM,
    -DL*value(LFBumper)*MotTBOA*(LargeRetract+value(RM)));

  add_value(LM,
    -DR*value(RFBumper)*MotTBOA*(LargeRetract+value(LM)));
  add_value(RM,
    -DR*value(RFBumper)*MotTBOA*(Retract+value(RM)));

/*If one of the back-bumpers is pressed and its motivation (MotTBOA)
  is on, the motor-values are set to the default speed DS.*/

  add_value(LM, value(LBBumper)*MotTBOA*(DS-value(LM)));
  add_value(RM, value(LBBumper)*MotTBOA*(DS-value(RM)));
```

```
   add_value(LM, value(RBBumper)*MotTBOA*(DS-value(LM)));
   add_value(RM, value(RBBumper)*MotTBOA*(DS-value(RM)));

}

/*Rotation with RotateSpeed in direction of MotRot.
   If MotRot=1, then robot turns right.
   If MotRot=-1, then robot turns left.*/

void rotate(void){
   add_value(LM,MotRot*(RotateSpeed-value(LM)));
   add_value(RM,-MotRot*(RotateSpeed+value(RM)));
}


/*Active IR Obstacle Avoidance (AOA) and IR-taxis
   Since the IR modulation for AOA is the inverse of IR-taxis,
   the same process is used. So, if MotIRT=1, then IR-taxis is
   applied, and if MotIRT=-1, AOA is applied.

   The IR modulation is regulated in the IR emission module ...

   inv_sigmoid dampens the difference between the left and right IR,
   so that large differences in IR don't give too large differences
   in motorvalues.
*/

float inv_sigmoid(float x){
   float Alpha=2.5,Beta=0.3;
   return (1/(1+exp(Alpha*(x-Beta))));
}

void IRTaxis(void){
   float F=inv_sigmoid(abs((value(RightIR)-value(LeftIR)))/255.0);
   add_value(LM,0.1*F*MotIRT*(value(RightIR)-value(LeftIR)));
   add_value(RM,-0.1*F*MotIRT*(value(RightIR)-value(LeftIR)));
}

/*When MotFW is on, the robot will try to accelerate towards default speed.
   The motor-values increase asymptotically towards this DS.*/

void towards_default(void){
   add_value(LM,MotFW*(DS-value(LM))/20.0);
   add_value(RM,MotFW*(DS-value(RM))/20.0);
}

/*If MotStop=1, the motor-values become zero.*/
```

B PDL code

```
void stopMotors(void){
  add_value(LM,-MotStop*value(LM));
  add_value(RM,-MotStop*value(RM));
}

/*Pulsing the IR. During their default behavior the robots emit pulses
  of IR so that the robots can detect each other's presence.*/

void pulse_IR(void){
  if (PulseIR){
    if ((Timer%(Pulse+NoPulse))>Pulse)
      IR=ON;
    else
      IR=OFF;
  }
}

/*Emitting the IR. The modulation of the IR is set to 1
  if the IR=1 (this means the IR is OFF), then the robot
  can detect other IR sources.
  If the IR > 1, the modulation is set to 95, so the robot
  can AND emit IR AND detect its own IR.
*/

void emitIR(void){
  if (IR>1)
    SMB2IRModDc(95);
  else
    SMB2IRModDc(1);
  add_value(IREm0,(IR-value(IREm0)));
  add_value(IREm1,(IR-value(IREm1)));
  add_value(IREm2,(IR-value(IREm2)));
  add_value(IREm3,(IR-value(IREm3)));
}


/*Sending radio messages.

  The 0 gives the reliability bit (i.e. unreliable transmission)
  receipient is the identity of the receiving robot.
  strlngth is the length of the message in bytes.
  out_buffer is the message to be send. This is specified where
  necessary.*/

void send_message(void){
  if (SEND){
```

```
    radio_link_tx(0,receipient,strlngth,(unsigned char *)out_buffer);
    SEND=0;
  }
}

/*timing increments the Timer and evaluates whether or not the
  robot is in a particular state too long. If so, the robot will
  stop its current behavior and will return to the default state.
*/

void timing(void){
  Timer++;
  if ((Timer>MaxTime)&&((StateHearer)||(StateSpeaker))){
    StateSpeaker=0;
    StateHearer=0;
    Timer=0;
  }
}

/*Reading radio linked messages */

void read_message(void){
  int i;
  Expression=0;
  while (radio_link_rx((unsigned char *)in_buffer)){
    message_length=(int)in_buffer[0];
    who_from=(int)in_buffer[1];
    for (i=1;i<=message_length;i++)
      message[i-1]=(char)in_buffer[i+1];
    Expression=1;
  }
}

/*Segmentation: In the actual implementation, the sensor-data is
  transmitted to a radio base station, connected to a PC.
  How the segmentation is done is discussed extensively in chapter 3.
  The actual segmentation takes place off-line and the implementation
  details are left out here for readability reasons.
*/

void segmentation(){
  if (SEGMENTATION){
    /*Read and process values of quantities L0, L1, L2 and L3.
      This process includes sensing and featue extraction.
      For each segment found, the feature values are calculated,
      the segment is added to the context and NrOfSegments is
      incremented.
```

B PDL code

```
      */
   }
}

/*The processes discrimination_game, production, understanding and
  feedbackadaptation are all processed off-board. They are given
  for completeness, however the implementation details are left out.
  For the details, see chapter 4.
*/

void discrimination_game(){
   if (DG){
      set_of_concepts=discriminate(Topic);
      Discriminated=1;
      DG=0;
   }
}

void production(){
   if (Produce){
      Utterance=production(Topic);
      Produced=1;
      Produce=0;
   }
}

void understanding(){
   if (Decode){
      Association=decode(Utterance);
      Decoded=1;
      Decode=0;
   }
}

void feedbackadaptation(){
   if (FeedbackAdaptate){
      Feedback=interpret(Association);
      adapt_lexicon(Association);
      Adapted=1;
      FeedbackAdaptate=0;
   }
}

/*So far (for now) the cognitive processes, which are mentioned for
  completeness. The code continues with on-board processing.

  maximize() detects a maximum in the IR flow of the front IR sensor.
```

```
   Note that it is a function and not a process.*/

int maximize(){
  int N=0;
  float diff;
  diff=value(FrontIR)-PreviousIR;

  if ((diff<=0)&&(Previous>0)&&
      (value(FrontIR)>IRClose))
    N=1;
  Previous=diff;
  PreviousIR=value(FrontIR);
  return N;
}

/*speaker() implements the finite state automaton of the speaker.

  Each state is divided in a set op actions and final conditions.
  The actions are executed by the basic behaviors or processes as
  defined above.

  The basic behaviors are activated by setting the motivations to
  their appropriate values. The motivations are specified with MotXX,
  where XX refers to the particular behavior.

  For reasons of clarity not all motivations are continously given.
  Unless otherwise specified, all motivations are initially set to 0.
  After changes, when a motivation is not given, its values is as
  last specified.

  The final conditions of one state are either the pre-conditions of
  the next state, or the pre-condition of state 0 in which the
  default_behavior process (see below) take over. The latter type of
  final condition is modeled by MaxTime and the process timing.

  MaxTime specifies how long a robot may remain in a particular state.

*/

void speaker(void){
  int i,j,m,Flag;
  switch(StateSpeaker){
  case 0:{/*Default state. See default_behavior().*/
    break;
  }
  case 1:{
    /*Waiting for confirmation and after the IR-switch has been
```

B PDL code

```
      relaxed, the speaker can determine in which direction to
      turn. Orienting towards the hearer helps finding it.*/
   //Actions.
   MotStop=1;
   IR=OFF;
   MotTBOA=1;

   if (Expression)
     if (strcmp(message[0],"confirm")==0)
       Confirm=1;

   //Final conditions
   MaxTime=RotationTime;
   if ((Timer>Relax)&&(Confirm)){
     if (value(LeftIR)>value(RightIR))
       MotRot=-1; /*Turning left*/
     else
       MotRot=1;  /*Turning right*/
     StateSpeaker=2;
     Timer=0;
   }
   break;
}
case 2:{/*Initial orientation*/
   //Actions
   IR=OFF;
   MotStop=0;
   MotTBOA=0; /*If robot rotates, obstacle avoidance is nasty side-effect*/

   //Final conditions
   if (Timer>(RotationTime-1)){
     /*If robot has not found other robot yet,
       keep searching using taxis in next state.
       Since the MaxTime in this state is
       RotationTime, the transition has to be made
       before, otherwise the state will be
       timed-out by the process 'timing'*/
     StateSpeaker=2;
     Timer=0;
   }
   if (maximize()){
     if (value(FrontIR)<IRCloseEnough)
       StateSpeaker=3;/*Distance to hearer is too big.*/
     else
       StateSpeaker=4;/*Distance to hearer is ok.*/
     MotStop=1;/*Setting motor-values to 0.*/
     Timer=0;
```

```
      }
      break;
    }
    case 3:{/*Get closer to the hearer by using IR taxis.*/
      //Actions
      MotFW=1;
      MotIRT=1;
      MotStop=0;
      MotRot=0;
      IR=OFF;
      MotTBOA=1;

      //Final condition
      MaxTime=SearchTime;
      if (value(FrontIR)>IRCloseEnough){
        StateSpeaker=4;
        Timer=0;
      }
      break;
    }
    case 4:{/*Final alignment back-to-back*/
      //Actions
      MotFW=0;
      MotIRT=0;
      MotStop=0;
      MotTBOA=0;
      MotRot=1;
      IR=OFF;

      //Final conditions
      MaxTime=RotationTime;

      /*If the robot detects enough IR with its LeftBackIR sensor,
        it stops. It stands still approximately when it is facing
        the opponent robot backwards.
        Using taxis would be more sophistigated, but takes longer and
        is more error-prone.
        Since the hearer must transfer to the next state simultaneously,
        the speaker also sends a message.*/

      if (value(LeftBackIR)>IRCloseEnough){
        StateSpeaker=5;
        strcpy(out_buffer,"aligned");
        SEND=1;
        Timer=0;
      }
      break;
```

B PDL code

```
    }
    case 5:{/*The hearer does its alignment. The speaker waits while
              emitting IR.*/
      //Actions
      MotStop=1;
      MotRot=0;
      IR=ON;
      MotTBOA=1;

      //Final condition
      MaxTime=2*RotationTime;
      if ((Expression)&&(strcmp(message,"aligned")==0)){
        /*There is a message saying the hearer aligned successfully.
          The speaker can start the sensing.*/
        MotStop=1;
        StateSpeaker=6;
        Timer=0;
      }
      break;
    }
    case 6:{/*The speaker does its sensing, segmentation and feature
              extraction.
              Here starts the process as described in the book.*/
      //Actions
      MotStop=0;
      MotRot=1;
      IR=0.0f;
      MotTBOA=0;

      SEGMENTATION=1;

      //Final condition
      MaxTime=2.5*RotationTime;

      /*After a particular time, the speaker stops rotating when it
        again detects the IR with its LeftBack sensor.*/

      if ((Timer>(1.75*RotationTime))&&
          (value(LeftBack)>IRCloseEnough)){
        StateSpeaker=7;
        strcpy(out_buffer,"perceived");
        SEND=1;//This way the hearer transits state as well.
        Timer=0;
      }
      break;
    }
    case 7:{/*Now the hearer does its sensing, segmentation and
```

```
            feature extraction.*/
   //Actions
   MotStop=1;
   MotRot=0;
   IR=ON;
   MotTBOA=1;

   //Final conditions
   MaxTime=3*RotationTime;

   /*Hearer finished sensing. The cognitive part can start.*/

   if ((Expression)&&(strcmp(message,"perceived")==0)){
     StateSpeaker=8;
     Timer=0;
   }
   break;
}
case 8:{/*The rest of the speaker's FSA is how it would look like
           if the cognitive part is processed on-board.
           For clarity the details are left out. See chapters 3 and 4
           for details.*/
   //Actions
   MotStop=1;

   if (!Discriminated){
     Topic=random(NrOfSegments);
     DG=1;
   }
   else{//Final condition
     Discriminated=0;
     if (NrOfConcepts>0)
       StateSpeaker=9; /*Discimination game was success.*/
     else{/*Discimination game was a failure.
             Language game ends in failure.
             Ontology adapted during discrimination game.*/
       StateSpeaker=0;
       strcpy(out_buffer,"failure");
       SEND=1;
       LG++;
     }
     Timer=0;
   }
   break;
}
case 9:{/*The speaker's word-form production.*/
   //Actions
```

B PDL code

```
      MotStop=1;

      if (!Produced)
        Produce=1;
      else{//Final condition
        Produced=0;
        if (strcmp(Utterance,"nil")){
          strcpy(out_buffer,Utterance);
          /*The speaker produced an meaningful utterance*/
          StateSpeaker=10;
        }
        else{/*The speaker could not produce an utterance.
              Adaptation (word-creation) has already been
              done during production.*/
          strcpy(out_buffer,"failure");
          StateSpeaker=0;
          LG++;
        }
        SEND=1;
      }
      break;
    }
    case 10:{/*Feedback and Adaptation.*/
      //Actions
      MotStop=1;
      if (Expression){
        /*Hearer provided feedback, which needs to be interpreted.
          After that the lexicon can be adapted.*/
        FeedbackAdaptate=1;
      }

      //Final condition
      if (Adapted){
        StateSpeaker=0;
        LG++;
        Adapted=0;
      }
      break;
    }
  }
}

/*hearer() implements the finite state automaton of the hearer.*/

void hearer(void){
  int i,j,Flag;
  switch(StateHearer){
```

```
case 0:{/*Default state. See default_behavior().*/
  break;
}
case 1:{/*Hearer starts waiting until speaker aligned.*/
  //Actions
  MotStop=1;
  MotTBOA=1;
  IR=ON;

  //Final conditions
  MaxTime=AlignTime;
  if ((Expression)&&(strcmp(message[0],"aligned")==0)){
    StateHearer=2;
    Timer=0;
  }
  break;
}
case 2:{/*The hearer has to wait for the IR to relaxate.
         Otherwise the robot cannot detect IR of the other.*/
  //Actions
  MotStop=1;
  MotTBOA=1;
  IR=OFF;

  //Final condition
  if (Timer>Relax){
    Timer=0;
    StateHearer=3;
  }
  break;
}
case 3:{/*Rotation for alignment.*/
  //Actions
  MotRot=1;
  MotStop=0;
  MotTBOA=0;
  IR=OFF;

  //Final conditions
  MaxTime=RotationTime;
  if (value(LeftBackIR)>IRCloseEnough){
    StateHearer=4;
    strcpy(message,"aligned");
    SEND=1;//The speaker has to transit state as well.
    Timer=0;
  }
  break;
```

B PDL code

```
    }
    case 4:{/*The speaker does its sensing, segmentation and
              feature extraction; the hearer waits.*/
      //Actions
      MotStop=1;
      MotRot=0;
      MotTBOA=1;
      IR=ON;

      //Final conditions
      MaxTime=3*RotationTime;
      if ((Expression)&&(strcmp(message,"perceived")==0)){
        StateHearer=5;
        Timer=0;
      }
      break;
    }
    case 5:{/*The hearer does its sensing, segmentation and
              feature extraction.*/
      //Actions
      MotStop=1;
      MotRot=1;
      IR=OFF;
      MotTBOA=0;
      SEGMENTATION=1;

      //Final conditions
      MaxTime=2.5*RotationTime;
      if ((Timer>(1.75*RotationTime))&&
          (value(LeftBack)>IRCloseEnough)){
        StateHearer=6;
        strcpy(out_buffer,"perceived");
        SEND=1;//The speaker has to transit state as well.
        Timer=0;
      }
      break;
    }
    case 6:{/*The hearer plays discrimination games for each segment
              in its context.*/
      //Actions
      MotStop=1;

      if (Topic<NrOfSegments){
        Topic++;
        DG=1;
      }
      else{//Final condition
```

```
      StateHearer=7;
      Timer=0;
    }
    break;
  }
  case 7:{/*The hearer waits for the speaker's utterance.*/
    //Actions
    MotStop=1;

    //Final conditions
    MaxTime=ProductionTime;
    if (Expression){
      if (strcmp(message,"failure")){
        /*The speaker produced an utterance.*/
        strcpy(Utterance,message);
        StateHearer=8;
      }
      else{/*The speaker failed either to produce or discriminate
             hence the language game fails and is finished for the hearer.*/
        StateHearer=0;
        LG++;
      }
      Timer=0;
    }
    break;
  }
  case 8:{/*The hearer tries to understand the speaker's utterance.*/
    //Actions
    MotStop=1;

    if (!Decoded)
      Decode=1;
    else{//Final condition
      Decoded=0;
      StateHearer=9;
    }

    break;
  }
  case 9:{/*Feedback and adaptation.*/
    //Actions
    //No physical actions are specified.

    if (!Adapted)
      FeedbackAdaptate=1;
    else{//Final condition
      Adapted=0;
```

B PDL code

```
            strcpy(out_buffer,Feedback);
            StateHearer=0;
            LG++;
        }
        break;
      }
    }
}

/*default_behavior describes the robots' behavior when they are
  exploring their environment 'arbitrary' in order to find each
  other.
  When one robot finds another contact is made, and the robots
  enter the first state in either the speaker- or hearer mode.
*/

void default_behavior(void)
{
  if ((!StateSpeaker)&&(!StateHearer)){
    //Actions
    MotStop=0;
    MotFW=1;
    MotIRT=-1;/*Inverse IR-taxis is Active Obstacle Avoidance*/
    MotRot=0;
    Pulse=1;/*The robots pulse IR to detect each other.*/
    MotTBOA=1;

    //Final conditions
    if ((value(FrontIR)>Threshold)&&
        ((Timer%(Pulse+NoPulse)>(Pulse+Relax)))){
      /*The robot is sure it does not detect reflected IR of itself*/
      strcpy(message,"communicate");
      SEND=1;
      StateSpeaker=1;
    }
    if ((Expression)&&(strcmp(message,"communicate")==0)){
      strcpy(message,"confirm");
      SEND=1;
      StateHearer=1;
      Timer=0;
    }
  }
}

/* Initializing the robot and some of its variables */

void initialize(void)
```

```c
{
  if (Init>0){
    if (value(Identity)==1){
      //Each robot has its own identity, which is automatically detected.
      Pulse=25;
      //Some other initializations.
    }
    else{
      //Each robot has its own identity, which is automatically detected.
      Pulse=25;
      //Some other initializations.
    }
    StateSpeaker=0;
    StateHearer=0;
    //Some other initializations.
    Init++;
  }
}

/*The main program of PDL. Here the PDL network is initialized,
  defined and constructed.
*/

void main(void){

  printf("Starting Execution\n\r");
  init_pdl();

  /*Quantities are added to the network.
    Each quantity has a name, an upper value,
    a lower value and an initial value.
  */

  //Sensors:
  Identity = add_quantity("Identity", 1.0,0.0,0.0);
  LFBumper = add_quantity("LeftFrontBumper", 1.0,0.0,1.0);
  RFBumper = add_quantity("RightFrontBumper", 1.0,0.0,1.0);
  LBBumper = add_quantity("LeftBackBumper", 1.0,0.0,1.0);
  RBBumper = add_quantity("RightBackBumper", 1.0,0.0,1.0);
  L0 = add_quantity("WhiteLight0",255.0,0.0,0.0);
  L1 = add_quantity("WhiteLight1",255.0,0.0,0.0);
  L2 = add_quantity("WhiteLight2",255.0,0.0,0.0);
  L3 = add_quantity("WhiteLight3",255.0,0.0,0.0);
  LeftIR = add_quantity("LeftIR",255.0,0.0,0.0);
  FrontIR = add_quantity("FrontIR",255.0,0.0,0.0);
  RightIR = add_quantity("RightIR",255.0,0.0,0.0);
  LeftBackIR = add_quantity("LeftBackIR",255.0,0.0,0.0);
```

B PDL code

```
//Actuators:
LM = add_quantity("LeftMotor",100.0,-100.0,0.0);
RM = add_quantity("RightMotor",100.0,-100.0,0.0);
IREm0 = add_quantity("IREm0",200.0,0.0,0.0);
IREm1 = add_quantity("IREm1",200.0,0.0,0.0);
IREm2 = add_quantity("IREm2",200.0,0.0,0.0);
IREm3 = add_quantity("IREm3",200.0,0.0,0.0);

//Connections with the SMBII are made.

connect_sensor(SID_BIN1, LFBumper);
connect_sensor(SID_BIN2, RFBumper);
connect_sensor(SID_BIN3, LBBumper);
connect_sensor(SID_BIN7, RBBumper);
connect_sensor(SID_BIN4, Identity);

connect_sensor(SID_AN0,L0);
connect_sensor(SID_AN1,L1);
connect_sensor(SID_AN2,L2);
connect_sensor(SID_AN3,L3);

connect_sensor(SID_IR1,LeftIR);
connect_sensor(SID_IR2,FrontIR);
connect_sensor(SID_IR3,RightIR);
connect_sensor(SID_IR4,LeftBackIR);

connect_actuator(AID_MOTOR2,RM);
connect_actuator(AID_MOTOR1,LM);

connect_actuator(AID_IREM0,IREm0);
connect_actuator(AID_IREM1,IREm1);
connect_actuator(AID_IREM2,IREm2);
connect_actuator(AID_IREM3,IREm3);

//Processes are added to the network.

add_process("initialize",initialize);
add_process("touch_based_obstacle_avoidance",
            touch_based_obstacle_avoidance);
add_process("rotate",rotate);
add_process("IRTaxis",IRTaxis);
add_process("towards_default",towards_default);
add_process("stopMotors",stopMotors);
add_process("emitIR",emitIR);
add_process("read_message",read_message);
add_process("send_message",send_message);
```

```
add_process("timing",timing);
add_process("segmentation",segmentation);
add_process("discrimination_game",discrimination_game);
add_process("production",production);
add_process("understanding",understanding);
add_process("feedbackadaptation",feedbackadaptation);
add_process("speaker",speaker);
add_process("hearer",hearer);
add_process("default_behavior",default_behavior);

/*The PDL program is run. This program is implemented as
  an infinite loop.*/

run_pdl(-1L);

}
```

Appendix C: Sensory data distribution

To investigate some properties of real-world experiments, it is interesting to know how the frequency of segments corresponding to light sources is distributed. Figure C.1 shows how this distribution is found in the recorded data set. It is interesting to note that light source L0 is detected most often; r1 segmented L0 on the average even more than once a situation. Figure C.2 shows the distribution of context size frequencies. It should be clear that contexts are not always of equal size within one situation, nor can one observe a normal distribution of set sizes.

Figures C.3 and C.4 show how the data is distributed after segmentation and feature extraction has been applied on the basic data set. The figures show the distributions of features for dimensions (a) wL0, (b) wL1, (c) wL2 and (d) wL3 after perceiving light sources L0 and L3. The x-axes show the intervals between 0 and 1 with step-sizes of 0.1. The lower bound is included in the intervals and the upper bound is not. The last "interval" shows the frequency of feature value 1.0. The figures should be read as follows: When a certain sensory channel reads feature value 1.0, this sensory channel corresponds with the light source at the same height (e.g. $sc0$ corresponds with L0). The relative frequency of reading feature value 1.0 for this referent is 1. The relative frequencies of all other sensory channels is distributed on the sensory space. It should be clear that most feature values of other sensory channels read values in the interval $[0.0, 0.1)$. However, there are more sensory channels that are not directly adjacent. Between 0.1 and 1.0, the distribution is low and not structurally distributed. Hence the data shows no clear laws in the distribution. This indicates the noisy perception of the robots. Noise that cannot directly be simulated.

C Sensory data distribution

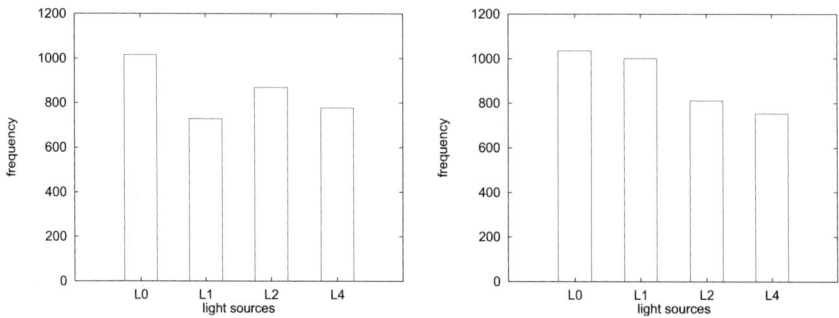

Figure C.1: The distribution of the frequency of corresponding segments in the data set for robots *r0* (a) and *r1* (b).

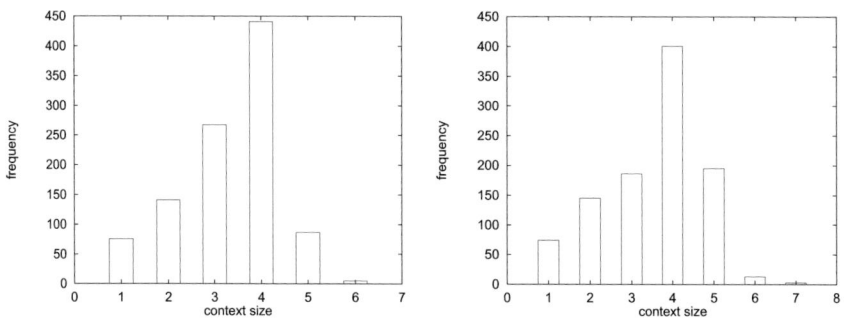

Figure C.2: The frequency distribution of context sizes of robots *r0* (a) and *r1* (b).

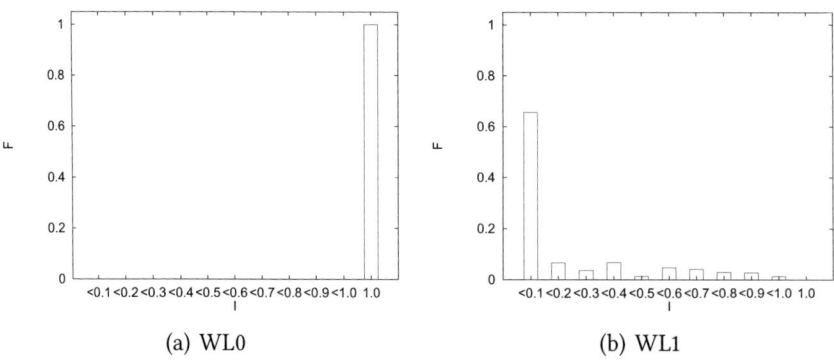

(a) WL0

(b) WL1

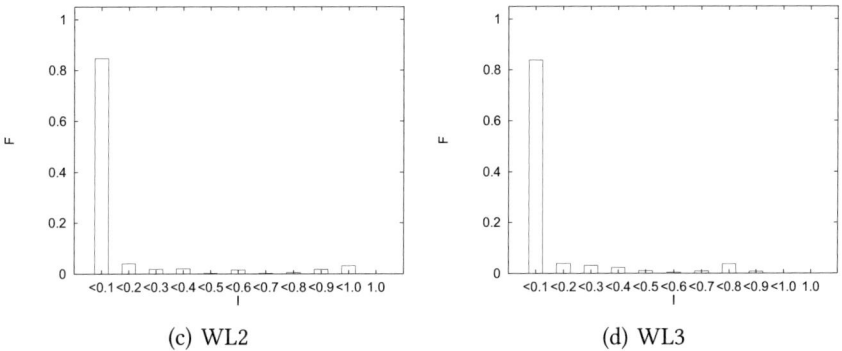

Figure C.3: The distribution of feature values observed for light source L0.

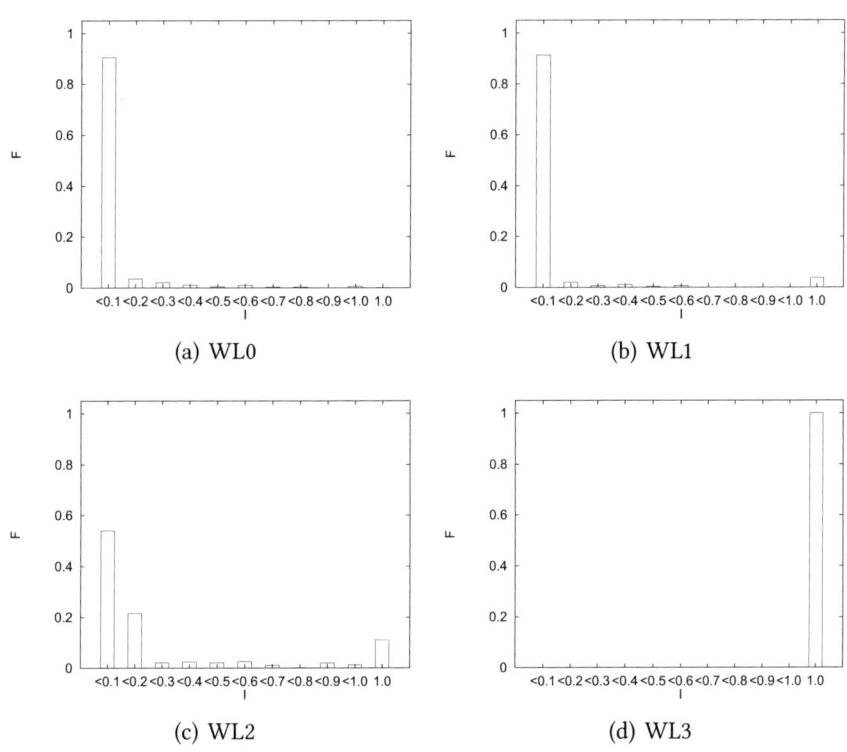

Figure C.4: The distribution of feature values observed for light source L3.

Appendix D: Lexicon and ontology

In this appendix the lexicon and ontology of the basic experiment (Chapter 4) is given. Of some additional meanings the legend is given (Tables D.5 and D.6). The lexicons (Tables D.1 and D.2) and ontologies (Tables D.3 and D.4) give weighted conditional probabilities based on co-occurrences of word and meaning or meaning and referent. These probabilities $P(c_i|b_j)$ are calculated as follows:

$$(\text{D.1}) \qquad P(c_i|b_j) = \frac{P(c_i)}{\sum_{j=1}^{n} P(c_i \wedge b_j)} \cdot \frac{P(c_i)}{P(b_j)}$$

where c_i are word-forms and b_j are the concepts when calculating the lexical entries $P(F|C)$. When calculating the probabilities for the ontologies c_i are the referents and b_j are the concepts, yielding $P(R|C)$. The tables only show a part of the lexicon and ontology. Entries that have probabilities ≤ 0.01 are left out.

The legends of some occurring meanings for robots $r0$ and $r1$ are given in tables D.5 and D.6.

D Lexicon and ontology

Table D.1: Lexicon of robot r0. The cells of the table give the weighted conditional probabilities that a word-form is used to name a meaning. These probabilities are based on the occurrence frequencies in one of the experiments after 5,000 language games. Associations with probabilities lower than 0.01 are left out for clarity.

C-F	huma	xomu	wosa	kyga	vyqa	guhu	lyzu	poma	pugu	wely
M53	0.58	—	—	—	—	—	—	—	—	—
M67	0.08	—	—	—	—	—	—	—	—	—
M30	0.02	0.37	—	—	—	—	—	—	—	—
M39	0.01	—	—	—	—	—	—	—	—	—
M18	—	0.14	—	—	—	—	—	—	—	—
M20	—	0.09	—	—	—	—	—	—	—	—
M17	—	0.04	—	—	—	—	—	—	—	—
M22	—	0.03	—	—	—	—	—	—	—	—
M43	—	0.03	—	—	—	—	—	—	—	—
M16	—	0.02	—	—	—	—	—	—	—	—
M26	—	—	0.37	—	—	—	—	0.11	—	—
M5	—	—	—	0.40	—	—	—	—	—	—
M27	—	—	—	0.07	—	—	—	—	—	—
M33	—	—	—	0.04	—	—	—	—	—	—
M15	—	—	—	0.02	—	—	—	—	—	—
M58	—	—	—	—	0.51	—	—	—	—	—
M393	—	—	—	—	0.08	—	—	—	—	—
M211	—	—	—	—	0.04	—	—	—	—	—
M484	—	—	—	—	0.04	—	—	—	—	—
M23	—	—	—	—	—	0.80	—	—	—	—
M61	—	—	—	0.08	—	—	0.44	0.01	—	—
M55	—	—	—	0.01	—	—	0.11	—	—	—
M394	—	—	—	—	—	—	0.02	—	—	—
M46	—	—	—	—	—	—	0.01	—	—	—
M169	0.01	—	—	—	—	—	—	—	0.46	—
M238	—	—	—	—	—	—	—	—	0.26	—
M121	—	—	—	—	—	—	—	—	—	1.00

Table D.2: Lexicon of robot *r*1.

C-B	huma	xomu	wosa	kyga	vyqa	guhu	lyzu	poma	pugu	wely
M4	0.44	—	0.02	—	0.01	—	—	—	0.01	—
M51	0.12	—	—	—	—	—	—	—	—	—
M55	0.08	—	—	—	—	—	—	—	—	—
M37	0.03	—	—	—	—	—	—	—	—	—
M1	0.02	—	—	—	—	—	—	—	—	—
M69	0.01	—	—	—	—	—	—	—	—	—
M91	0.01	—	—	—	—	—	—	0.03	—	—
M5	—	0.33	—	—	—	—	—	—	—	—
M39	—	—	0.40	—	—	—	—	—	—	—
M81	—	—	0.10	—	—	—	—	0.12	—	—
M13	—	—	0.05	—	—	—	—	—	—	—
M96	—	—	0.03	—	—	—	—	—	—	—
M40	—	—	0.02	—	—	—	—	—	—	—
M16	—	—	0.02	—	—	—	—	—	—	—
M65	—	—	0.02	—	0.07	—	—	—	—	—
M46	—	—	0.02	—	—	—	—	—	—	—
M21	—	—	0.01	—	—	—	—	—	—	—
M242	—	—	0.01	—	0.04	—	—	—	—	—
M0	—	—	—	0.30	—	—	—	—	—	—
M22	—	—	—	0.18	—	—	—	—	—	0.01
M78	—	—	—	0.09	—	—	—	—	—	—
M68	—	—	—	0.08	0.01	—	—	0.01	—	—
M75	—	—	—	0.06	—	—	—	—	—	—
M85	—	—	—	—	0.04	—	—	—	—	—
M389	—	—	—	—	—	0.08	—	—	—	—
M42	—	—	—	—	—	0.07	—	—	—	—
M44	—	—	—	—	—	—	0.81	—	—	—
M363	—	—	—	—	—	—	—	0.12	—	—
M102	—	—	—	—	—	—	—	0.03	—	—
M287	—	—	—	—	—	—	—	0.01	—	—
M62	—	—	—	—	—	—	—	—	0.19	—

D Lexicon and ontology

Table D.3: Ontology of robot *r0* in relation to the referents for which they have been used. The weighted frequencies give the relative frequency that a given meaning co-occurs with the particular referent.

C-B	0	1	2	3
M53	0.68	—	—	—
M55	0.10	—	—	—
M67	0.03	—	—	—
M169	0.03	—	—	—
M33	0.01	—	0.01	—
M128	0.01	—	—	—
M187	0.01	—	—	—
M43	0.01	0.01	—	—
M46	0.01	—	—	—
M30	—	0.68	—	—
M18	—	0.18	—	—
M16	—	0.03	—	—
M5	—	—	0.45	—
M20	—	—	0.21	—
M27	—	—	0.13	—
M23	—	—	0.03	—
M22	—	—	0.03	—
M26	—	—	0.02	—
M15	—	—	0.02	—
M89	—	—	0.02	—
M37	—	—	0.01	—
M233	—	—	0.01	—
M61	—	—	—	0.84
M58	—	—	—	0.08
M394	—	—	—	0.02
M90	—	—	—	0.01
M393	—	—	—	0.01

Table D.4: Ontology of robot $r1$.

C-B	0	1	2	3
M4	0.70	—	—	—
M55	0.07	—	—	—
M65	0.05	—	—	—
M51	0.04	0.02	—	—
M37	0.03	—	—	—
M39	—	0.58	—	—
M81	—	0.17	—	—
M13	—	0.06	—	—
M96	—	0.03	—	—
M94	—	0.02	—	—
M16	—	0.01	—	—
M1	—	0.01	—	—
M0	—	—	0.46	—
M22	—	—	0.27	—
M75	—	—	0.08	—
M78	—	—	0.05	0.01
M44	—	—	—	0.73
M68	—	—	—	0.15
M40	—	—	—	0.03
M242	—	—	0.05	—

D Lexicon and ontology

Table D.5: Additional legend of meanings of robot $r0$. See also Table 4.4.

M15	$(0.02, 0.31, 1.00, 0.02)_1$
M16	$(0.02, 0.99, 0.30, 0.02)_1$
M17	$(0.56, 0.99, 0.30, 0.02)_1$
M22	$(0.02, 0.01, 1.00, 0.99)_1$
M23	$(0.56, 0.31, 1.00, 0.44)_1$
M26	$(0.02, 0.31, 1.00, 0.99)_1$
M33	$(1.00, 0.99, 1.00, 0.99)_1$
M39	$(1.00, 0.31, 1.00, 0.44)_1$
M43	$(1.00, 0.99, 0.30, 0.02)_1$
M46	$(1.00, 0.31, 0.30, 0.44)_1$
M89	$(0.00, 0.00, 0.01, 0.00)_4$
M121	$(1.00, 0.01, 0.30, 0.44)_1$
M128	$(1.00, 0.01, 0.30, 0.02)_1$
M169	$(1.00, 0.00, 0.00, 0.00)_2$
M187	$(0.00, 0.00, 0.00, 0.00)_4$
M211	$(0.69, 1.00, 0.00, 0.00)_2$
M233	$(0.00, 0.00, 1.00, 0.00)_2$
M238	$(0.02, 0.99, 1.00, 0.99)_1$
M394	$(0.00, 0.00, 0.00, 0.01)_5$
M484	$(1.00, 0.99, 1.00, 0.44)_1$

Table D.6: Legend of meanings of robot r1.

M0	$(0.02, 0.02, 1.00, 0.01)_1$
M1	$(0.02, 0.02, 0.46, 0.01)_1$
M4	$(1.00, 0.02, 0.03, 0.01)_1$
M5	$(0.31, 0.02, 1.00, 0.01)_1$
M13	$(0.00, 0.00, 0.00, 0.00)_3$
M16	$(0.00, 0.00, 0.01, 0.00)_3$
M21	$(0.00, 0.00, 0.00, 0.00)_5$
M22	$(0.02, 0.02, 1.00, 0.53)_1$
M37	$(0.00, 0.00, 0.00, 0.00)_4$
M39	$(0.02, 1.00, 0.03, 0.01)_1$
M40	$(0.00, 0.00, 0.00, 0.00)_4$
M42	$(1.00, 1.00, 1.00, 1.00)_1$
M44	$(0.02, 0.02, 0.03, 1.00)_1$
M46	$(1.00, 1.00, 0.46, 0.01)_1$
M51	$(1.00, 1.00, 0.03, 0.01)_1$
M55	$(1.00, 0.58, 0.03, 0.01)_1$
M62	$(0.02, 1.00, 1.00, 0.53)_1$
M65	$(1.00, 0.02, 0.03, 0.53)_1$
M68	$(0.02, 0.02, 0.46, 1.00)_1$
M69	$(0.02, 1.00, 1.00, 0.01)_1$
M75	$(0.02, 0.58, 1.00, 0.01)_1$
M78	$(0.02, 0.02, 1.00, 1.00)_1$
M81	$(0.31, 1.00, 0.03, 0.01)_1$
M85	$(0.31, 1.00, 0.46, 0.53)_1$
M91	$(1.00, 1.00, 0.46, 1.00)_1$
M94	$(0.02, 1.00, 0.46, 0.01)_1$
M96	$(0.31, 1.00, 0.46, 0.01)_1$
M102	$(0.02, 0.58, 1.00, 1.00)_1$
M242	$(0.02, 0.58, 1.00, 0.53)_1$
M287	$(0.01, 0.01, 0.00, 0.00)_4$
M363	$(0.31, 0.02, 0.03, 1.00)_1$
M389	$(0.02, 0.02, 0.00, 0.00)_5$

References

Aczel, Amir D. 1989. *Complete business statistics*. Toronto: Irwin.

Aha, David W., Dennis Kibler & Marc K. Albert. 1991. Instance-based learning algorithms. *Machine Learning* 6 (1). 37–66.

Aitchison, Jean. 1987. *Words in the mind: An introduction to the mental lexicon*. 2nd edition. Cambridge, MA: Blackwell Publishers.

Aitchison, Jean. 1996. *The seeds of speech: Language origin and evolution*. Cambridge, UK: Cambridge University Press.

Banks, S. 1990. *Signal processing, image processing and pattern recognition*. UK: Prentice Hall International, Ltd.

Barnes, D. P. 1996. A behavior synthesis architecture for co-operant mobile robots. In J. O. Gray & D. G. Caldwell (eds.), *Advanced robotics and intelligent machines*, 295–314. IEE Control Engineering Series 51.

Barnes, D. P., R. S. Aylett, A. M. Coddington & R. A. Ghanea-Hercock. 1997. A hybrid approach to supervising multiple co-operant autonomous mobile robots. In *Proceedings of the International Conference on Advanced Robotics*.

Baronchelli, Andrea, Maddalena Felici, Emanuele Caglioti, Vittorio Loreto & Luc Steels. 2006. Sharp transition towards shared lexicon in multi-agent systems. *Journal of Statistical Mechanics* June 2006. P06014.

Barrett, M. 1995. Early lexical development. In P. Fletcher & B. MacWhinney (eds.), *The handbook of child language*, 362–392.

Belpaeme, Tony. 1999. Evolution of visual feature detectors. In *Evolutionary computation in image analysis and signal processing and telecommunications. first European Workshops in Göteborg, Sweden, EvoIASP99 and EuroEcTel99 Joint Proceedings*, vol. 1596 (LNCS). Berlin: Springer-Verlag.

Belpaeme, Tony, Luc Steels & J. van Looveren. 1998. The construction and acquisition of visual categories. In A. Birk & J. Demiris (eds.), *Learning robots, proceedings of the ewlr-6, lecture notes on artificial intelligence 1545*. Springer.

Berthouze, L. & Y. Kuniyoshi. 1998. Emergence and categorization of coordinated visual behavior through embodied interaction. *Machine Learning* 31/1,2,3. 187–200.

References

Billard, Aude. 1998. *Drama, a connectionist model for robot learning: Experiments on grounding communication through imitation in autonomous robots.* University of Edingburgh PhD thesis.

Billard, Aude & G. Hayes. 1997. Robot's first steps, robot's first words ... In Sorace & Heycock (eds.), *Proceedings of the GALA '97 Conference on Language Acquisition in Edingburgh.* Human Communication Research Centre: University of Edinburgh.

Billard, Aude & G. Hayes. 1999. Drama, a connectionist architecture for control and learning in autonomous robots. *Adaptive Behaviour* 7(1).

Bowerman, M. 1988. The "no negative evidence" problem: How do children avoid constructing an overly general grammar. In J. A. Hawkins (ed.), *Explaining language universals*, chap. 4, 73–101. Oxford, UK: Basil Blackwell.

Braine, M. D. S. 1971. The acquisition of language in infant and child. In C. Reed (ed.), *The learning of language*, 153–186. New York: Scribners.

Braitenberg, V. 1984. *Vehicles, experiments in synthetic psychology.* Cambridge, MA: The MIT Press.

Brentano, Franz. 1874. *Psychology from an empirical standpoint.* Leipzig: Duncker & Humblot.

Brooks, Rodney A. 1986. A robust layered control system for a mobile robot. *IEEE Journal of Robotics and Automation* 2. 14–23.

Brooks, Rodney A. 1990. Elephants don't play chess. *Robotics and Autonomous Systems* 6. 3–15.

Brooks, Rodney A. 1991. Intelligence without representation. *Artificial Intelligence* 47. 139–159.

Cangelosi, A., A. Greco & S. Harnad. 2000. From robotic toil to symbolic theft: Grounding transfer from entry-level to higher-level categories. *Connection Science* in press.

Cangelosi, A. & D. Parisi. 1998. The emergence of "language" in an evolving population of neural networks. *Connection Science* 10. 83–93.

Chandler, D. 1994. *Semiotics for Beginners.* http://www.aber.ac.uk/media/Documents/S4B/semiotic.html.

Chapman, D. & L. P. Kaebling. 1991. Input generalization in delayed reinforcement learning: an algorithm and performance comparisons. In J. Mylopoulos & R. Reiter (eds.), *Proceedings of the twelfth international joint conference on artificial intelligence (IJCAI-91)*, 726,731. San Mateo, CA: Morgan Kauffmann.

Chomsky, Noam. 1956. Three models for the description of language. *IRE Transactions on Information Theory IT* 2(3). 13–54.

Churchland, Patricia S. 1986. *Neurophilosophy.* Cambridge, MA: The MIT Press.

Clancey, W. J. 1997. *Situated cognition*. Cambridge, UK: Cambridge Univsity Press.

Clark, E. V. 1993. *The lexicon in acquisition*. Cambridge, UK: Cambridge University Press.

Clark, H. H. & E. V. Clark. 1977. *Psychology and language*. San Diego, CA: Harcourt Brace Jovanovich.

Cotter, J. R. 1990. The visual pathway: An introduction to structure and organization. In K. N. Leibovic (ed.), *Science of vision*. Springer-Verlag.

Damper, R. I. 2000. Ontogenetic versus phylogenetic learning of the emergence of phonetic categories. In J.-L. Dessalles & L. Ghadakpour (eds.), *The evolution of language: 3rd International Conference, Paris 2000*. Paris: ENST.

Darwin, Charles. 1968. *The origin of species*. London, UK: Penguin Books.

Dawkins, R. 1976. *The selfish gene*. Oxford: Oxford University Press.

de Boer, Bart. 1997. Generating vowels in a population of agents. In C. Husbands & I. Harvey (eds.), *Proceedings of the Fourth European Conference on Artificial Life*, 503–510. Cambridge, MA & London: MIT Press.

de Boer, Bart. 1999. *Self-organisation in vowel systems*. Vrije Universiteit Brussels PhD thesis.

de Boer, Bart & Paul Vogt. 1999. Emergence of speech sounds in changing populations. In D. Floreano, J.-D. Nicoud & F. Mondada (eds.), *Advances in Artificial Life: Proceedings of 5th European Conference ECAL'99*. Springer.

de Jong, Edwin D. 1999a. Analyzing the evolution of communication from a dynamical systems perspective. In D. Floreano, J.-D. Nicoud & F. Mondada (eds.), *Proceedings of the fifth european conference on artificial life ecal'99*. Berlin: Springer-Verlag.

de Jong, Edwin D. 1999b. Autonomous concept formation. In *Proceedings of the Sixteenth International Joint Conference on Artificial Intelligence IJCAI'99*.

de Jong, Edwin D. 2000. *The development of communication*. VUB AI Lab PhD thesis.

de Jong, Edwin D. & Luc Steels. 1999. Generation and selection of sensory channels. In *Evolutionary Computation in Image Analysis and Signal Processing and Telecommunications. First European Workshops in Göteborg, Sweden, EvoIASP99 and EuroEcTel99 Joint Proceedings*, vol. 1596 (LNCS). Berlin: Springer-Verlag.

de Jong, Edwin D. & Paul Vogt. 1998. How should a robot discriminate between objects? In R. Pfeifer, B. Blumberg, J-A. Meyer & S. Wilson (eds.), *From animals to animats 5, Proceedings of the fifth internation conference on simulation of adaptive behavior*. Cambridge, MA: MIT Press.

de Saussure, F. 1974. *Course in general linguistics*. New York: Fontana.

References

Demetras, M. J., K. Nolan Post & C. E. Snow. 1986. Feedback to first language learners: The role of repetitions and clarification questions. *Journal of Child Language* 13. 275–292.

Dennett, Daniel C. 1991. *Consciousness explained.* Boston: Little, Brown.

Dessalles, J.-L. 2000. Two stages in the evolution of language use. In J.-L. Dessalles & L. Ghadakpour (eds.), *The evolution of language: 3rd International Conference, Paris 2000.* Paris: ENST.

Dircks, C. & S. C. Stoness. 1999. Effective lexicon change in the absence of population flux. In D. Floreano, J.-D. Nicoud & F. Mondada (eds.), *Advances in Artificial Life: Proceedings of 5th European Conference ECAL'99.* Springer.

Eco, Umberto. 1976. *A theory of semiotics.* Bloomington: Indiana University Press.

Eco, Umberto. 1986. On symbols. In J. Deely, B. Williams & F. E. Kruse (eds.), *Frontiers in semiotics*, 153–180. Bloomington: Indiana University Press.

Edelman, G. M. 1987. *Neural darwinism.* New York: Basic Books Inc.

Edelman, G. M. 1992. *Bright air, brilliant fire.* New York: Basic Books Inc.

Fodor, Jerry A. 1975. *The language of thought.* Hassocks: Harvester Press.

Fu, K. S. (ed.). 1976. *Digital Pattern Recognition.* Berlin: Springer-Verlag.

Gärdenfors, P. 1996. Conceptual spaces as a basis for cognitive semantics. In A. Clark et al (ed.), *Philosophy and cognitive science.* Dordrecht: Kluwer.

Gardner, B. T. & R. A. Gardner. 1969. Teaching sign language to a chimpanzee. *Science* 165. 664–672.

The Grounding of Word Meaning: Data and Models, Papers from the 1998 Workshop. 1998. Tech. rep. Technical Report WS-98-06. AAAI Press.

Gilbert, Nigel, Matthijs den Besten, Akos Bontovics, Bart G. W. Craenen, Federico Divina, A. E. Eiben, Robert Griffioen, Gyorgy Hévízi, Andras Lõrincz, Ben Paechter, Stephan Schuster, Martijn C. Schut, Christian Tzolov, Paul Vogt & Lu Yang. 2006. Emerging artificial societies through learning. *Journal of Artificial Societies and Social Simulation* 9 (2). 9. http://jasss.soc.surrey.ac.uk/9/2/9.html.

Greco, A., A. Cangelosi & S. Harnad. 1998. A connectionist model for categorical perception and symbol grounding. In *International conference on artificial neural networks.*

Harnad, S. 1990. The symbol grounding problem. *Physica D* 42. 335–346.

Harnad, S. 1993. Grounding symbols in the analog world with neural nets. *Think* 2. 12 –78.

Harnad, S., H. Steklis & J. Lancaster (eds.). 1976. *Origins and evolution of language and speech.* Vol. 280. (Annals of the New York Academy of Sciences). The New York Academy of Sciences.

Harris, M., D. Jones & J. Grant. 1983. The nonverbal context of mothers' speech to infants. *First Language* 4. 21–30.

Harris, M., D. Jones & J. Grant. 1984. The social interactional context of maternal speech to infants: an explanation for the event-bound nature of early word use? *First Language* 5. 89–100.

Jaeger, H. & T. Christaller. 1998. Dual dynamics: designing behavior systems for autonomous robots. *Artificial Life and Robotics* 2. 108–112.

Kaplan, Frédéric. 2000. *L'émergence d'un lexique dans une population d'agent autonomes*. Université Pierre-et-Marie-Curie (Paris 6) PhD thesis.

Kirby, Simon & James R. Hurford. 1997. Learning, culture and evolution in the origin of linguistic constraints. In C. Husbands & I. Harvey (eds.), *Proceedings of the Fourth European Conference on Artificial Life*. Cambridge, MA & London: MIT Press.

Kirby, Simon & James R. Hurford. 2002. The emergence of linguistic structure: An overview of the iterated learning model. In Angelo Cangelosi & Domenico Parisi (eds.), *Simulating the evolution of language*, 121–148. London: Springer.

Kröse, Ben, Roland Bunschoten, Nikos Vlassis & Yoichi Motomura. 1999. Appearance based robot localization. In G. Kraetzschmar (ed.), *IJCAI-99 workshop on adaptive spatial representations of dynamic environments*, 53–58.

Labov, W. 1973. The boundary of words and their meanings. In C.-J. N. Bailey & R. W. Shuy (eds.), *New ways of analyzing variation in english*. Washington, DC: Georgetown University Press.

Lakoff, G. 1987. *Women, fire and dangerous things*. The University of Chicago Press.

LeDoux, J. 1996. *The emotional brain*. New York: Simon & Schuster.

MacLennan, B. 1991. Synthetic ethology: An approach to the study of communication. In C. G. Langton, C. Taylor & J. D. Farmer (eds.), *Artificial Life II, Vol. X of SFI Studies in the Sciences of Complexity*. Redwood City, CA: Addison-Wesley Pub. Co.

Maturana, H. R. & F. R. Varela. 1992. *The tree of knowledge: The biological roots of human understanding*. Boston: Shambhala.

Mitchell, Tom M. 1997. *Machine learning*. New York City: McGraw-Hill.

Moore, A. W. & C. G. Atkeson. 1995. The parti-game algorithm for variable resolution reinforcement learning in multidimensional state-spaces. *Machine Learning* 21(3). 199–233.

Nagel, Thomas. 1974. What is it like to be a bat? *The Philosophical Review* 83. 435–450.

Newell, A. 1980. Physical symbol systems. *Cognitive Science* 4. 135–183.

References

Newell, A. 1990. *Unified theories of cognition*. Cambridge, MA: Harvard University Press.

Nöth, W. 1990. *Handbook of semiotics*. Bloomington: Indiana University Press.

Oates, T. 1999. Identifying distinctive subsequences in multivariate time series by clustering. In *Proceedings of the Fifth International Conference on Knowledge Discovery and Data Mining*.

Oates, T., Z. Eyler-Walker & P. R. Cohen. 1999. *Using syntax to learn semantics: An experiment in language acquisition with a mobile robot*. Tech. rep. Technical Report 99-35. Amherst: University of Amherst.

Oja, Erkki. 1983. *Subspace methods of pattern recognition*. Letchworth: Research Studies Press Ltd.

Oliphant, Mike. 1997. *Formal approaches to innate and learned communication: laying the foundation for language*. University of California, San Diego PhD thesis.

Oliphant, Mike. 1998. Rethinking the language bottleneck: Why don't animals learn to communicate? In Chris Knight & James R. Hurford (eds.), *The evolution of language (selected papers from the 2nd International Conference on the Evolution of Language, London, April 6–9 1998)*.

Oliphant, Mike. 1999. The learning barrier: Moving from innate to learned systems of communication. *Adaptive Behavior* 7(3/4). 371–384.

Oudeyer, P.-Y. 1999. *Experiment in emergent phonetics*. Rapport de stage de deuxième année. Magistère informatique et modélisation, ENS Lyon.

Peirce, C. S. 1931–1958. *Collected papers*. Vol. I-VIII. Cambridge, MA: Harvard University Press.

Pfeifer, R. & C. Scheier. 1999. *Understanding intelligence*. Cambridge, MA: MIT Press.

Piaget, J. 1996. *La naissance de l'intelligence chez l'enfant*. Neufchatel: Delachaux et Netlé.

Pinker, Steven. 1984. *Learnability and cognition*. Cambridge, MA: MIT Press.

Popescu-Belis, A. 1997. Design of an adaptive multi-agent system based on the "neural darwinism" theory. In *First International Conference on Autonomous Agents*, 484–485. Marina del Rey, California.

Premack, D. 1971. Langauge in chimpanzee? *Science* 172. 808–822.

Prigogine, I. & I. Strengers. 1984. *Order out of chaos*. New York: Bantam Books.

Pylyshyn, Z. W. (ed.). 1987. *The Robot's Dilemma*. New Jersey: Ablex Publishing Corporation.

Rosch, Eleanor, C. B. Mervis, W. D. Gray, D. M. Johnson & P. Boyes-Braem. 1976. Basic objects in natural categories. *Cognitive Psychology* 8. 382–439.

Rosenstein, M. & P. R. Cohen. 1998a. Concepts from time series. In *Proceedings of the Fifteenth National Conference on Artificial Intelligence*. Menlo Park Ca.: AAAI Press.

Rosenstein, M. & P. R. Cohen. 1998b. Symbol grounding with delay coordinates. In *Working notes of the AAAI-98 workshop on: The Grounding of Word Meaning*. Menlo Park Ca.: AAAI Press.

Schaffer, H. R., A. Hepburn & G. Collis. 1983. Verbal and non-verbal aspects of mothers' directives. *Journal of Child Language* 10. 337–355.

Searle, John R. 1980. Minds, brains and programs. *Behavioral and Brain Sciences* 3. 417–457.

Searle, John R. 1984. *Minds, brains and science*. Cambridge, MA: Harvard University Press.

Shannon, C. 1948. A mathematical theory of communication. *The Bell System Technical Journal* 27. 379–423, 623–656.

Siskind, Jeffrey M. 1996. A computational study of cross-situational techniques for learning word-to-meaning mappings. *Cognition* 61. 39–91.

Smith, Kenny, Andrew D. M. Smith, Richard A. Blythe & Paul Vogt. 2006. Cross-situational learning: A mathematical approach. In Paul Vogt, Yuuya Sugita, Elio Tuci & Chrystopher Nehaniv (eds.), *Symbol grounding and beyond*, vol. 4211 (Lecture Notes in Artificial Intelligence). Springer.

Steels, Luc. 1992. *The PDL Reference Manual*. AI Lab Memo 92-05.

Steels, Luc. 1994a. A case study in the behaviour-oriented design of autonomous agents. In *Proceedings of the third Simulation of Adaptive Behavior Conference*. Cambridge, MA: The MIT Press.

Steels, Luc. 1994b. Artificial life roots of artificial intelligence. *Arificial Life Journal* 1(1). 89–125.

Steels, Luc. 1994c. Building agents with autonomous behavior systems. In Luc Steels & Rodney A. Brooks (eds.), *The "artificial life" route to "artificial intelligence". Building situated embodied agents*. New Haven: Lawrence Erlbaum Associates.

Steels, Luc. 1996a. A self-organising spatial vocabulary. *Artificial Life Journal* 2(3). 319–332.

Steels, Luc. 1996b. Discovering the competitors. *Journal of Adaptive Behavior* 4(2). 173–199.

Steels, Luc. 1996c. Emergent adaptive lexicons. In P. Maes (ed.), *From Animals to Animats 4: Proceedings of the Fourth International Conference On Simulating Adaptive Behavior*. Cambridge, MA: The MIT Press.

References

Steels, Luc. 1996d. Perceptually grounded meaning creation. In M. Tokoro (ed.), *Proceedings of the International Conference on Multi-Agent Systems*. Menlo Park Ca.: AAAI Press.

Steels, Luc. 1996e. The spontaneous self-organization of an adaptive language. In S. Muggleton (ed.), *Machine intelligence 15*. Oxford: Oxford University Press.

Steels, Luc. 1997a. Language learning and language contact. In W. Daelemans, A. Van den Bosch & A. Weijters (eds.), *Workshop Notes of the ECML/MLnet Familiarization Workshop on Empirical Learning of Natural Language Processing Tasks*, 11–24. Prague.

Steels, Luc. 1997b. Synthesising the origins of language and meaning using co-evolution, self-organisation and level formation. In James R. Hurford, C. Knight & M. Studdert-Kennedy (eds.), *Evolution of human language*. Edingburgh: Edingburgh University Press.

Steels, Luc. 1997c. The synthetic modeling of language origins. *Evolution of Communication* 1(1). 1–34.

Steels, Luc. 1999. *The Talking Heads experiments. Volume 1. Words and meanings*. Special pre-edition for LABORATORIUM, Antwerpen.

Steels, Luc. 2000. The emergence of grammar in communicating autonomous robotic agents. In W. Horn (ed.), *Proceedings of ECAI-2000*. Amsterdam: IOS Press.

Steels, Luc (ed.). 2012. *Experiments in cultural language evolution*. Vol. 3 (Advances in interaction studies). Amsterdam & Philadelphia: John Benjamins.

Steels, Luc & Rodney A. Brooks. 1995. *The "artificial life" route to "artificial intelligence". Building situated embodied agents*. New Haven: Lawrence Erlbaum Ass.

Steels, Luc & Joachim De Beule. 2006. Unify and merge in Fluid Construction Grammar. In Paul Vogt, Yuuya Sugita, Elio Tuci & Chrystopher Nehaniv (eds.), *Symbol grounding and beyond: Proceedings of the Third International Workshop on the Emergence and Evolution of Linguistic Communication* (Lecture Notes in Computer Science), 197–223. Springer.

Steels, Luc & Frédéric Kaplan. 1998. Stochasticity as a source of innovation in language games. In *Proceedings of Alive VI*.

Steels, Luc & Frédéric Kaplan. 1999. Situated grounded word semantics. In *Proceedings of IJCAI 99*. Morgan Kaufmann.

Steels, Luc & Frédéric Kaplan. 2000. AIBO's first words. The social learning of language and meaning. *Evolution of Communication* 4 (1). 3–32.

Steels, Luc & A. McIntyre. 1999. Spatially distributed naming games. In *Advances in complex systems*.

Steels, Luc & Paul Vogt. 1997. Grounding adaptive language games in robotic agents. In C. Husbands & I. Harvey (eds.), *Proceedings of the Fourth European Conference on Artificial Life*. Cambridge, MA & London: MIT Press.

Steels, Luc, Frédéric Kaplan, A. McIntyre & Joris Van Looveren. 2002. Crucial factors in the origins of word-meaning. In Alison Wray (ed.), *The transition to language*, 252–271. Oxford, UK: Oxford University Press.

Sutton, R. S. & A. G. Barto. 1998. *Reinforcement learning: An introduction*. Cambridge, MA: The MIT Press (A Bratford Book).

Tani, J. & S. Nolfi. 1998. Learning to perceive the world as articulated: An approach for hierarchical learning in sensory-motor systems. In R. Pfeifer, B. Blumberg, J-A. Meyer & S. Wilson (eds.), *From animals to animats 5, Proceedings of the fifth internation conference on simulation of adaptive behavior*. Cambridge, MA: MIT Press.

Tomasello, M. & M. Barton. 1994. Learning words in nonostensive contexts. *Developmental Psychology* 30(5). 639–650.

Tomasello, M., S. Mannle & A. Kruger. 1986. The linguistic environment of one to two year old twins. *Developmental Psychology* 22. 169–176.

Tomasello, M. & J. Todd. 1983. Joint attention and lexical acquisition style. *First Language* 4. 197–212.

Van Looveren, J. 1999. Multiple word naming games. In E. Postma & M. Gyssens (eds.), *Proceedings of the Eleventh Belgium-Netherlands Conference on Artificial Intelligence*. University of Maastricht.

Vereertbrugghen, D. 1996. *Design and implementation of a second generation sensor-motor control unit for mobile robots*. Vrije Universiteit Brussel MA thesis.

Vogt, Paul. 1997. *A perceptual grounded self-organising lexicon in robotic agents*. School of Cognitive Science & Engineering, University of Groningen MA thesis.

Vogt, Paul. 1998a. Perceptual grounding in robots. In A. Birk & J. Demiris (eds.), *Learning robots, proceedings of the EWLR-6*, vol. 1545 (Lecture Notes on Artificial Intelligence). Springer.

Vogt, Paul. 1998b. The evolution of a lexicon and meaning in robotic agents through self-organization. In H. La Poutré & J. van den Herik (eds.), *Proceedings of the Netherlands/Belgium Conference on Artificial Intelligence*. Amsterdam: CWI Amsterdam.

Vogt, Paul. 1998c. *The evolution of a lexicon and meaning in robotic agents through self-organization*. VUB AI Memo 98-09, Presented at the 2nd Evolution of Language Conference, April 1999. London.

References

Vogt, Paul. 1999. Grounding a lexicon in a coordination task on mobile robots. In E. Postma & M. Gyssens (eds.), *Proceedings of Eleventh Belgium-Netherlands Conference on Artificial Intelligence*. Univ. of Maastricht.

Vogt, Paul. 2000a. Bootstrapping grounded symbols by minimal autonomous robots. *Evolution of Communication* 4 (1). 89–118.

Vogt, Paul. 2000b. Grounding language about actions: Mobile robots playing follow me games. In Meyer, Bertholz, Floreano, Roitblat & Wilson (eds.), *SAB2000 Proceedings Supplement Book*. Honolulu: International Society for Adaptive Behavior.

Vogt, Paul. 2002. The physical symbol grounding problem. *Cognitive Systems Research* 3 (3). 429–457.

Vogt, Paul. 2003a. Anchoring of semiotic symbols. *Robotics and Autonomous Systems* 43 (2). 109–120.

Vogt, Paul. 2003b. THSim v3.2: the Talking Heads simulation tool. In Wolfgang Banzhaf, Thomas Christaller, Peter Dittrich, Jan T. Kim & Jens Ziegler (eds.), *Advances in Artificial Life – Proceedings of the 7th European Conference on Artificial Life (ECAL)*, 535–544. Berlin & Heidelberg: Springer Verlag.

Vogt, Paul. 2005a. On the acquisition and evolution of compositional languages: Sparse input and the productive creativity of children. *Adaptive Behavior* 13 (4). 325–346.

Vogt, Paul. 2005b. The emergence of compositional structures in perceptually grounded language games. *Artificial Intelligence* 167 (1–2). 206–242.

Vogt, Paul. 2006. Language evolution and robotics: Issues in symbol grounding and language acquisition. In Angelo Loula, Ricardo Gudwin & João Queiroz (eds.), *Artificial cognition systems*, 176–209. Hershey, PA: Idea Group Publishing.

Vogt, Paul. 2007. Variation, competition and selection in the self-organisation of compositionality. In Brendan Wallace, Alastair Ross, John B. Davies & Tony Anderson (eds.), *The mind, the body and the world: Psychology after cognitivism?*, 233–256. Exeter: Imprint Academic.

Vogt, Paul. 2012. Exploring the robustness of cross-situational learning under Zipfian distributions. *Cognitive Science* 36 (4). 726–739.

Vogt, Paul & Hans Coumans. 2003. Investigating social interaction strategies for bootstrapping lexicon development. *Journal for Artificial Societies and Social Simulation* 6 (1). http://jasss.soc.surrey.ac.uk/6/1/4.html.

Vogt, Paul & Bart de Boer. 2010. Language evolution: Computer models for empirical data. *Adaptive Behavior* 18 (1). 5–11.

Vogt, Paul & Federico Divina. 2007. Social symbol grounding and language evolution. *Interaction Studies* 8 (1). 31–52.

Vogt, Paul & Evert Haasdijk. 2010. Modelling social learning of language and skills. *Artificial Life* 16 (4). 289–309.

Vogt, Paul & Elena Lieven. 2010. Verifying theories of language acquisition using computer models of language evolution. *Adaptive Behavior* 18 (1). 21–35.

Vogt, Paul & J. Douglas Mastin. 2013. Anchoring social symbol grounding in children's interactions. *Künstliche Intelligenz* 27 (2). 145–151.

Werner, G. M. & M. G. Dyer. 1991. Evolution and communication in artificial organisms. In C. G. Langton, C. Taylor & J. D. Farmer (eds.), *Artificial Life II, Vol. X of SFI Studies in the Sciences of Complexity*. Redwood City, CA: Addison-Wesley Pub. Co.

Winograd, T. 1972. *Understanding natural language*. Orlando, FL: Academic Press.

Wittgenstein, Ludwig. 1958. *Philosophical investigations*. Oxford, UK: Basil Blackwell.

Yanco, H. & L. Stein. 1993. An adaptive communication protocol for cooperating mobile robots. In J-A. Meyer, H. L. Roitblat & S. Wilson (eds.), *From Animals to Animats 2. Proceedings of the Second International Conference on Simulation of Adaptive Behavior*, 478–485. Cambridge, MA: The MIT Press.

Zlatev, J. 1997. *Situated embodiment*. Sweden: Stockholm University PhD thesis.

Name index

Aczel, Amir D., 104
Aha, David W., 76
Aitchison, Jean, 19, 122, 126
Albert, Marc K., 76
Atkeson, C. G., 82

Banks, S., 73
Barnes, D. P., 15, 51, 202, 203
Baronchelli, Andrea, vii
Barrett, M., 25, 83, 140, 199
Barto, A. G., 76, 94
Barton, M., 25, 198, 199
Belpaeme, Tony, 21, 71, 186, 189
Berthouze, L., 15
Billard, Aude, 2, 3, 15, 16, 28–31, 186, 208
Bowerman, M., 24, 83, 91, 140, 198
Braine, M. D. S., 25, 198, 199
Braitenberg, V., 46, 202
Brentano, Franz, 1
Brooks, Rodney A., 3, 10, 12–15, 17, 49, 190, 201

Cangelosi, A., 17, 20, 28, 30, 31
Chandler, D., 8, 9, 84
Chapman, D., 82
Chomsky, Noam, 18
Christaller, T., 49, 51, 202
Churchland, Patricia S., 5
Clancey, W. J., 2, 25, 190, 198, 201
Clark, E. V., 25, 198, 200
Clark, H. H., 198

Cohen, P. R., 15–17, 29, 30, 213, 214
Collis, G., 199
Cotter, J. R., 189
Coumans, Hans, viii

Damper, R. I., 189
Darwin, Charles, 26
De Beule, Joachim, vii
de Boer, Bart, ix, 21, 53
de Jong, Edwin D., 21, 23, 24, 28, 31, 71, 72, 78, 80, 82, 99–102, 145, 149, 161, 189, 190, 198, 209, 210, 212
de Saussure, F., 9, 20
Demetras, M. J., 25, 198, 199
Dennett, Daniel C., 1, 6
Dessalles, J.-L., 199, 214
Dircks, C., 215
Divina, Federico, viii, ix
Dyer, M. G., 20

Eco, Umberto, 8
Edelman, G. M., 6
Eyler-Walker, Z., 17

Fodor, Jerry A., 4
Fu, K. S., 69

Gärdenfors, P., 210
Gardner, B. T., 20
Gardner, R. A., 20
Gasser, M., 17
Gilbert, Nigel, viii

Name index

Grant, J., 199
Greco, A., 17

Haasdijk, Evert, ix, x
Harnad, S., vii, 1, 8, 10, 11, 15, 17, 19, 61, 62, 186, 189, 190, 192
Harris, M., 199
Hayes, G., 2, 3, 15, 16, 28–31, 186, 208
Hepburn, A., 199
Hurford, James R., 20

Jaeger, H., 49, 51, 202
Jones, D., 199

Kaebling, L. P., 82
Kaplan, Frédéric, vii, 21, 23, 53, 71, 85, 90, 145, 149, 152, 161, 203, 206, 208, 210–212, 214
Kibler, Dennis, 76
Kirby, Simon, 20
Kröse, Ben, 15
Kruger, A., 25, 199
Kuniyoshi, Y., 15

Labov, W., 126
Lakoff, G., 2, 126, 190
Lancaster, J., 19
LeDoux, J., 60
Lieven, Elena, ix
Looveren, J. van, 21, 71, 186

MacLennan, B., 20
Mannle, S., 25, 199
Mastin, J. Douglas, x
Maturana, H. R., 2
McIntyre, A., 21
Mitchell, Tom M., 76
Moore, A. W., 82

Nöth, W., 8

Nagel, Thomas, 3
Newell, A., 1, 8, 14, 15
Nolan Post, K., 25, 198, 199
Nolfi, S., 15

Oates, T., 17
Oja, Erkki, 79
Oliphant, Mike, 11, 20, 24, 28–31, 85, 145, 149, 198
Oudeyer, P.-Y., 21

Parisi, D., 17, 20, 28, 30, 31
Peirce, C.S., 8–10, 84, 193
Peirce, C. S., 8
Pfeifer, R., 1, 15, 187
Piaget, J., 1
Pinker, Steven, viii, 85
Popescu-Belis, A., 215
Premack, D., 20
Prigogine, I., 54
Pylyshyn, Z. W., 1, 15

Rosch, Eleanor, 192
Rosenstein, M., 15, 16, 29, 30, 213, 214

Schaffer, H. R., 199
Scheier, C., 1, 15, 187
Searle, John R., 1, 5–8
Shannon, C., 99, 100
Siskind, Jeffrey M., viii, 85
Smith, Kenny, viii
Snow, C. E., 25, 198, 199
Steels, Luc, vii, 3, 9, 11, 12, 15, 18, 20–22, 23, 23, 26, 28, 31, 33, 41, 46, 47, 49, 51, 53–55, 60, 62, 70–72, 75, 78, 80, 83–85, 88, 90, 93, 100, 104, 132, 145, 149, 157, 158, 186, 189–191, 201–203, 208–210, 212, 213, 215, 221

Stein, L., 2, 3, 15, 16, 20, 28–31
Steklis, H., 19
Stoness, S. C., 215
Strengers, I., 54
Sutton, R. S., 76, 94

Tani, J., 15
Todd, J., 199
Tomasello, M., 25, 198, 199

Van Looveren, J., 21
Varela, F. R., 2
Vereertbrugghen, D., 33, 38, 40
Vogt, Paul, vii–x, 3, 17, 21, 22, 24, 26, 31, 33, 36, 53, 55, 60, 70, 72, 78, 80, 85, 87, 88, 92, 102, 104, 132, 150, 185, 190, 203, 209, 213, 214, 221

Werner, G. M., 20
Winograd, T., 2
Wittgenstein, Ludwig, 2, 11, 20, 53–54, 126, 193, 196

Yanco, H., 2, 3, 15, 16, 20, 28–31

Zlatev, J., 190

Subject index

a priori success, 107
actual success, 102, 197, 217
adaptation, 92–94, 206
adaptive subspace method, 80, 209
AIBO, 23, 212

basic experiment, 107, 193
behaviour synthesis architecture, 51
behaviour-based
    architecture, 26, 47, 201
    cognitive architecture, 47–51, 56–61, 201–203
binary
    subspace, 78–82, 209, 217
    subspace method, 78–82, 129
    tree method, 78, 205, 209

categorisation, 72–82, 125–131, 190, 210, 217
category, 72–82, 84, 125–131, 217
    fuzzy, 126, 129, 191
    prototypical, 73, 74, 190, 192, 219
    static, 129
Chinese Room, 5–8
co-evolution, 11, 196
communicative success, 94, 101, 193, 197, 217
competition diagram, 115–120, 171, 210
consistency, 102, 217
context, 70, 201, 208, 217
correspondence, 38, 64–65, 87, 91, 107, 173

coupling, 94–98
cultural evolution, 13, 26

data set
    basic, 106
    gearing, 133
discrimination, 71, 190, 217
discrimination game, 71–72, 110, 190, 205
discriminative success, 100, 191, 218
distinctive category, 71, 77, 218
distinctiveness, 100, 192, 218
dual dynamics, 51

entropy, 100
evolutionary linguistics, 20
extra-linguistic information, 27, 185

family resemblance, 126, 196
feature, 69, 218
    extraction, 69–71, 188, 218
    space, 69, 73, 76, 218
    vector, 69, 218
feedback, 24, 85, 91–92, 140–145, 197–200, 218
follow me game, 60, 213
form, 9, 86, 193, 218
    adoption, 93, 94, 157, 159, 194, 198, 207
    creation probability, 93, 108, 145, 150–153, 194, 206, 207, 211
form-meaning association, 86

gearing, 132, 138
guessing game, 85, 140–145, 163

identification game, 213
instance-based learning, 76
invariance, 10, 173, 188, 193–195, 205, 209

joint attention, 25, 85–88, 140–145, 177–182, 198, 201, 218

k-nearest neighbour algorithm, 73

language
    acquisition, 24–25, 197, 199
    game, 11, 20, 54–98
    of thought, 4
    origins, 19
lateral inhibition, 145, 194, 198, 210
learning rate, 94, 108, 153–157, 194
lexicon, 86, 120–123, 169, 219
    growth, 121–123, 169

Mann-Whitney U test, 103
meaning, 9, 75, 77, 84, 89, 193, 219
memes, 26
mismatch in reference, 93

naming game, 84–94, 206
no negative feedback evidence, 24, 197–200

object constancy, 197
observational game, 85, 140–150, 177–182, 198
ontology, 71, 113, 115, 248, 249
    growth, 121–123, 169
ostensive game, 85, 140–145

parsimony, 101, 192, 219
PDL, 41–51, 56–61

phototaxis, 41–46
physical
    grounding hypothesis, 11–14
    symbol grounding problem, 14–18
    symbol system, 12, 14
pointing, 203
polysemy, 119, 121, 172, 174–175, 180, 182, 194, 199, 219
Process Description Language, *see* PDL
production, 88–89
prototype, 72–78, 113–115, 190, 209, 219
    dynamics, 113–115
    effect, 192
    method, 72–78

referent, 9, 193, 219
region of interest, 65
reinforcement learning, 76

saliency, 192, 205, 209
score, 74, 206
    association, 93, 94, 194, 210
    categorisation, 74
    depth, 75
    effectiveness, 74
    meaning, 75
    sucsess, 91
    topic, 93
segment, 68, 219
segmentation, 67–69, 188, 204, 219
self-organisation, 26, 194, 210
semiotic landscape, 62, 63, 120, 121, 165–168, 195
semiotics, 8–10, 84, 193
sensing, 64–67, 188, 204–206, 219
sensors light, 37–38, 133
sensory channel, 219

Subject index

sign, *see* symbol
situated embodiment, 14, 200
situation, 105
SMBII, 40
specificity, 102, 194, 219
structural coupling, 195
subsumption architecture, 14, 51, 201
symbol, 8–10, 84, 193, 220
symbol grounding problem, 8–11, 14, 24, 27, 185, 186, 197
    discrimination, 10, 186, 189–193, 217
    iconisation, 10, 186–189, 218
    identification, 10, 62, 186, 193–195, 218
synonymy, 119, 152, 170, 181, 182, 194, 199, 220

Talking Heads, 21–23, 203
topic, 88, 89, 220

understandability, 106–107, 200, 208
    potential, *see* understandability
understanding, 89–90
Universal Grammar, 19

Wilcoxon rank sum test, *see* Mann-Whitney U test
word-form, *see* form

XSL game, 85, 140–145

Subject index